NEW ORDINARY CAUSE RULES

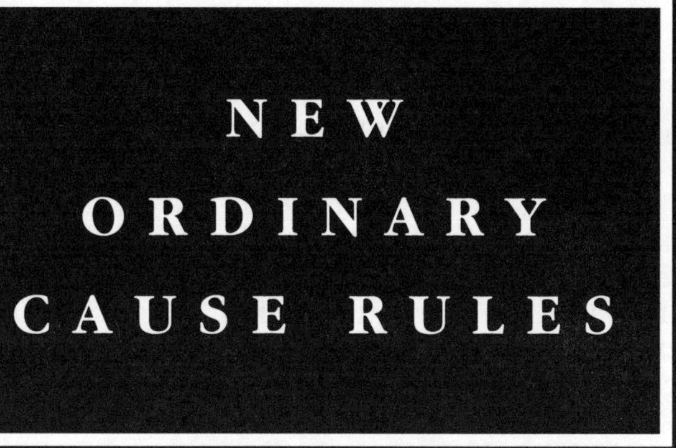

NEW ORDINARY CAUSE RULES

by

William McCulloch
BA (Hons), MSc
Sheriff Clerk, Dunfermline

and

Evelyn Laing
Secretary of the Sheriff Court Rules Council

CLT PROFESSIONAL PUBLISHING
A DIVISION OF CENTRAL LAW TRAINING LTD

Published by
CLT Professional Publishing
A Division of Central Law Training Ltd
Wrens Court
52-54 Victoria Road
Sutton Coldfield
Birmingham B72 1SX

ISBN 1 85811 027 0

Typeset by Dorchester Typesetting Group Ltd, Dorchester, Dorset
Printed in Great Britain by The Lavenham Press

Contents

List of Abbreviations

AS	Act of Sederunt
OCR	Ordinary Cause Rules[1]
RCS	Rules of the Court of Session[2]
GWD	Greens Weekly Digest
SCLR	Scottish Civil Law Reports
SLT	Scots Law Times

[1]Ordinary Cause Rules, contained in The Sheriff Courts (Scotland) Act 1907, Schedule 1, as substituted by SI 1983 No 747 and subsequently amended.

[2]Rules of the Court of Session in AS (Rules of Court) (Consolidation and Amendment) 1965 [SI No 321].

Table of Derivations

Rule no.	Derivation
Chapter 1	
1.1	New provision
1.2	
(1), (5)	New provision
(2)	OCR 72(3)
(3)	New provision
(4)	OCR 2(3)
1.3	OCR 2(1), (2)
1.4	New provision
Chapter 2	
2.1	OCR 1
Chapter 3	
3.1	OCR 3(1)–(4), 4
3.2	RCS 76
3.3	OCR 5(1), (5), (6)
3.4	OCR 6
3.5	OCR 42
3.6	OCR 7, 138(6)–(8)
Chapter 4	
4.1	RCS 68H
4.2(1), (2)	RCS 68I
(3)	New provision
Chapter 5	
5.1	OCR 8, 130(2)
5.2	OCR 9(1), 2(A), (3)–(6)
5.3	OCR 15, 138(4), (5)
5.4	OCR 10; RCS 74A(3)
5.5	OCR 12, 139
5.6	OCR 11
5.7	OCR 14
5.8	OCR 16
5.9	OCR 17
5.10	OCR 18

Rule no.	Derivation
Chapter 6	
6.1	OCR 111
6.2	OCR 112
6.3	New provision
Chapter 7	
7.1	New provision
7.2	OCR 21(1), 21A
7.3	OCR 21B
7.4	OCR 24
7.5	OCR 26
7.6	OCR 27
Chapter 8	
8.1	OCR 28
Chapter 9	
9.1	OCR 33
9.2	New provision
9.3	New provision
9.4	New provision
9.5	New provision
9.6(1)	New provision
(2)	OCR 44
9.7	OCR 45
9.8	New provision
9.9	New provision
9.10	OCR 47
9.11	New provision
9.12	New provision
9.13	OCR 151C, 188K
9.14	OCR 151D, 188L
9.15	OCR 57A

Rule no.	*Derivation*
Chapter 10	
10.1	New provision
10.2	New provision
10.3	New provision
10.4	New provision
10.5	New provision
10.6	New provision
Chapter 11	
11.1	New provision
11.2(1)	New provision
(2), (3)	OCR 38
11.3	OCR 39
11.4	OCR 40
11.5	OCR 41
11.6	New provision
11.7	New provision
11.8	New provision
Chapter 12	
12.1	RCS 93A
12.2	OCR 89
Chapter 13	
13.1	OCR 50A
13.2	New provision
Chapter 14	
14.1	New provision
14.2	New provision
14.3	New provision
Chapter 15	
15.1	New provision
15.2	New provision
15.3	New provision
15.4	New provision
Chapter 16	
16.1	New provision
16.2	OCR 59(1), (2)
16.3	OCR 59(3)

Rule no.	*Derivation*
Chapter 17	
17.1	OCR 59A(1)
17.2	OCR 59A(2)–(5)
17.3	OCR 59A(6)
Chapter 18	
18.1	OCR 48
18.2	OCR 64(1)(a)–(d)
18.3	Court of Session Practice Note, 27 March 1986
18.4	New provision
18.5	OCR 64(1)(c)
18.6	OCR 64(2)
18.7	OCR 64(3)
18.8	New provision
Chapter 19	
19.1	RCS 84(a)
19.2	OCR 53
19.3	OCR 55(1), (2)
19.4	OCR 54
Chapter 20	
20.1	OCR 50(1), (2), (4), (11)
20.2	OCR 50(1), (3)
20.3	OCR 50(7), (8)
20.4	OCR 50(5), (6)
20.5	OCR 50(4), (5)
20.6(1)	New provision
(2), (3)	OCR 50(9), (10)
Chapter 21	
21.1	New provision
21.2	New provision
21.3	OCR 68
Chapter 22	
22.1	New provision
Chapter 23	
23.1	OCR 58
23.2	OCR 55(4), (5)

Rule no.	Derivation
Chapter 24	
24.1	New provision
24.2	New provision
24.3	New provision
Chapter 25	
25.1	RCS 106
25.2	OCR 60
Chapter 26	
26.1	OCR 19
26.2	OCR 20
26.3	OCR 20A(1)
Chapter 27	
27.1	New provision
27.2	New provision
27.3	New provision
27.4	New provision
27.5	New provision
27.6	New provision
27.7	New provision
27.8	New provision
27.9	New provision
Chapter 28	
28.1	New provision
28.2	OCR 78(2), (3); RCS 95 OCR 84(1)–(3); RCS 95A OCR 84A(1)–(3)
28.3	OCR 81; RCS 96
28.4	RCS 98
28.5	New provision
28.6	New provision
28.7	New provision
28.8	OCR 82
28.9	OCR 83
28.10(1)(a)	OCR 71
(1)(b)	OCR 70
(2)–(5)	New provisions
28.11	New provision
28.12	New provisions
28.13	New provisions
28.14	CAS 1913, Chap II; RCS 102
28.15	New provision
Chapter 29	
29.1	OCR 67
29.2	OCR 69
29.3	OCR 72(2), 72A(1), (3)
29.4	OCR 65
29.5	OCR 66
29.6	RCS 108
29.7	OCR 74(1), 75; RCS 106A
29.8	RCS 106B
29.9	OCR 76
29.10	OCR 74(2), 77
29.11	OCR 79; RCS 107
29.12	New provision
29.13	RCS 107
29.14	RCS 99
29.15	OCR 73(1)
29.16	OCR 73(3)
29.17	OCR 85
29.18	OCR 73, 86; RCS 113
29.19	OCR 87
20.20	OCR 88
Chapter 30	
30.1	New provision
30.2	SR&O 1936 No 780 (Amendment to CAS); RCS 36
30.3	New provision
30.4	OCR 25, 90
30.5	New provision
30.6	Sheriff Courts (Scotland) Extracts Act 1892, ss 4 and 5; OCR 90A
30.7	New provision
30.8	New provision
30.9	OCR 13A

Rule no.	*Derivation*
Chapter 31	
31.1	OCR 91
31.2	OCR 92
31.3	OCR 93
31.4	OCR 94
31.5	New provision
31.6	OCR 95
31.7	OCR 96
Chapter 32	
32.1	OCR 97
32.2	OCR 97
32.3	OCR 98(1)–(3)
32.4	OCR 98(4), (5)
Chapter 33	
33.1	New provision
33.2	OCR 3(5), (7)
33.3	OCR 132C
33.4	New provision
33.5	OCR 132G
33.6	OCR 150, 151
33.7	OCR 11A(1)–(3), 130(1), (4)–(11)
33.8	OCR 130(2), (3)
33.9	OCR 3(9)
33.10	OCR 5(2)
33.11	OCR 9(2), (3)
33.12	New provision
33.13	OCR 11A(4), (5)
33.14	OCR 131
33.15	New provision
33.16	OCR 133
33.17	OCR 3(8)
33.18	OCR 132
33.19	OCR 3(11); RCS 170B(14)(a), (b), 260D(2), (3)
33.20	RCS 260D(6), (8)
33.21	RCS 260D(4), (6)–(8)
33.22	OCR 132F
33.23	OCR 132D
33.24	OCR 132B, E
33.25	New provision
Chapter 33—*Contd*	
33.26	OCR 34(6), 56(3)
33.27	New provision
33.28	OCR 23(1), (2), 72(1)(b)
33.29	OCR 72(1)(a)
33.30	OCR 25
33.31	OCR 22
33.32	OCR 73(4)
33.33	New provision
33.34	New provision
33.35	New provision
33.36	New provision
33.37	OCR 59
33.38	New provision
33.39	New provision
33.40	OCR 130(7)(a)
33.41	OCR 130(7)(b)
33.42	New provision
33.43	New provision
33.44	OCR 129(1), (2)(e); RCS 170B(10)
33.45	OCR 129(1), (2)(a); RCS 170B(10)
33.46	New provision
33.47	New provision
33.48	OCR 132A
33.49	New provision
33.50	New provision
33.51	OCR 129(1), (2)(f); RCS 170D(3), 7(a), (8)
33.52	OCR 132A; RCS 170D(4), (7)(c)
33.53	New provision
33.54	New provision
33.55	RCS 170M
33.56	New provision
33.57	New provision
33.58	OCR 129(1), (2)(a); RCS 170B(10)
33.59	OCR 132A(1), (2)
33.60	New provision
33.61(a), (b)	New provision
(c)	RCS 170C(2)
33.62	New provision
33.63	New provision

Rule no.	*Derivation*
Chapter 33—*Contd*	
33.64	OCR 130(7)(a)
33.65	OCR 129(1), (2)(e); RCS 170B(10)
33.66 33.68 33.69 33.70	AS (Matrimonial Homes) (Family Protection) (Scotland) Act 1981, 1982
33.71	RCS 188D(11)
33.72	AS (Matrimonial Homes) (Family Protection) (Scotland) Act 1981, 1982
33.73	OCR 135
33.74	OCR 136
33.75	OCR 137
33.76	OCR 138(1)–(3)
33.77	OCR 138(9)–(11)
33.78	OCR 140
33.79	New provision
33.80	OCR 141
33.81	OCR 142
33.82	OCR 143
33.83	New provision
33.84 33.85 33.86 33.87	AS (Variation and Recall of Orders in Consistorial Causes) 1984
33.88	OCR 150
33.89	OCR 152
33.90	OCR 153
33.91	OCR 154
Chapter 34	
34.1	OCR 99
34.2	OCR 100
34.3	OCR 101
34.4	OCR 102
34.5	OCR 103
34.6	OCR 104
34.7	OCR 105
34.8	OCR 106
34.9	OCR 107
34.10	OCR 107A
Chapter 35	
35.1	New provision
35.2	New provision
35.3	OCRS 113, 114
35.4	OCRS 116, 120
35.5	New provision
35.6	New provision
35.7	OCR 115
35.8	OCR 117
35.9	New provision
35.10	New provision
35.11	OCR 119
35.12	OCR 121
35.13	OCR 122
35.14	New provision
35.15(1), (2)	OCR 123
(3)	OCR 124
35.16	OCR 125
35.17	OCR 126
35.18	OCR 127
Chapter 36	
36.1	OCR 144
36.2	OCR 145(1)
36.3	OCR 145(2)
36.4	New provision
36.5	New provision
36.6	OCR 146(1)
36.7	OCR 146(2)
36.8	New provision
36.9	OCR 147
36.10	OCR 148
36.11	New provision
36.12	New provision
36.13	OCR 149
36.14	OCR 128(1)
36.15	New provision
36.16	New provision
36.17	OCR 128(4), (5)
36.18	AS (Proceedings under Sex Discrimination Act 1975) (No 2) 1976, para 2

Rule no.	*Derivation*
Chapter 37	
37.1	New provision
37.2	Partly based on para 2 of AS (Presumption of Death) Act 1978
37.3	New provision
37.4	New provision
37.5	New provision
37.6	New provision

Rule no.	*Derivation*
Chapter 38	
38.1	OCR 134(1)
38.2	OCR 134(2), (3)
38.3	OCR 134(4)
38.4	OCR 134(5)
38.5	OCR 134(6)

Foreword

1 January 1994 was indeed a Red Letter Day for all those involved in civil litigations in Scotland. That date saw the introduction of new Rules for the conduct of Ordinary Causes in the Sheriff Court. These Rules represented no mere tinkering with previous procedure,. but rather a radical re-think of how civil litigations should be conducted in our Courts. The Rules encourage early disclosure, discourage trial by ambush and envisage a radical pro-active role for the Sheriff with a view to him helping to ensure the efficient and expeditious disposal of ordinary civil business.

The Rules, promulgated by Act of Sederunt, were the product of a lengthy gestation involving the Sheriff Court Rules Council in widespread consultations, a drafting exercise of truly epic proportions and efforts in educating the profession as to the effect of these new Rules.

In all of this vast exercise the authors of this book were intimately involved in their capacity as successive Secretaries to the Rules Council. They brought to that task their significant experience and expertise gained through many years of experience in the Scottish Court Service.

The success of the new system depends upon the proper operation of the Rules whether by Sheriffs, Practitioners or Sheriff Clerks. All participants in the civil process as well as students will benefit from this lucid and comprehensive guide to the application of the new procedures set out in such an accessible and practical manner.

"Education" said Ambrose Bierce is "that which discloses to the wise and disguises from the foolish their lack of understanding." This book is truly an education to the wise and foolish alike.

Hugh Neilson, LLB (Hons), NP
Solicitor

Preface

The Act of Sederunt (Sheriff Court Ordinary Cause Rules) 1993 (referred to hereafter as 'the Rules') brought into force on 1 January 1994 important changes in the procedures regulating the conduct of proceedings in ordinary actions in the Sheriff Court. Written 18 months after the introduction of these new procedures, the book provides a practical guide to the new Rules. In looking at the more fundamental changes, particularly those which apply to defended actions, the background and policy issues, which prompted what is effectively a new approach to the control and management of contested actions, are examined. The book also identifies issues that have arisen in the first year, including points raised in reported cases.

This book does not set out to be a treatise on the law relating to ordinary cause litigation. It is a procedural guide which attempts to provide practical guidance on the application of the new procedures, and various checklists are provided throughout the text. While assuming a working knowledge of the practices and procedures of the civil courts, the book is intended to assist all who have an interest or are involved in this area, whether they are experienced court practitioners or clerks of court, or are about to embark on a traineeship or study law.

We are indebted to Mr H Neilson, Solicitor, Mrs M Liddell, Solicitor and Mr S Walker, Deputy Clerk of Session, who read drafts of the text at short notice and provided valuable comments. We, of course, are responsible for any errors in the text.

E Laing
W McCulloch
June 1995

Publisher's note: The Sheriff Court Ordinary Cause Rules 1993 are reproduced by kind permission of Her Majesty's Stationery Office.

CHAPTER 1

Introduction to the Rules

Chapters 1 and 2 of the Rules

1.1 This chapter considers the policy objectives relating to the overall structure of the Rules and the provisions in Chapters 1 and 2 of the Rules, including the important *dispensing power* in rule 2.1 (see para 1.6 below).

Structure of the Rules

1.2 The Rules are ordered in 38 separate chapters and are numbered to enable future amendments to be made without disturbing their logical sequence. Within each chapter procedures relating to specific stages in proceedings and to certain types of action are brought together in a coherent and logical fashion. While many of the rules are restatements of procedures which existed prior to the introduction of the new Rules, most of the provisions have been redrafted to provide greater clarity. There are also a number of new and radical procedures, especially those which regulate the conduct of defended actions covering the period from the lodging of a notice of intention to defend to the fixing of a proof or other hearing. In redrafting the Rules considerable advances have been made in terms of harmonising the procedures of the Court of Session and the Sheriff Court, and there are now significant areas of procedure where the Rules applicable to both courts are either identical or in similar form.

The basic structure of the Rules is that Chapters 1–32 and 38, which generally regulate the procedures from raising of an action until disposal, apply to all ordinary actions except where in a particular rule it is stated that the rule does not apply to a particular type of action. For example, a number of provisions do not apply to family actions or actions of multiplepoinding. The rules contained in Chapters 33–37, however, reflect differences in procedure that are specific to the type of action, as follows.

- Family actions (Chapter 33)
- Actions relating to heritable property (Chapter 34)
- Actions of multiplepoinding (Chapter 35)
- Actions of damages (Chapter 36)
- Causes under the Presumption of Death (Scotland) Act 1977 (Chapter 37).

These procedural differences are in some cases substantial, particularly in relation to actions of multiplepoinding where there is a different timetable. Chapter 33 (family actions) provides a code of procedures extending to some 91 rules, many of which have been introduced to meet the procedural requirements of family law. The rules in Chapters 33–37 do not, however, stand alone, but require to be applied alongside the general rules except where it is specified that a particular rule does not apply.

Prescribed forms

1.3 The prescribed forms which are referred to in various rules are found in Appendices 1 and 2 of the Rules. Each form is separately numbered and prefixed by a letter according to the particular type of action or proceedings in which it is to be used. The categories of prescribed forms are as follows:

Appendix 1: G—General form applicable to all types of action
F—Family actions
H—Actions relating to heritable property
M—Actions of multiplepoinding
D—Actions of damages
P—Causes under the Presumption of Death (Scotland) Act 1977
O—Forms applicable to ordinary actions except where an alternative form is provided for in any of the above types of action.
E—Request to European Court

Appendix 2: Forms for Extract Decrees.

The prescribed forms must be used in the terms in which they appear in the Appendix to the Rules, except where the circumstances dictate the need for a variation in a particular form in which case the form may be used "with such variations as circumstances may require"[1]. For example, forms of extract decree may require to be modified or combined to reflect the terms of the court's decree.

Interpretation

1.4 Rule 1.2 defines various terms used in the Rules, ie "document", "period of notice" and "affidavit"[2]. In addition it provides that where a rule states that intimation is to be given to a party, intimation may be sent to the

[1] r 1.4

[2] r 1.2(1), (2)

solicitor for that party[3]. Generally throughout the rules reference to a "party" can be taken to be a reference to the solicitor for the party, unless the context otherwise requires[4].

Representation

1.5 A party to an action may be represented by a solicitor or advocate. However, rule 1.3 makes provision for a party being represented by someone other than a solicitor or advocate in proceedings relating to an application for a time to pay direction under the Debtors (Scotland) Act 1987[5]. The representative may be a friend or relative or a volunteer from a Citizen's Advice Bureau. A representative, sometimes referred to as a lay representative, may appear in these proceedings provided the sheriff is satisfied as to the suitability of the person and that the lay representative is authorised to appear on behalf of the party[6]. This relaxation of the general rules relating to representation does not extend to an appeal to the sheriff principal in respect of proceedings under the 1987 Act[7].

Relief from compliance with the Rules

1.6 Rule 2.1 provides the sheriff with the power, often referred to as the sheriff's dispensing power, to relieve a party who has failed to comply with any of the provisions of the Rules from the consequences of such a failure where it is shown that this was due to "a mistake, oversight or other excusable cause"[8].

The consequences of a failure to comply with the rules can be serious, *i.e.* decree by default may be granted. Moreover, it would appear that the court is not likely to exercise the dispensing power lightly, particularly where there has been a failure to comply with the time limits provided in the Rules. This approach is evident particularly in decisions made in relation to the late lodging of the certified copy record for an Options Hearing (for further discussion of which see Chap 4 to this book). Since the introduction of this provision a number of decisions have been reported, following appeal, which indicate that sheriffs principal, and the Court of Session, are taking a strong line in relation to such defaults and the exercise of the dispensing power. In an appeal against a sheriff's decision to dismiss an action as a consequence of the pursuer's failure to

[3] r 1.2(3)
[4] r 1.2(4)
[5] see para 3.8 for further discussion on procedure relating to time to pay applications
[6] r 1.3(1)
[7] r 1.3(2)
[8] r 2.1(1)

lodge a record timeously, due to an administrative error in the office of the pursuer's solicitor, the Court of Session held that there were no compelling reasons in the interests of justice for granting relief and that the sheriff was entitled to dismiss the action. It was, however, observed that a sheriff would be entitled grant relief under rule 2.1 where "the failure was due to something for which the pursuer or his solicitor could not reasonably be held responsible or a serious injustice would result from dismissing the action"[9].

In another case,where an appeal by a defender against the decision of the sheriff not to allow him to lodge defences late was refused, it was observed that: "there comes a time when the interests of justice require that the rules be applied firmly. There is undoubtedly an attitude abroad that mistakes in operating the rules of court do not matter and can be rectified automatically on payment of an appropriate amount of expenses. This is not so and from time to time agents require to be reminded of that."[10]

[9] *DTZ Debenham Thorpe* v *I Henderson Transport Services*, 1st Division, 27 January 1995 (I.H.) 1995 SCLR, 345. See also *Welsh* v *Thornehome Services* (Sh Ct) 1994 SCLR 1021; *Mahoney* v *Officer* (Sh Ct) 1994 SCLR 1059; and *Morran* v *Glasgow District Council of Tenants' Associations* (Sh Ct) 1994 SCLR 1065

[10] 1994 SCLR, Quotations, 5 April 1994.

CHAPTER 2

Commencement of Proceedings

Chapters 3–6 of the Rules

Introduction

2.1 Chapters 3–6 of the Rules regulate the procedure for commencing proceedings by ordinary cause. These rules are in the main derived from rules which were in force prior to the 1993 Act of Sederunt, but they do contain some new procedures and innovative reforms. For example, there are new rules prescribing the form in which initial writs must be presented and regulating, for the first time, caveat procedure. These rules are examined in this chapter, as are the rules for service, citation and intimation.

Initial writs

Form of initial writ

2.2 An initial writ must be presented on "A4 paper of durable quality and shall not be backed or folded"[1]. On first reading, it may appear somewhat odd that the type of paper to be used and whether writs should be backed or folded should be prescribed. This, however, is one of a number of rules which implement the recommendations of a committee (established by the Scottish Courts Administration) which concluded that the old style of process, with backings and folded parts of process held together by tape or elastic bands, should be replaced with a modern flat file process.[2]

Additional averments

2.3 In addition to including averments in the initial writ relating to the subject matter of the action, the Rules impose certain requirements for special averments to be included in initial writs. Rule 3.1 contains two new provisions: one which makes provision in relation to averments about the ground of jurisdiction and the other about averments where the defender's address or whereabouts is not known.

[1] r 3.1(2)
[2] Scottish Courts Administration, *Report on Civil Court Processes*, 1991; see also para 4.6 and Chap 5 of this book for further provisions relating to the process folder.

Ground of jurisdiction The pursuer must not only specify the ground of jurisdiction but must also include the facts upon which the averment as to the ground of jurisdiction is based[3]. Thus where the ground of jurisdiction is the defender's domicile, averments must be inserted which establish that the defender is domiciled in the Sheriff Court district where the action is to be raised.

Defender's whereabouts unknown In this instance the pursuer must, in addition to making a statement to this effect in the initial writ, include averments detailing the steps taken in an attempt to trace the defender[4] (*i.e.* details of enquiries made by a sheriff officer).

Other special averments There are other special averments which must be included in an initial writ, such as those required where the pursuer seeks warrant to arrest to found jurisdiction or relating to matters such as an agreement to prorogate jurisdiction or about any related proceedings pending before another court. These and the other averments referred to above are as follows:

- *Rule 3.1(3)* Details of any agreement prorogating jurisdiction to another court.
- *Rule 3.1(4)* Details of any proceedings pending before another court involving the same parties and the same cause of action.
- *Rule 3.1(5)* The ground of jurisdiction and facts upon which it is based.
- *Rule 3.1(6)* Steps taken to ascertain the whereabouts of a defender whose address is not known.
- *Rule 3.4(2)* Where warrant is sought to found jurisdiction, averments justifying warrant.

Actions relating to heritable property

2.4 In actions relating to heritable property the holder of a security over the property (*e.g.* a bank or building society) may have an interest in the action. Rule 3.2 provides that, where the action relates to a heritable right or title over the property, the holder of a security need not be called as a defender but must receive intimation of the action. To this extent the new rule brings Sheriff Court procedure into line with that in the Court of Session. The Sheriff Court rule, however, further stipulates that in other actions relating to heritable property, where the holder of a security over the property might not have a direct interest, intimation need only be given if the sheriff considers it appropriate.

[3] r 3.1(5)

[4] r 3.1(6)

Intimation to heritable creditor Rule 3.2 does not provide a procedural mechanism either for applying for a warrant to intimate to a heritable creditor or for dispensing with intimation. It is suggested that in the absence of such a provision the procedure which applies in other types of action (*e.g.* in family actions) where intimation is to be given to a person who is not a party to the action might be adopted. This would involve the pursuer including an appropriate crave in the initial writ.

Application by heritable creditor to appear A heritable creditor who, on receipt of intimation under this rule, wishes to respond to the initial writ may apply by minute to appear in the proceedings (see Chap 6 of this book).

Citation and intimation

Warrant to cite defender

2.5 When an initial writ is lodged in court the sheriff clerk checks that it is *ex facie* competent and the court has jurisdiction. If so satisfied, a warrant to cite[5] the defender is prepared and signed by the sheriff clerk, except in the circumstances detailed in para 2.6. The warrant is attached to the initial writ and they are returned to the pursuer for service. Depending on the type of action, one of the following prescribed forms of warrant is issued by the sheriff clerk.

- F1—family actions
- M1—actions of multiplepoinding
- O1—all other actions
- O2—actions where the defender may apply for a time to pay direction under section 1(1) of the Debtors (Scotland) Act 1987.[6]

Signature of warrant to cite

2.6 Warrants to cite are normally signed by a sheriff clerk except in the following circumstances when the warrant is signed by a sheriff[7]:

- Where a shortened or extended period of notice is sought
- Where a warrant to arrest on the dependence is sought in a family action in respect of a claim for aliment or financial provision
- Where a warrant to intimate is sought on a person in a family action against whom allegations of an improper association are made or
- Where an order which may only be granted by a sheriff is sought, for example an order for interim interdict

[5] r 3.3

[6] s 1(1) of the 1987 Act provides that an individual debtor may apply to pay the sum claimed by instalments or by a lump sum where this does not exceed £10,000 (exclusive of interest and expenses)

[7] r 5.1

A sheriff might also be called on to sign a warrant where a sheriff clerk is not satisfied that a warrant should be granted where the view is taken that the court does not have jurisdiction[8]. In these circumstances the case is referred to a sheriff. If the sheriff is satisfied, after consideration or having heard the pursuer's solicitor, that a warrant should be granted he will sign the warrant. If not so satisfied the sheriff may refuse to issue a warrant to cite.

Period of notice

2.7 The period of notice given to a defender following service of an initial writ is specified in the warrant to cite. The period to be fixed depends on where the defender is resident or has a place of business. If the defender is within Europe the period is 21 days; if outwith Europe the period is 42 days. The sheriff has power to reduce the period of notice on application made by the solicitor for the pursuer, but not to less than two days[9]. An application to reduce the period of notice is usually considered by the sheriff in chambers.

Documents to be served on defender

2.8 The defender must be sent a copy of the initial writ and warrant of citation together with forms of citation and notice of intention to defend (Forms O4, O7). The citation advises the defender of the procedure for lodging a notice of intention to defend and the time within which it must be lodged. The solicitor for the pursuer must complete Part A of the notice of intention to defend which provides details of the case and, in particular, the dates of expiry of the period of notice and service. This not only alerts the defender to the time limit for lodging a notice of intention to defend but enables the sheriff clerk to check whether the notice, when lodged, is timeous.

Time to pay application form

2.9 In an action where it is competent for a defender to make an application for a time to pay direction a form of application (Form O3) is served on the defender along with notice of citation and intention to defend (Forms O5, O7). The application form provides the defender with information about how to apply for a time to pay direction should the defender admit the claim and wish to pay the sum due by instalments or in a lump sum.

Forms to be served on defender with the copy initial writ and warrant

Ordinary actions:

Form O4—Citation
Form O7—Notice of intention to defend

[8] r 5.1(3)

[9] r 3.6(3)

Ordinary action in which the defender may apply for a time to pay direction:

Form O3—Application for time to pay direction
Form O5—Citation
Form O7—Notice of intention to defend

Certificate of citation

2.10 Following service, a certificate of citation (Form O6) is completed certifying that service has been effected and providing details of the method of service and any forms of notice or intimation served with the initial writ. The certificate is signed by the solicitor or sheriff officer who effected service.

Methods of service

2.11 In the following paragraphs reference is made to service of an initial writ. The rules relating to service, however, apply also to the service or intimation of other documents, including service of a charge following decree and intimation of a motion. In considering the various methods of service, it is useful to examine these under the following four headings:

- Postal service
- Service by sheriff officer
- Service on a person outwith Scotland
- Service on a person whose address is not known

Postal service

2.12 Postal service is the most commonly used method of service. It may be used by either a solicitor or a sheriff officer against defenders who are resident or have a place of business in Scotland, and also on defenders outwith Scotland; provided that postal service is a competent method of service both in terms of the Rules and in the country where the citation is to be sent. A citation served by post on a defender at an address in Scotland may be sent by either first class recorded delivery or registered post. However, where the defender is outwith Scotland the Rules provide for service by post to be made only by registered post[10].

Commencement of period of notice When using postal service it must be borne in mind that the period of notice runs not from the date of posting but from "the beginning of the day after the date of posting"[11]. The

[10] see para 2.14 for further discussion about service on defenders outwith Scotland.

[11] r 5.3(2)

pursuer's solicitor must take this into account when calculating the date of expiry of the period of notice outlined in para 2.7 above.

Notice on envelope The envelope in which the copy initial writ and other forms are sent must have on the outside a notice to the effect that it contains a citation which must be returned to the court immediately if it cannot be delivered[12].

Translations If the letter is to be posted to a defender abroad the notice on the envelope must be translated into the official language of the country, unless that is English[13]. Moreover, all the documents to be sent in the envelope must be translated on the same basis[14]. Where a translation is necessary, a certificate must be obtained from the person making the translation certifying that it is correct and also providing details of the translator's name, address and qualifications[15]. This certificate must be lodged in process after service.

There is no provision in the Rules to enable a translation to be dispensed with, for example in a case where the defender is a UK national living in a country where the official language is not English. This would appear to be an unnecessary expense, and it may be that in these circumstances a motion to dispense with a translation should be considered.

Service by sheriff officer

2.13 A sheriff officer may serve an initial writ anywhere in Scotland without the warrant being endorsed by the sheriff clerk[16]. Service may be effected in the following ways:

- Personally
- By leaving it with a resident at the defender's residence or with an employee at his place of business
- By depositing it in the defender's residence or place of business, or
- By affixing it to the door of the defender's residence or place of business[17]

Certain conditions attach to these methods of service[18]. First, where service is effected by leaving, details of the person with whom the initial writ is left must be included in the certificate of citation. Secondly, depositing or affixing may only be used where attempts to serve personally or by leaving have not been successful. Moreover, where depositing or affixing is the method used the sheriff officer must also send the defender a letter containing the copy initial writ and other forms by ordinary post to the address at which he thinks the defender is most likely to be found.

[12] r 5.3(3)
[13] r 5.5(6)
[14] r 5.5(6)
[15] r 5.5(7)
[16] r 5.8
[17] r 5.4(1), (3)
[18] r 5.4(2)–(4)

Service on defenders outwith Scotland

2.14 The method of service which may be employed where a defender is outwith Scotland depends on:

- The provisions in the ordinary cause rules
- The law of the country in which service is to be executed
- Whether the country is a "convention" country
- Whether the country has a bilateral convention on service of writs with the United Kingdom

The conventions mentioned above are the Hague, Brussels and Lugano conventions; see the Appendix to this chapter for a list of convention countries and of countries with which the UK has a bilateral convention on service of writs.

Further guidance on service abroad Guidance on service in particular countries is available from the Scottish Courts Administration, Hayweight House, 23 Lauriston Street, Edinburgh EH3 9DQ and from the Foreign and Commonwealth Office, Nationality and Treaty Department, Clive House, Petty France, London SW1H 9HD. The Scottish Courts Administration also publishes a booklet, *Service of Documents Abroad—Guidance on Procedures in the Court of Session and Sheriff Court,* which may be obtained on request. In many instances it will be necessary to contact these authorities directly to ascertain the methods of service available in the country in which service is to be executed. Accordingly, in the following paragraphs, it is only possible to provide guidance on the procedural matters that need to be considered.

Defender in another part of the UK, the Isle of Man or the Channel Islands Service may be made either by post or by personal service[19]. Where service is by post, registered mail may be used but not (according to the Rules) recorded delivery letter. Personal service must be in accordance with the domestic law of the country concerned; it is necessary to check what rules are applicable in the place where service is to be executed and make arrangements for service to be carried out by a process server.

Defender in a country with which the UK does not have a convention Service can be made either by post or in accordance with the rules for personal service in that country[20]. As mentioned in the previous paragraph service by post must be by registered mail. If personal service is to be used arrangements must be made with the relevant officials or authorities to effect service in terms of the laws of the country in question. After service, a certificate, by a person who is conversant with the law of the country and who practises, or has practised, law or is an accredited representative of the

[19] r 5.5(1)(a)

[20] r 5.5(1)(a)

government of the country, must be lodged with the initial writ stating (a) the method of service used, and (b) that service has been effected in accordance with the law of that country[21].

Defender in Hague, Brussels or Lugano convention country There are a number of methods of service[22] available in an action in which the defender resides or has a place of business in a convention country. These are:

- Any method prescribed by that country
- By or through a central authority (eg Ministry of Justice) at the request of the Foreign Office
- By or through a British Consular Office at the request of the Foreign Office
- Where the country permits it, by posting in Scotland to the defender's residence
- Where the country permits it, by a *huissier* (sheriff officer equivalent) or other judicial officer or official.

If service is to be made by or through a central authority or British Consular Office a copy initial writ and warrant to cite, together with other relevant forms, must be sent to the Foreign Office with a request for service to be made in the relevant country[23]. Further information and a style of "request" can be found in the Scottish Courts Administration booklet, referred to above. A certificate by the appropriate authority which executed service must be lodged with the initial writ when it is returned to court after service certifying (a) that service has been effected and (b) the method of service[24]. A certificate[25] is also required when the method of service used is one which is prescribed by the country's internal law. This certificate must be provided by someone who practises, or has practised, law and is conversant with the law of the country or is a government official. The certificate must confirm that the method of service used is acceptable in that country.

The arrangments referred to in the preceding paragraph, in relation to a request for service and certification of the method used, also apply where service is to be made by a *huissier* or other such officer or official[26].

Defender in country with which the UK has a bilateral convention Service may be by any method approved in the particular convention[27]. Information about the approved methods may be obtained from the Scottish Courts Administration or Foreign and Commonwealth Office.

Translations The requirements relating to the translation of documents and notices detailed in para 2.12 apply where service is to be effected in any country where the official language is not English[28].

[21] r 5.5(5)
[22] r 5.5(1)(b)
[23] r 5.5(3)(a)
[24] r 5.5(3)(b)
[25] r 5.5(5)
[26] r 5.5(4)
[27] r 5.5(1)(c)
[28] r 5.5(6) and (7)

Service on person whose address is not known

2.15 If the defender's address or whereabouts is not known, service may be effected either by newspaper advertisement or by displaying a notice on the walls of the Sheriff Court. (In family actions there are additional requirements where a defender's address is not known and these are explained in Chap 13 of this book.) Application for warrant to serve by either advertisement or on the walls of court may be made when seeking a warrant to cite and is normally considered by the sheriff in chambers. If warrant is granted the period of notice starts to run from the date of publication of the newspaper advertisement or display on the walls of court[29].

Newspaper advertisement Warrant for service by newspaper advertisement is usually granted by the sheriff without enquiry, provided there are appropriate averments in the initial writ relating to the steps taken to ascertain the defender's whereabouts. Advertisement is made in a newspaper circulating in the area where the defender was last known to reside, and the form of advertisement is prescribed in the Rules[30]. A copy initial writ and relevant forms of citation and notices must be supplied to the sheriff clerk for issue to the defender should he respond to the newspaper advertisement. After service by advertisement, the pursuer must lodge in court a full copy of the newspaper[31]. An extract or copy of the advertisement is not sufficient.

Intimation on the walls of court Warrant to cite by notice on the walls of court is not normally granted unless the sheriff is satisfied that there are good reasons why advertisement should not be ordered. If the application is granted, the Rules provide that the pursuer's solicitor must prepare a notice in the prescribed form[32] and supply this to the sheriff clerk together with a certified copy of the instance of the initial writ, the crave and warrant of citation. These documents are displayed by the sheriff clerk on a notice board in a public area within the Sheriff Court house. In addition, the pursuer's solicitor also provides the sheriff clerk with a full copy of the initial writ and other relevant forms for uplift by the defender.

Defender's address subsequently becomes known If, after service under this rule, the defender's address subsequently becomes known, the pursuer's solicitor must lodge a motion to amend the initial writ and obtain warrant to re-serve the action or have it transferred to another court where the defender's address is outwith the court's jurisdiction[33].

[29] r 5.6(1)
[30] Form G3
[31] r 5.6(4)
[32] Form G4
[33] r 5.6(3)

Other matters affecting service

Person carrying on business under a trading or descriptive name

2.16 A defender carrying on business under a trading or descriptive name may sue or be sued in that name alone[34]. Where service is to be effected on such a defender it may be made at any place or office at which the business is being carried out if within the sheriffdom of the Sheriff Court where the action is raised. If the defender does not have a place of business within the sheriffdom, service may be made at any place where the defender is carrying on business.[35]

Re-service and objections to service

2.17 The sheriff has power to order re-service where there has been a "failure or irregularity" in service[36], although in practice this power is rarely invoked. Where service has failed (*e.g.* recorded delivery letter is returned by the post office) or where the sheriff clerk identifies some irregularity (*e.g.* service made at incorrect address) the solicitor for the pursuer will be advised and will arrange for re-service to be effected without a formal court order (see para 3.11 – amendment of initial writ).

Entering appearance in an action, usually by lodging a notice of intention to defend, cures any defect in service. Accordingly, a person who appears in an action cannot then state an objection to the regularity of service. This, of course, does not preclude a plea of no jurisdiction being stated by the defender.[37]

Arrestment

2.18 *Service of schedule of arrestment* Chapter 6 of the Rules contains a number of provisions relating to service of arrestments. In particular, it is provided that where an arrestee does not receive an arrestment by personal service it will only be effective if a copy of the schedule of arrestment is also sent to the arrestee by registered or recorded delivery letter[38].

Arrestment on the dependence before service An arrestment on the dependence made prior to service of the initial writ ceases to have effect if the initial writ is not served within 20 days of the date of the arrestment[39]. In an undefended case, an arrestment ceases to have effect if decree in absence is not granted within 20 days after the expiry of the period of notice following citation[40].

A report of the execution of an arrestment on the dependence used

[34] r 5.7(1)
[35] r 5.7(2)
[36] r 5.9
[37] r 5.10
[38] r 6.1
[39] r 6.2(1)(a)
[40] r 6.2(1)(b)

before service must be lodged with the sheriff clerk forthwith after execution[41].

Movement of arrested property Rule 6.3 is a new provision introduced to harmonise Sheriff Court and Court of Session procedures. It provides for an application to be made by motion by any party having an interest in the movement of a vessel or cargo which has been arrested either to found jurisdiction or on the dependence. This procedure might be used where a third party is experiencing difficulty because the arrested vessel is causing an obstruction.

Interim interdicts, interim orders and caveats

Application of Rules on caveats

2.19 The procedure for obtaining interim interdict, either before or after service, is not regulated by the Rules. However, caveat procedure, which was formerly a matter of practice, is now prescribed[42]. The procedure discussed here applies to applications for interim interdict and other interim orders. These rules, however, apply only to proceedings which are regulated by the Ordinary Cause Rules and not to summary applications or other civil proceedings[43].

Application for interim interdict or interim order

2.20 *No caveat lodged* An application for interim interdict or an interim order made before service of the initial writ is heard by the sheriff in chambers. The sheriff, having heard the solicitor for the pursuer either grants or refuses the application and issues a warrant to cite the defender. A date for a further hearing will usually be fixed to take place after service of the initial writ, in practice 7–10 days after the first hearing. The second hearing is also held in chambers, with solicitors for parties appearing at the hearing having the opportunity to address the sheriff.

Caveat lodged The purpose of a caveat is to obtain notice of any application for interim interdict or an interim order made before service of the initial writ. The Rules provide that a caveat is effective against an application for interim interdict sought at any time before the defender lodges a notice of intention to defend[44] and against an interim order if sought before the expiry of the period of notice for lodging a notice of

41 r 6.2(2)
42 r 4.1, 4.2
43 Caveat procedure in relation to summary applications is prescribed in the Act of Sederunt (Sheriff Court Summary Application Rules) 1993.
44 r 4.1(a)

intention to defend[45]. If the defender lodges a notice of intention to defend the caveat effectively becomes redundant, as in a defended action the defender will receive notification of any application for interim interdict or an interim order by written motion.

Form of caveat

2.21 The form of caveat (prescribed in Form G2) must include details of the application to which the caveat is to apply[46] and also the telephone and fax numbers of the solicitor for the caveator (including out of hours numbers) to enable the sheriff clerk to make contact when an application for interim interdict or an interim order is made. If the sheriff clerk is unable to contact the caveator or his solicitor the sheriff may grant the application provided he is satisfied that all reasonable steps have been taken to contact and give the caveator or his solicitor an opportunity of being heard. The sheriff may, however, continue the hearing to enable further attempts to be made to contact the solicitor or caveator[47].

Duration of caveat

2.22 A caveat remains in force for one year but may be renewed, on payment of the relevant court fee, for a further period of one year and yearly thereafter[48].

[45] r 4.1(b)
[46] See Stewart Alexander Nicolson and another (Notes) 1995 SCLR, 389.
[47] r 4.2(3)
[48] r 4.2(2)

APPENDIX 2.1

Conventions on Service Abroad

1 Hague Convention on the Service Abroad of Judicial and Extrajudicial documents in Civil or Commercial Matters (Cmnd. 3986 (1969))

Antigua and Barbuda
Barbados
Belgium
Botswana
Canada
China
Cyprus
Czech Republic
Denmark
Egypt
Finland
France
Germany
Greece
Israel
Italy
Japan
Luxembourg
Netherlands (and Aruba)
Norway
Pakistan
Portugal
Spain
Slovak Republic
Seychelles
Sweden
Turkey
USA (and dependent territories)*
UK (and dependent territories)**

*USA dependent territories: Guam, Puerto Rico and the US Virgin Islands.

**UK dependent territories: Anguilla, Bermuda, Cayman Islands, Falkland Islands, Gibraltar, Guernsey, Hong Kong, Isle of Man, Jersey, Montserrat, Pitcairn, Saint Helena and dependencies, South Georgia and the South Sandwich Islands, Turks and Caicos Islands and the British Virgin Islands.

2 Brussels Convention (Art IV of the Annexed Protocol to the 1968 Brussels Convention which is inserted in Schedule 1 to the Civil Jurisdiction and Judgments Act 1982)

Belgium
Denmark
France
Germany
Greece
Ireland
Italy
Luxembourg
Netherlands
Portugal
Spain
UK

3 Lugano Convention (Art IV of Protocol No 1 to the Lugano Convention which is inserted in Schedule 3C to the Civil Jurisdiction and Judgments Act 1982)

Finland
France
Italy
Luxembourg
Netherlands
Norway
Portugal
Sweden
Switzerland
UK

4 Countries with which the UK has bilateral conventions

Austria
Belgium
Czech and Slovak Republics
Denmark
Finland
France
Germany
Greece
Iraq
Israel
Italy
Laos
Lebanon
Netherlands
Norway
Poland
Portugal
Romania
Spain
Sweden
Syria
Turkey
Yugoslavia
Hungary

CHAPTER 3

Undefended Causes

Chapters 7 and 8 of the Rules

Introduction

3.1 In Chapter 7 provision is made for (a) obtaining decree in absence in those types of action where decree may be granted without evidence and (b) amendment of the initial writ in undefended cases. Chapter 8 regulates the procedure for reponing (recall) of decrees granted in absence.

Decrees in absence

3.2 This part of the chapter focuses on the basic procedure which applies to the vast majority of actions in which decree in absence may be obtained. The procedure is relatively straightforward, and decree in absence may be applied for, without any attendance at court, by the pursuer's solicitor completing a simple minute for decree and submitting this to the court along with the initial writ after service on the defender.

Application of procedure for obtaining decree in absence

3.3 The rules in Chapter 7 apply to all ordinary actions in which decree in absence may be granted without evidence. This, therefore, excludes actions raised under the Presumption of Death (Scotland) Act 1977 and most family actions.[1] Decree in absence procedure also applies to actions such as division and sale and sequestration for rent. However, in these actions some further procedure will be necessary before final decree is granted; for example in an action of division and sale before finally disposing of the craves in the initial writ the sheriff is likely to remit to a surveyor to report of the feasibility of division of the property.

The procedure in actions where it is competent for the defender to apply for a time to pay direction under section 1(1) of the Debtors (Scotland) Act 1987 also differs from the basic procedure outlined in para 3.2 above, and is considered separately in para 3.9.

[1] r 7.1; see also r 33.28–r 33.31 (procedure in undefended family actions) and Chap 13 of this book.

Conditions to be met before applying for decree in absence

3.4 Before the solicitor for the pursuer can apply for decree in absence, service of the initial writ must have been successfully effected and the period of notice following service must have expired without the defender lodging a notice of intention to defend. The solicitor for the pursuer can find out whether the defender has lodged a notice of intention to defend by contacting the sheriff clerk's office after the expiry of the period of notice.

Minute for decree

3.5 If the conditions mentioned above have been met, the solicitor for the pursuer may apply for decree in absence by completing the minute for decree which is included in some of the standard pro-forma warrants to cite issued by the sheriff clerk's office. Alternatively the pursuer's solicitor may prepare and lodge a separate form of minute in similar terms to the pro-forma.

In the minute for decree the pursuer's solicitor should request that decree be granted as craved or in a restricted form (*e.g.* decree for a reduced sum) and seek expenses. The expenses sought by the pursuer will in most cases be the inclusive fee and outlays[2]. The pursuer may, however, seek expenses as taxed by the auditor of court. When completed, the minute is attached to the initial writ and returned to the court with the execution of service. Thereafter, the sheriff clerk checks that no notice of intention to defend has been lodged, completes a certificate to that effect, and prepares an interlocutor, which is submitted to the sheriff for consideration along with the initial writ.

Granting of decree in absence and issue of extract decree

3.6 Decree in absence may be granted by the sheriff without requiring the attendance in court of the pursuer's solicitor[3]. Before granting a decree the sheriff must be satisfied on the following matters: first, that *ex facie* there is a ground of jurisdiction; and secondly, that the action is one to which the "undefended cause" procedure applies (*i.e.* it is not a case that requires evidence before decree in absence may be granted or a case to which rule 33.31 (undefended family action for parental rights) applies)[4]. The sheriff also must be satisfied that any conditions relating to service, for example in another part of the United Kingdom or in a convention country, have been met[5]. If satisfied with regard to these matters the sheriff may grant decree in absence, including expenses, against the defender[6]. Following the

[2] Act of Sederunt (Fees of Solicitors in the Sheriff Court) (Amendment and Further Provisions) 1993
[3] r 7.2(1)
[4] r 7.2(2)
[5] r 7.2(3), (4)
[6] r 7.4

granting of a decree in absence an extract decree may be issued by the sheriff clerk to the pursuer's solicitor after the expiry of 14 days from the date of decree[7].

Procedure in action for payment of solicitor's fees

3.7 If the action is one in which the pursuer is a solicitor suing for professional fees the sheriff should remit the case to the auditor of court for taxation, and decree may not be granted until the pursuer's account has been taxed[8].

Application for time to pay direction

3.8 *Making application* If an action is for payment of a sum of money not exceeding £10,000 (exclusive of interest and expenses) the defender may (if he or she is a private individual) admit the claim and apply to the court to grant a time to pay direction. If granted the defender is permitted to pay the sum due by instalments or in a lump sum within a specified period. Application is made by lodging Form O3 (which is served on the defender along with the initial writ) with the sheriff clerk before the expiry of the period of notice[9]. The Rules do not require the defender to inform the pursuer that an application has been made and lodged. In practice, the pursuer finds out about the application by contacting the sheriff clerk after the expiry of the period of notice, at the same time as checking whether a notice of intention to defend has been lodged.

Pursuer not objecting to application If the pursuer does not object to the defender's application, the pursuer's solicitor should in the minute for decree intimate that the pursuer does not object to the application. The procedure for obtaining decree in absence applies thereafter. If the sheriff decides to make a time to pay direction in terms of the defender's application and the pursuer's minute for decree this will be incorporated into the interlocutor granting decree[10].

Pursuer objecting to application If the pursuer objects to a defender's application for a time to pay direction, the solicitor for the pursuer may intimate the objection in the minute for decree. On receipt of the initial writ and objection, the sheriff clerk fixes a hearing and intimates this by sending a letter to each of the parties.[11] At the hearing the application is determined by the sheriff, after hearing parties or their representatives (see para 1.5 re "lay representation"), and decree granted including a time to

[7] r 30.4(1)

[8] The procedure for taxation of a solicitor's account for professional fees is regulated by the Act of Sederunt (Solicitor and Client Accounts in the Sheriff Court) 1992.

[9] r 7.3(2)

[10] r 7.3(3)

[11] r 7.3(4)

pay direction if the sheriff considers this to be appropriate. The sheriff may determine the application and grant decree whether or not any party appears[12].

Finality of decree in absence

3.9 A decree in absence becomes final[13] and has the same effect as a decree in a defended action on the expiry of six months from the date of decree, or the date of service of a charge following decree, provided there has been personal service of the initial writ or charge[14]. In any other case decree in absence becomes final after 20 years from the date of decree[15].

Amendment of initial writ

3.10 An initial writ in an undefended case may be amended in any way permitted in rule 18.2 (see Chap 8 of this book). The procedure outlined in Chapter 18 of the Rules, however, applies only in defended actions. There is no procedure prescribed in Chapter 7. Accordingly, in undefended actions the procedure for amending initial writs is a matter for the sheriff's discretion and will depend on the nature and extent of the amendment sought. Where the amendment is extensive, radically alters the action or introduces new parties, a minute of amendment will be necessary. Where such an amendment is allowed re-service of the initial writ will be ordered on the defender. However, if the amendment is simply to correct the defender's address this may in some courts be allowed by application made in the minute for decree or by motion without the necessity of a minute of amendment, and decree may be granted provided the sheriff is satisfied that service has been duly effected. However, in other courts the practice is to insist on a minute of amendment and order re-service[16]. Accordingly, it will be necessary for solicitors to check on local practice.

The expenses of an amendment in an undefended action will normally be borne by the pursuer; indeed the Rules provide that the defender should not be liable for the expenses of such an amendment unless the sheriff orders otherwise[17].

12 r 7.3(5)

13 An exception to this rule is a decree granted in certain actions of removing under s 9(7) of the Land Tenure (Scotland) Reform Act 1974 where decree is final when extract recorded in Register of Sasines.

14 r 7.5(a). See also *Rae and others* v *Calor Gas and Timbermills* (I.H.) 1995 SCLR, 261.

15 r 7.5(b)

16 r 7.5(1); see also commentary in *Sleaford Trading Co* v *R D Norman and another*, (Notes) 1994 SCLR 1093

17 r 7.6(2)

Reponing

Application of procedure for reponing (recall of decree)

3.11 Reponing is the procedure available to a defender to recall a decree in absence granted under the provisions of Chapter 7. As such the procedure does not apply to most family actions and to causes under the Presumption of Death (Scotland) Act 1977.[18]

Reponing note

3.12 An application for reponing is made by lodging with the sheriff clerk a reponing note "at any time before implement in full" of the decree. There is no prescribed form of reponing note but it must contain both a statement of the defender's defence and an explanation of the failure to lodge a notice of intention to defend[19].

Fixing hearing

3.13 When the reponing note is lodged, the sheriff clerk fixes a date for hearing. Thereafter a copy of the reponing note must be served[20] on the pursuer by the defender's solicitor together with a notice of the date for the hearing. The reponing note when lodged with the sheriff clerk and served acts as a sist of any diligence which has been or is about to be used to enforce the decree[21].

Sheriff's powers

3.14 The sheriff's powers in relation to recall of a decree are discretionary. In this respect the Sheriff Court provisions differ from those in the Court of Session[22] where recall is mandatory if the application is made timeously. Although rule 8.1(1) stipulates that the reponing note should set out the defender's proposed defence and explain the failure to enter appearance in the action, it has been held by a Court of Five Judges that the sheriff does not first require to be satisfied that there is a reasonable excuse for non-appearance before going on to consider whether the defender has a stateable defence. The sheriff is entitled to take all circumstances into account and to balance one consideration against another in deciding whether to allow a reponing note. This decision supersedes earlier dicta.[23]

If, after hearing parties, the sheriff grants the reponing note and recalls the decree the defender may be found liable for the expenses of the

[18] r 8.1(1)(a) and (b). *Note:* r 8.11(a) provides that reponing does not apply to those family actions listed in r 33.1(1)(a)–(h).

[19] r 8.1(1)

[20] r 8.1(2)

[21] r 8.1(4)

[22] Court of Session Rule of Court 19.2

[23] *Forbes* v *Johnstone*, 1995 SLT 158

reponing procedure. If the reponing note is refused, the decree in absence stands, although there is provision for an appeal against the sheriff's decision (see para 3.16).

Procedure following recall of decree

3.15 After recall, the procedure applicable to defended actions comes into play with the date of recall of the decree replacing the date of expiry of the period of notice as the effective date from which the defended cause timetable starts to run[24]. This procedure, which is discussed in Chapter 4 of this book, requires the sheriff clerk, on the recall of a decree in absence, to fix a date for an Options Hearing and intimate this together with the defended cause timetable to all parties in the action.

Appeal against sheriff's decision

3.16 An order granting a reponing note and recalling a decree in absence cannot be appealed, the sheriff's decision being final[25]. Refusal of a reponing note may, however, be appealed to the sheriff principal or the Court of Session without leave[26].

[24] r 8.1(3)
[25] r 8.1(5)
[26] ss 27 and 28 of the Sheriff Courts (Scotland) Act 1907

CHAPTER 4

Standard and Additional Procedures

Chapters 9, 10 and 19–22 of the Rules

Introduction and policy background

4.1 Chapters 9 and 10 of the Rules contain the core procedures introduced to regulate the conduct of proceedings in defended ordinary actions. The basis of these new procedures is found in the Rules Council's Report (issued in April 1991) in which the Council outlined its proposals for a new framework for defended ordinary causes[1]. The rules which were drafted to bring this new procedural framework into force are intended to implement a number of policy objectives including the following:

- That cases should call in court only when necessary
- There should be targets in the rules for completion of procedural stages, such as adjustment of pleadings, and
- That the court should manage and control the pace of litigation.

These policy objectives are embodied in the Standard Procedure, which the Rules Council intended should be suitable for the majority of defended actions, and the Additional Procedure for cases involving issues of difficulty or complexity. The structure of the procedural framework is outlined in the flowchart opposite.

Except for actions of multiplepoinding[2], the Standard and Additional Procedures apply to all defended ordinary actions, including family actions. There are, however, some procedural differences in relation to family actions and these are identified both in this chapter and in Chapter 13 of this book.

Consideration is also given in this chapter to the rules in Chapters 19 (counterclaims), 20 (third party procedure), 21 (documents founded on) and 22 (preliminary pleas) as these are linked to the Standard and Additional Procedures.

[1] *Report on Proposals for New Procedures for Defended Ordinary Causes and Family Actions*, Sheriff Court Rules Council.

[2] See Chapter 14 of this book and para 14.5 for those rules in Chapter 9 which do apply to actions of multiplepoinding.

Framework of new procedures for defended ordinary causes and family actions

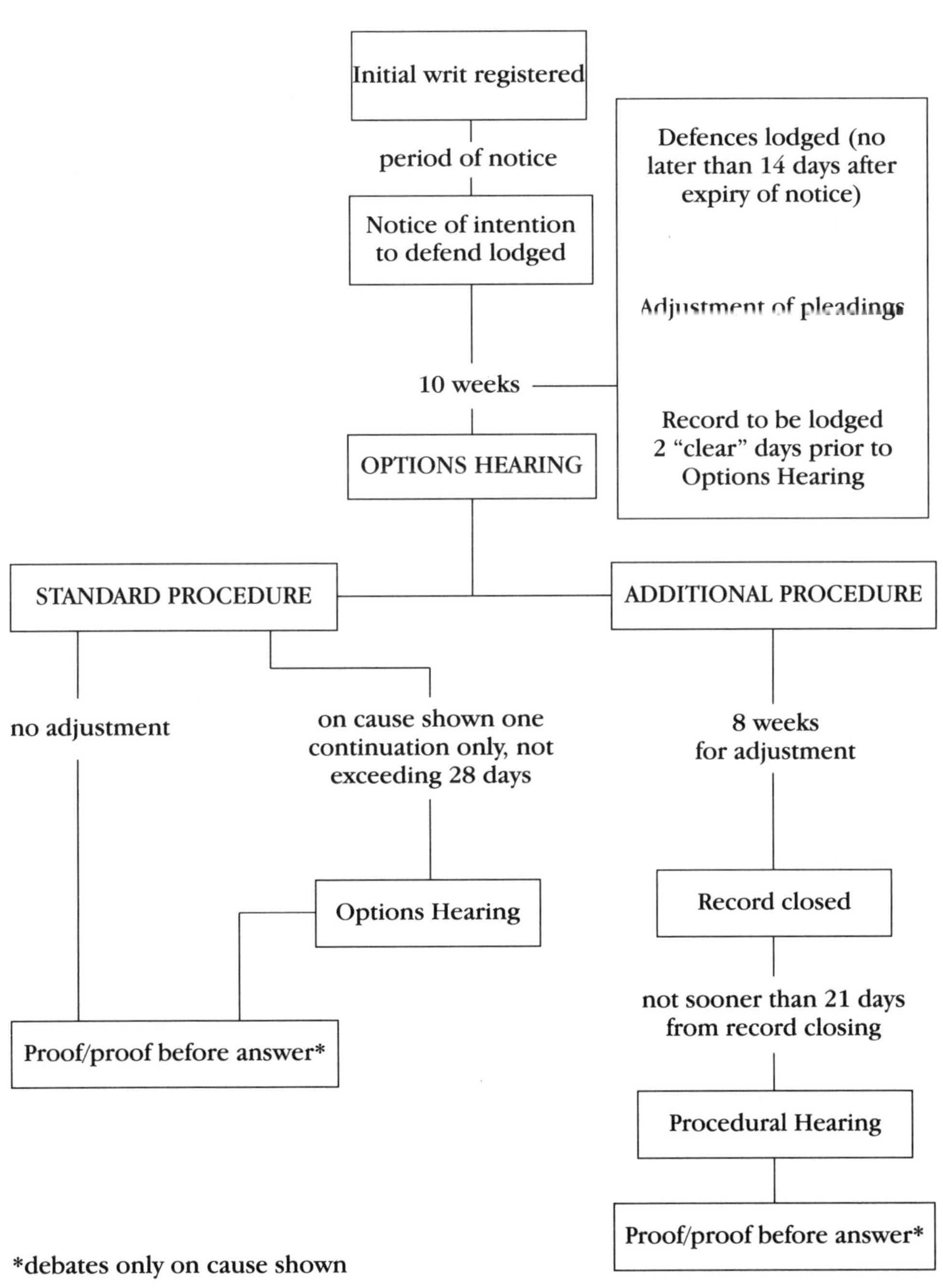

Standard Procedure

4.2 The Standard and Additional Procedures are not optional and initially parties do not have a say in which procedure should apply. The way that the rules are structured means that all defended actions proceed in the first instance under the Standard Procedure, and it is only at the Options Hearing that a decision may be made to remit a case to proceed under the Additional Procedure. A decision to remit may only be made if the sheriff is satisfied that because of the "difficulty or complexity" of the case it is unsuitable to continue under the Standard Procedure.

Notice of intention to defend

4.3 *Time for lodging notice* Although, there may have been some correspondence about possible litigation between the pursuer and defender or their solicitors prior to the commencement of proceedings, the first official notice that the defender receives about the commencement of proceedings is the service copy initial writ with accompanying forms and notices. Following service, the defender has just 21 days (42 days if the defender is outwith Europe) to lodge a notice of intention to defend and 14 days thereafter in which to lodge defences.

Procedure for lodging notice Rule 9.1 provides that a defender who wishes to challenge the jurisdiction of the court, state a defence or make a counterclaim must lodge with the sheriff clerk a notice of intention to defend before the expiry of the period of notice[3]. This the defender does by completing and lodging the form of notice of intention to defend which is served with the copy initial writ and citation. This particular rule does not apply to family actions and actions of multiplepoinding. The equivalent procedural rules which apply to these types of action are considered in Chapters 13 and 14 of this book.

Form of notice The form of notice of intention to defend (Form O7) contains details of the dates of service and of expiry of the period of notice. The dates are inserted in this form, by the pursuer's solicitor prior to service, and perform two functions. The first is to provide the defender with clear notice of the time within which a response must be made to the initial writ. The second is to enable the sheriff clerk to check whether a notice of intention to defend, when lodged, is timeous. In addition to lodging a notice of intention to defend the defender must pay the relevant court fee, details of which must also be inserted in the form of citation by the pursuer's solicitor prior to service.

[3] r 9.1(1)

Starting point for timetable for defended actions The lodging of the notice of intention to defend is an important stage in proceedings, for not only does the action now become a defended cause but it marks the starting point of the timetable for defended actions. The effect of this is that a date will be fixed for an Options Hearing[4] which, as discussed below, has a bearing on the time available for adjustment. Accordingly, if, for example, a defender finds it necessary to apply for legal aid, he would be well advised to move the court to sist the cause at this stage. A delay in moving for a sist will result in the loss of time available for adjustment, as any period of adjustment which has elapsed prior to the sist will be discounted when the sist is subsequently recalled.

Notice of intention to defend—late lodging Although there is no specific rule dealing with the question of late lodging of a notice of intention to defend, the sheriff may be asked to use the dispensing power[5] to excuse a failure to comply with the Rules. This matter must be resolved before the action can proceed as a defended cause. In practice, application to allow late lodging is sought by lodging a motion at the same time as the notice of intention to defend.

Motion to allow late lodging If, after intimation and hearing, the motion is granted a date will be fixed by the sheriff clerk for the lodging of defences, adjustment and an Options Hearing. It should be noted, however, that the dates to be fixed are determined by the date of expiry of the period of notice and not the date of granting the motion. The effect of this is that say, for example, the notice of intention to defend is late by 14 days, the time for lodging defences will have expired (*i.e.* 14 days after the expiry of the period of notice) and the time available for adjustment will have been curtailed. Accordingly, the solicitor for the defender, when framing a motion for late lodging, would be well advised to seek additional time for lodging defences and for adjustment if required.

Intimation of timetable for lodging defences and for adjustment

4.4 When a notice of intention to defend is lodged (or a motion for late lodging is granted) the sheriff clerk fixes a date for the Options Hearing and intimates this together with the last date for lodging defences and adjustment to all parties to the action[6]. The time limits fixed by the Rules are:

- *lodging defences:* 14 days after expiry of period of notice[7]
- *adjustment:* until 14 days before the Options Hearing[8]

[4] r 9.2(1)
[5] r 2.1
[6] r 9.2(1), (2); Form G5
[7] r 9.6(1)
[8] r 9.8(1)

Date for Options Hearing

4.5 The date which the sheriff clerk fixes for the Options Hearing is the "first suitable court day occurring not sooner than 10 weeks" after the period of notice has expired[9]. The actual date fixed may in fact be the first available court day when civil business is heard or the regular day for the "ordinary court". However, the wording of the rule (*i.e.* the "first suitable court day") introduces an element of flexibility so that instead of putting all hearings down for the first available court day, hearings may be scheduled on a quota basis to ensure that sufficient time is allocated to enable hearings to be conducted as intended.

Process folder

4.6 As discussed in Chapter 2 of this book, the process rules implement recommendations that individual parts of process should be housed in a purpose designed process folder to be supplied by the sheriff clerk's office. These rules provide that the process folder should be made up following the lodging of a notice of intention to defend, and should at this stage contain the notice of intention to defend, interlocutor sheets (and duplicates), production files for both pursuer and defender, a motion file and an inventory of process[10]. The initial writ is lodged in process when subsequently returned by the pursuer (within seven days after the period of notice has expired)[11], and other parts of process such as defences are entered in the process folder when lodged (see Chapter 5 of this book for further information about processes).

Defences: lodging and format

4.7 The defences must be lodged within 14 days after the expiry of the period of notice. It should be noted that, in addition to lodging the defences in process, the defender must send an intimation copy to all other parties in the case and this should be done at the same time as lodging the defences. Defences must be presented in the form of answers to the articles of condescendence in the initial writ followed by a note of the defender's pleas-in-law. The answers should be numbered and correspond to the numbers in the condescendence[12].

Counterclaims

4.8 Where a defender wishes to make a counterclaim this must be stated in the defences and, under the new Rules, may not be lodged as a separate document. This provision was introduced to provide that all the defender's pleadings are contained in a single document. As such a counterclaim must

[9] r 9.21
[10] r 9.5
[11] r 9.3
[12] r 9.6(2)

be lodged 14 days after the expiry of the period of notice, although it may be introduced at a later stage either by adjustment or, where the time for adjustment has expired, by amendment. A counterclaim introduced by minute of amendment (after the adjustment period) may only be accepted with leave of the sheriff and may result in the defender being found liable for the expense occasioned by the counterclaim being introduced at this stage in proceedings[13].

Defences including a counterclaim commence with a crave representing the defender's counterclaim, followed by the defender's answers to the articles of condescendence in the initial writ, a statement of the facts supporting the counterclaim (in numbered paragraphs), and finally the pleas-in-law in relation to the principal action and the counterclaim[14].

Format of Defences including Counterclaim

- Defender's Crave (counterclaim)
- Answers to articles in the condescendence of the initial writ
- Statement in support of the counterclaim
- Pleas in law in relation to initial writ
- Pleas in law in relation to counterclaim

A counterclaim may be made in an action where the subject matter of the counterclaim could have been raised as a separate action and provided that the defender in that action is the pursuer in the action in which the counterclaim is to be lodged[15]. In addition the following must apply:

- The counterclaim must form part of the pursuer's action or arise out of the grounds of the action,
- The issue in the counterclaim must be a matter the decision of which is necessary for the determination of the question at issue between the parties, or
- If the pursuer had not otherwise been subject to the jurisdiction of the court, the subject matter of the counterclaim could have been the basis of an action against the pursuer in which jurisdiction would have arisen by reconvention.[16]

Rule 19.1 brings the Sheriff Court provisions for counterclaims into line with those of the Court of Session[17]. Previously the grounds for making counterclaims were quite different. The rules in Chapter 19 do not apply to family actions and actions of multiplepoindings as there are different rules (in Chaps 33 and 36) regulating the procedure where a defender or party

[13] r 19.1(2)(b)
[14] r 19.1(3)
[15] r 19.1(1)(a)
[16] r 19.1(1)(b)
[17] Court of Session Rule of Court 25.1

wishes to make a claim in these types of proceedings.

When lodging a counterclaim, the defender may apply for warrant to arrest on the dependence in much the same way as a pursuer applies for warrant in an initial writ. Procedurally, application is made by inserting the words "Warrant for arrestment on the dependence applied for"[18] before the crave in the counterclaim. The Rules provide that the application may be disposed of by the sheriff clerk writing on the defences, adjusted defences or minute of amendment the words "Warrant granted as craved". This is followed by the date of the warrant and the signature of the sheriff clerk.[19]

If the pursuer in the course of proceedings abandons the action, and the defender wishes to continue with the counterclaim, the counterclaim may continue as if it was a separate action[20].

Third party procedure

4.9 The object of the third party procedure is to enable issues arising out of the same subject matter to be disposed of in one action, and the Rules provide that a third party may be brought into an action where it is claimed that:

- The defender has a right of contribution, relief or indemnity against a person who is not a party to the action, or
- A person whom the pursuer is not bound to call as a defender should be made a party to the action along with the defender on the basis that this person is:
  - (i) liable, or liable along with the defender, to the pursuer, or
  - (ii) liable to the defender in respect of a claim arising from or in connection with the liability of the defender to the pursuer[21]

In the following paragraphs reference is made to the circumstances where a defender seeks to convene a third party. However, the procedure applies also where a pursuer against whom a counterclaim has been made or a third party convened in an action seeks to make a claim against a person who is not a party to the action[22].

Procedure for making application Before the record is closed, a defender may bring in a third party by including in his defences averments, or a separate statement of facts setting out the grounds for calling the third party and also the appropriate pleas-in-law[23]. If these matters are not included in the defences when lodged they may be introduced at a later stage by adjustment. In either event there must be appropriate averments in the defender's pleadings relating to the third party before a motion may

[18] r 19.2(2)
[19] r 19.2(3)
[20] r 19.3(2)
[21] r 20.1(1)
[22] r 20.1(2)
[23] r 20.2(1)

be lodged seeking an order for service of a third party notice.

Application to introduce a third party after the record has been closed must be made by minute of amendment, and this should be lodged along with a motion seeking an order for service on the third party[24]. The Rules provide that a motion for service of a third party notice must be lodged before the start of "the hearing of the merits of the cause"[25] which suggests that this is the latest time for making such an application.

Warrant to found jurisdiction or to arrest on the dependence A defender may, when applying for an order for service on the third party, or at a later date, apply by motion for a warrant for diligence to found jurisdiction or to arrest on the dependence[26]. The Rules further provide that the defender must include averments in support of such an application in the pleadings[27].

Service of third party notice and lodging answers Service of a third party notice must be effected within the period stipulated in the Rules, *i.e.* within 14 days after the date of the interlocutor granting the order[28], and it should be noted that the order for service ceases to have effect if the notice is not served within the prescribed period. If service has not been effected within this period and the defender subsequently wishes to serve a notice it will be necessary to re-apply by motion for a new order[29]. The form of notice[30] provides the third party with details of the case, the grounds on which the claim is made and time for lodging answers. In addition to the notice a copy of the pleadings is served on the third party[31]. After service the defender must lodge in process a copy of the notice with a certificate of service[32].

If the third party wishes to resist the claim, answers must be lodged with the sheriff clerk within 28 days (or such other period fixed by the sheriff) of the date of service of the notice[33]. The answers must be headed "Answers for [EF] Third Party in the action at the instance of [AB] Pursuer against [CD] Defender" and include answers to the defender's averments or statement of facts in the form of numbered paragraphs corresponding to the paragraphs in the defender's averments or statement, and appropriate pleas-in-law[34].

Fixing of Options Hearing where third party lodges answers If answers are lodged, the sheriff clerk fixes a new date for an Options Hearing and the date of lodging answers replaces the date of expiry of the period of

24 r 20.2(2)
25 r 20.2(3)
26 r 20.3(1), (3)
27 r 20.3(2)
28 r 20.4(1)
29 r 20.4(2)
30 Form O10
31 r 20.4(3)
32 r 20.5(1)2
33 r 25.5(1)
34 r 20.5(2)

notice[35] as the operative date for fixing the Options Hearing. No matter what stage the case has reached, if a third party is brought into an action, the defended cause timetable starts again as it is necessary to provide parties with time to adjust their pleadings in light of matters introduced by, or in relation to, the third party.

Implied admissions

4.10 Parties must answer statements of fact made by other parties in their pleadings, and where a statement of a fact, which is within the knowledge of a party, is not denied the Rules provide that it will be deemed to have been admitted[36].

Adjustment of pleadings

4.11 *Adjustment period* The actual period within which parties may adjust their pleadings is not specified in the Rules, but is, in fact, determined by the period of time between the date when the defender lodges defences and the date fixed by the sheriff clerk for the Options Hearing. Adjustment cannot begin until the defender lodges defences (*i.e.* 14 days after the expiry of the period of notice) and must be concluded 14 days before the date of the Options Hearing[37]. The effect of this is that the period of time available for adjustment in most cases will be six weeks, although where the defender lodges defences early and/or where the Options Hearing is fixed for a date which is more than 10 weeks after the expiry of the period of notice the adjustment period will be a little longer.

Late lodging of defences and effect on adjustment period The calculation of the adjustment period in the previous paragraph assumes that the defender lodges defences within the prescribed period. However, if the defender is late in lodging defences this will clearly reduce the period available for adjustment. Each day that the defences are late is a day less for adjustment. The pursuer's remedy in this situation is to apply for decree by default[38]. However, on the basis that the pursuer does not invoke the default procedures a defender who has not lodged defences timeously should seek leave by motion either to allow defences to be lodged late or to prorogate the time for lodging defences[39]. It is for consideration also, depending on how late the defences are, whether the motion should also seek a new date for the Options Hearing with a view to allowing a full period for adjustment.

35 r 20.6(1)
36 r 9.7
37 r 9.8(1)
38 rr 16.2, 33.37 (family)
39 rr 2.1, 16.3; see r 33.37(4) for procedures for family actions.

Late adjustment Any adjustments made after the end of the adjustment period may be accepted with leave of the court. As there is unlikely to be sufficient time to enrol a motion seeking leave an oral motion must be made at the Options Hearing. It is suggested that a copy of the adjustments should be submitted to the court prior to the Options Hearing in order that they may be considered by the sheriff along with the certified copy record prior to the hearing. The adjustment should not be incorporated into the record, however, until leave has been granted[40].

alongfdd time allows a written motion seeking leave to allow late adjustments should be lodged before the Options Hearing so that the motion and the adjustments can be considered by the sheriff prior to the Options Hearing. If there is not sufficient time to enrol such a motion an oral motion must be made at the Options Hearing. In this event it is suggested that the adjustments should be submitted to the court prior to the Options Hearing in order that they may be considered by the sheriff, along with the certified copy record.

Effect of sist on adjustment period If an action is sisted during the adjustment period, any part of the adjustment period which has expired prior to the action being sisted is deducted when the sist is subsequently recalled[41]. When a sist is recalled the sheriff clerk will fix, and intimate to parties, a new date for an Options Hearing, taking into account any period of the adjustment period which has elapsed[42].

Method of adjusting pleadings Adjustments are exchanged between parties and not lodged in process[43], as was the case under the old Rules. This provision was introduced to take account of developments in new technologies, such as word processors, on the basis that solicitors could more effectively maintain a record of their adjusted pleadings in their own offices. The rules place a duty on solicitors for parties to maintain such a record[44].

Lodging certified copy record

4.12 *Content of record* At the end of the adjustment period (*i.e.* 14 days before the Options Hearing) the pursuer's solicitor must prepare a record containing a copy of the pleadings, as adjusted, and any amendments[45]. The record must also include the pleadings in relation to any counterclaim lodged by the defender or answers by a third party. The Rules do not, however, make any provision for including copies of interlocutors, as was the practice under the old procedures.

[40] r 9.8(4); see also *Taylor* v *Stakis*, 1995 SLT (Sh Ct)14
[41] r 9.9(1)
[42] r 9.9(2)
[43] r 9.8(2)
[44] r 9.8(3)
[45] r 9.11(1)

Time for lodging record The pursuer has from the end of the adjustment period until not later than two days before the Options Hearing to lodge in process a certified copy of the record[46]. At the same time as lodging the certified copy record the pursuer must send an intimation copy to all parties in the case[47]. It has been held that "not later than 2 days before" the Options Hearing means two clear days[48]. The policy objective of the record being lodged in advance of the Options Hearing is to provide the sheriff, and indeed all parties, with a full and up-to-date record of the pleadings in good time for the Options Hearing. Since the introduction of this provision a number of decisions have been reported, following appeal, which indicate that sheriffs principal and the Court of Session regard the late lodging of a record for an Options Hearing as a serious default and not to be lightly excused. In particular, the First Division of the Court of Session has held that "It is crucial to the performance by the sheriff of his functions at the options hearing that he should have the record in his hands when he has time to prepare for the hearing by reading it."[49]

Lodging of pleadings for continued Options Hearing It has been held that there is no requirement in the Rules for the lodging of a second certified copy record for a continued Options Hearing, where a continuation has been allowed for adjustment[50]. In these circumstances it is suggested that a copy of any adjustments made, after the lodging of the record for the first Options Hearing, should be lodged in good time for them to be considered by the sheriff prior to the continued Options Hearing. When the sheriff closes the record at this hearing he may order that the adjustments be included in a closed record to be lodged within seven days of the hearing[51].

Lodging of adjusted pleadings for other hearings

4.13 In line with the policy objective of ensuring that the sheriff and parties are provided with a full set of pleadings for hearings, the Rules also provide that where there is a hearing prior to an Options Hearing (*e.g.* a motion roll hearing) each party must lodge in process a copy of their pleadings, as adjusted to date. This must be done not later than two days before the hearing[52].

[47] r 11.6(1)

[48] *Ritchie* v *The Maersk Co* (Sh Ct) 1994 SCLR 1038

[49] *DTZ Debenham Thorpe* v *I Henderson Transport Services*, 1st Division, 27 January 1995 (I.H.) 1995 SCLR, 345. See also *Group 4 Total Security* v *Jaymarke Developments* (Sh Ct) 1995 SCLR, 303; *Welsh* v *Thornehome Services* (Sh Ct) 1994 SCLR 1021; *Mahoney* v *Officer* (Sh Ct) 1994 SCLR 1059; and *Morran* v *Glasgow District Council of Tenants' Associations* (Sh Ct) 1994 SCLR 1065

[50] *Gordon* v *Mayfair Homes Ltd* (Sh Ct) 1994 SCLR 862; *Mellor* v *Towle* (Sh Ct) 1994 SCLR 953

[51] r 9.12(6)(b)

[52] r 9.4

Open record

4.14 There is also provision in the Rules for the sheriff, before the closing of the record, to order that an open record be lodged[53]. This might be considered necessary, for example, in relation to a motion roll hearing in an action in which there have been fairly extensive adjustments.

Documents founded on or adopted in pleadings

4.15 *Lodging documents* Any document founded on, or adopted as incorporated, by a party in their pleadings must be lodged as a production, provided that it is in the party's possession and control. Such documents must be lodged at the same time as the part of process in which it is founded on is lodged in process or in the case of adjustments intimated.[54]

Failure to lodge documents Failure to lodge documents founded on or adopted in pleadings may result in the party being found liable for the expense of a commission and diligence granted on the motion of any other party in the action who seeks production of the documents[55]. Failure to lodge documents might also be held to be a default in terms of rule 16.2 (decree where party in default).

Objections to documents A party wishing to challenge any deed or writing founded on may do so by way of exception, without the necessity of raising an action to have it reduced. Where such an objection is stated the sheriff has power to order the party stating the objection to find caution or give security[56].

Note of basis of preliminary plea

4.16 A party intending to insist on a preliminary plea must lodge in process a note setting out the basis of the plea (and send a copy to the other parties) not later than three days before the Options Hearing[57]. The object of this procedure is to enable the sheriff to decide, at the Options Hearing, whether there is a preliminary matter of law which justifies a debate or, where the preliminary plea is directed to the relevancy and specification of the pleadings, whether the matter might be rectified by further adjustment or amendment. Failure to comply with this provision will result in the plea being repelled at the Options Hearing[58]. It has been held that such a failure should not result in the case being dismissed. The

[53] r 9.10
[54] r 21.1(1)
[55] r 21.2
[56] r 21.3
[57] r 22.1(1)
[58] r 22.1(2)

appropriate course of action in this situation is for the sheriff to repel the plea and fix a proof.[59]

The provisions relating to the lodging of a note are intended to sift out preliminary pleas which do not merit a debate. This procedure does not, however, preclude matters being raised at any proof before answer or debate in addition to those contained in the preliminary plea note; although it has been held that this does not permit a wholly new plea to be introduced or a plea which has previously been repelled to be resurrected.[60]

Options Hearing

4.17 *Preparation: parts of process and documents to be lodged prior to hearing* As will have become clear from the examination of the procedures leading up to the Options Hearing, there are a number of parts of process and documents to be lodged prior to the hearing and, moreover, there are strict time limits for so doing. Before the date for the Options Hearing arrives a check should be made to ensure that all the relevant parts of process or documents have been lodged. These are summarised as follows:

Parts of process and other documents to be lodged prior to Options Hearing

	Time for Lodging	*Rule No*
Defences	within 14 days after the expiry of period of notice	9.6(1)
Certified copy record	Not later than two days before Options Hearing	9.11(2)
Documents founded on	At the time of lodging initial writ, defences or intimating adjustment	21.1
Preliminary plea note	Not later than three days before Options Hearing	22.1

See opposite for a summary of the orders which may be sought and granted by the sheriff at the Options Hearing.

[59] *Strathclyde Business Park (Management) Ltd* v *Cochrane*, 1994 GWD 30–1834; see for further discussion on preliminary pleas at para 4.17, Debate.

[60] r 22.1(3); see also *Bell* v *John Davidson (Pipes)*, 1995 SLT (Sh Ct), 18.

Summary of orders which may be sought at Options Hearing

Order sought	*Provisions relating to sheriff's powers and conduct of hearing*	*Matters on which sheriff should be addressed/advised*
Proof [rule 9.12(3)(a)]	To identify matters on record which are in dispute [rule 9.12(1)]	Parties have duty to provide sheriff with sufficient information [rule 9.12(2)].
	Order parties to lodge minute of admissions or agreement	Parties should identify any matters which might be included in a minute.
	Close record and fix proof	Anticipated duration of proof, number of witnesses, dates to avoid.
Proof before answer [rule 9.12(3)(b)]	To hear parties on preliminary plea note lodged in terms of rule 22.1	Arguments in favour of maintaining preliminary plea and fixing proof before answer.
	[Otherwise as in "Proof" above]	
Debate [rule 9.12(3)(c)]	To hear parties on preliminary plea note lodged in terms of rule 22.1, and be satisfied that there is a preliminary matter of law which justifies a debate	Arguments justifying debate.
	Close record and fix debate	Anticipated duration of debate, and any dates to avoid.

Continued overleaf

Order sought	*Provisions relating to sheriff's powers and conduct of hearing*	*Matters on which sheriff should be addressed/advised*
Remit to Additional Procedure [rule 9.12(4)]	Sheriff may remit action if satisfied that it is not suitable for the Standard Procedure in view of the difficulty or complexity of the case	Arguments in favour of remit.
Continuation of Options Hearing [rule 9.12(5)]	Sheriff may, on cause shown, continue Options Hearing for one period only, not exceeding 28 days	Reasons why continuation necessary and period sought.
Other orders (i) Leave to allow late adjustments [rule 9.8(4)]	Adjustments made after adjustment period may only be permitted with leave of the sheriff	Arguments in favour of leave being exercised.
(ii) Leave to allow late lodging of part of process *e.g.* preliminary plea note, certified copy record	Sheriff may be asked to exercise the dispensing power in rule 2.1 or grant decree by default in terms of rule 16.2	Whether failure to comply with the Rules was due to "mistake, oversight or other excusable cause" and why sheriff should exercise dispensing power.

Note: In family actions the parties must attend in person, except on cause shown [rule 33.36].

Preparation: orders which may be sought at hearing In addition to ensuring that the certified copy record, preliminary plea note(s) and any other documents are lodged timeously the solicitor attending the hearing (if not the principal agent) must ensure that he has full instructions about the order sought, whether it be to fix a proof, proof before answer or debate, or some other order. These instructions should, of course, also deal with matters such as any preliminary pleas which are to be maintained, including arguments justifying a debate and, where appropriate, provide reasons in support of a motion for a continuation or remit to the additional procedure. These issues are discussed further in the following section which examines the orders which may be sought and the sheriff's powers at the hearing.

Conduct of Options Hearing by sheriff As outlined in the introduction to this chapter of the book, one of the key policies of the Rules Council was that the court should have a responsibility for the management and control of cases. The Rules Council took the view that it was in the public interest, as well as the parties', that once an action has commenced it should be brought to a conclusion with a minimum of delay. Up to the Options Hearing the timetable is largely controlled by the time limits prescribed in the Rules. At the Options Hearing, however, the sheriff takes control and is provided with important powers and, indeed, responsibilities. In particular, it is provided that "the sheriff shall seek to secure the expeditious progress of the cause by ascertaining from the parties the matters in dispute and information about any other matter referred to in paragraph(3)".[61] The "other matters" referred to include making orders relating to the extent of proof, the lodging of joint minutes of admission or agreement and deciding whether there are any preliminary matters of law which justify a debate. In short, the sheriff is being asked to intervene with a view to identifying the issues between parties and, thereafter, deciding the type and extent of hearing that is appropriate to resolve these issues.

Duty of parties It is not just the sheriff, however, who is given new reponsibilities. The Rules also assign the following duty to parties: "It shall be the duty of parties to provide the sheriff with sufficient information to enable him to conduct the hearing as provided for in this rule."[62]

Sheriff's powers at Options Hearing The Rules Council[63] envisaged that in the majority of cases adjustment of pleadings should be completed before the Options Hearing and that a proof or proof before answer would

[61] r 9.12(1)
[62] r 9.12(2)

[63] *Report on Proposals for New Procedures for Defended Ordinary Causes and Family Actions,* Sheriff Court Rules Council, April 1991

be fixed at that hearing. However, as the name given to the first hearing implies, the sheriff has a number of options with regard to the future conduct of cases. These options are now looked at in turn.

Fixing of proof The sheriff at the Options Hearing may, having heard parties on the matters in dispute, fix a proof and make any order with regard to the extent of the proof as he thinks fit, including ordering parties to lodge a joint minute of admissions or agreement[64]. This points to the need for solicitors for parties to be prepared to advise the sheriff at the hearing on the issues in dispute and on whether there are matters not admitted in the pleadings which could be the subject of a joint minute of admissions or agreement.

The same conditions apply to the fixing of a proof before answer[65]. In addition, however, the sheriff must hear parties on the preliminary plea note(s) lodged in terms of rule 22.1 (see para 4.16), with a view to deciding in this instance whether the relevant plea or pleas should be reserved until after proof.

Debate A debate on a preliminary plea may only be allowed where the sheriff is satisfied, after having considered the preliminary plea note and heard parties, that there is a preliminary matter of law which justifies a debate[66]. As regards the conduct the hearing in relation to preliminary pleas, it has been held that the sheriff is not required to hear full arguments on the substance of the pleas. Instead the sheriff should be provided with the basis of the arguments which would be put at any debate to enable a decision to be made as to the likelihood of there being a preliminary matter of law justifying a debate[67].

Closing the record at the Options Hearing The sheriff, when fixing a proof, proof before answer or debate, also makes an order closing the record[68]. If there have been no adjustments since the lodging of the record, for the Options Hearing that record becomes the closed record[69]. However, if there have been adjustments since the record was lodged (for example, where the Options Hearing has been continued for that purpose) the sheriff may order that a closed record including these adjustments be lodged within seven days of the interlocutor closing the record[70].

Remit to additional procedure The sheriff's power to remit to the additional procedure[71] is limited. The Rules provide that an action may

64 r 9.12(3)(a)
65 r 9.12(3)(b)
66 r 9.12(3)(c)
67 *Gracey* v *Sykes* (Sh Ct) 1994 SCLR 911; *The Blair Bryden Partnership* v *Adair* (Sh Ct) 1995 SCLR, 358
68 r 9.12(3)
69 r 9.12(6)(a)
70 r 9.12(6)(b)
71 r 9.12(4)

only be remitted if the sheriff is satisfied that the difficulty or the complexity of the issues makes it unsuitable for proceeding under the standard procedure. It was the intention of the Rules Council that the test to be applied would be strict and it was anticipated that only a limited number of actions would meet the criteria prescribed in the Rules.

A remit may be made at the instance of the sheriff or on the motion of any party to the action. In view of the terms of the remit provisions relating to remits a party intending to make such a motion at the Options Hearing must be well armed with arguments to satisfy the sheriff that there are issues of difficulty or complexity which make the action unsuitable for the Standard Procedure.

Continuation of the Options Hearing The final option available to the sheriff is to allow a continuation of the Options Hearing for a period not exceeding 28 days[72]. The sheriff may, provided cause is shown that a continuation is necessary, allow one continuation only. If the continuation is for adjustment, it should be noted that of the 28-day period only 14 days will be available for adjustment, as the Rules provide that adjustment may be made up to 14 days before the Options Hearing "or any continuation of it"[73].

Consequences of failure to appear at Options Hearing An Options Hearing is defined as a "diet" for the purposes of the rules relating to decree by default[74]. Accordingly, if a party does not appear or is not represented at an Options Hearing the sheriff may grant decree by default.

Intimation of list of documents and exchange of witness lists

4.18 In general the new defended cause procedure is designed to encourage early disclosure with a view to expediting progress and preventing "trial by ambush". Two specific provisions are introduced to regulate disclosure of evidence in cases where the sheriff has allowed a proof or proof before answer at the Options Hearings. These provide for:

- The intimation of a list of documents, and
- The exchange of witness lists.[75]

Specifically the Rules provide that a list of any documents which are intended to be put in evidence and of witnesses who are to be called to give evidence must be intimated to parties within 14 days of the interlocutor fixing a proof or proof before answer. Moreover, in relation to documents, the Rules provide that these may be inspected, if in the

[72] r 9.12(5)
[73] r 9.8(1)
[74] r 9.12(7)
[75] rr 9.13(1), 9.14(1)

possession or control of the party intimating the list, at a convenient time and place[76].

A party who fails to intimate any document or witness and subsequently seeks to use the document or call the witness at the proof may do so, provided no other party objects. If, however, there is an objection the evidence may only be led with leave of the sheriff[77].

Additional procedure

4.19 Procedurally the main differences between the Additional and Standard Procedures are that under the Additional Procedure

- There is an additional period for adjustment
- The sheriff has power to vary the adjustment period by either reducing or extending the period, and
- There is a further hearing (the Procedural Hearing) at the end of the adjustment period.

As discussed in the following paragraphs there are, however, a number of common features which the two procedures share.

Adjustment

4.20 When an action is remitted to the Additional Procedure it is continued by the sheriff for adjustment for a fixed period of eight weeks[78]. The rules relating to adjustment of pleadings under the Standard and Additional Procedures are similar. In particular, the procedures for making adjustments (*i.e.* exchange between parties) and the effect of a sist on the adjustment period are the same[79]. Moreover, under both procedures the sheriff has power at any time before the record is closed to order that an open record be lodged[80], for example for the hearing of a motion during the adjustment period.

A motion seeking an extension of the adjustment period should state the reasons for seeking an extension and the additional period required for adjustment; a copy of the record as adjusted should be lodged with the motion[81]. If satisfied with the explanation in the motion, the sheriff may grant the motion and extend the adjustment period[82].

[76] r 9.13(2)
[77] rr 9.13(3), 9.14(2)
[78] r 10.1(1)
[79] rr 10.1(2), 10.2
[80] r 10.4
[81] r 10.3(2), (3)
[82] r 10.3(2)

If parties wish to have the record closed early, they may lodge a motion to reduce the adjustment period. This motion may only be made of consent or jointly by parties, and this must be stated in the motion[83]. If granted the sheriff will close the record and thereafter the procedure discussed below will apply.

Closing of record

4.21 At the end of the adjustment period the record is closed automatically without the case calling in court and without the attendance of solicitors for parties. Forthwith thereafter the sheriff clerk must prepare and sign an interlocutor closing the record, fix a date for a Procedural Hearing and intimate the date of the hearing to parties[84]. After the record is closed, the pursuer has 14 days to prepare and lodge a certified copy of the closed record containing only the pleadings of parties[85].

Note of basis of preliminary pleas

4.22 Any party insisting on a preliminary plea must lodge a note setting out the basis of the plea not later than three days before the Procedural Hearing. The sheriff must at the Procedural Hearing hear parties on any such note before a proof before answer or debate may be fixed. In the case of a debate the sheriff has to be satisfied that there is a preliminary matter of law which justifies a debate.[86]

Procedural Hearing

4.23 *Parts of process to be lodged before Procedural Hearing* The following parts of process must be lodged before the hearing:

	Time for Lodging	*Rule No*
Closed record	Within 14 days after date of closing record	10.5(2)
Preliminary plea note	Not later than 3 days before hearing	22.1

See overleaf for a discussion of the orders which may be sought and granted by the sheriff at the Procedural Hearing.

83 r 10.3(1)

84 r 10.5(1)

85 r 10.5(2), (3). *Note*: under the old procedures a closed record included copies of all interlocutors. It is understood that the Rules Council took the view that this was unnecessary as the principal interlocutors are available for inspection from the process.

86 rr 22.1, 10.6(3)(b), (c). *Note:* see also discussion about preliminary pleas at paras 4.16 and 4.17 under *Debate*

Summary of orders which may be sought at Procedural Hearing

Order sought	*Provisions relating to sheriff's powers and conduct of hearing*	*Matters on which sheriff should be addressed/advised*
Proof [rule 10.6(3)(a)]	To identify matters on record which are in dispute [rule 10.6(1)]	Parties have duty to provide sheriff with sufficient information [rule 10.6(2)].
	Order parties to lodge minute of admissions or agreement	Parties should identify any matters which might be included in a minute.
	Close record and fix proof diet	Anticipated duration of proof, number of witnesses, dates to avoid.
Proof before answer [rule 10.6(3)(b)]	To hear parties on preliminary plea note lodged in terms of rule 22.1	Arguments in favour of maintaining preliminary plea and fixing proof before answer.
	[Otherwise as in "Proof" above]	
Debate [rule 10.6(3)(c)]	To hear parties on preliminary plea note lodged in terms of rule 22.1, and be satisfied that there is a preliminary matter of law which justifies a debate	Arguments justifying debate.
	Other matters connected with fixing debate	Anticipated duration of debate, and any dates to avoid.
Other orders Leave to allow late lodging of part of process, *e.g.* closed record	Sheriff may be asked to exercise the dispensing power in rule 2.1 or grant decree by default in terms of rule 16.2	Whether failure to comply with the Rules was due to "mistake, oversight or other excusable cause" and why sheriff should exercise dispensing power.

Sheriff's powers The purpose of the Procedural Hearing is to enable the sheriff to identify the issues in dispute and decide whether the action should proceed to proof, proof before answer or debate. The powers of the sheriff and the duties placed on parties at the Procedural Hearing are similar to those which apply at Options Hearings[87]. There is no provision, however, under the Additional Procedure permitting a continuation of a Procedural Hearing. This is on the basis that, parties having been provided with an additional period for adjustment, and with the opportunity to seek an extension of the adjustment period, there should be no need for any further continuation of the proceedings.

At the Procedural Hearing the sheriff is directed to "seek to secure the expeditious progress of the cause by ascertaining from the parties the matters in dispute and information about any other matter referred to in paragraph (3)".[88] The "other matters" referred to relate to the making of an order in connection with the extent of proof, the lodging of joint minutes of admission or agreement and deciding whether there are any preliminary matters of law which justify a debate.

Parties are assigned the following duty: "It shall be the duty of parties to provide the sheriff with sufficient information to enable him to conduct the hearing as provided for in this rule."[89]

Consequences of failure to appear at Procedural Hearing A party who fails to appear or be represented at a Procedural Hearing may be held to be in default and the sheriff may grant decree by default[90].

Further orders in relation to fixing proof, etc

4.24 As previously discussed the sheriff has power, in terms of Rules 9.12(3) and 10.6(3), at the Options Hearing or Procedural Hearing to fix a proof, proof before answer or debate. There are, however, other rules which are relevant to the fixing of such hearings, and these may be applied generally at any time after the closing of the record. These rules are found in Chapter 29 of the Ordinary Cause Rules under the heading of "Proof", and provide for the following orders:

- Renouncing of probation
- A separate proof on merits and quantum

These rules require to be read along with relevant rules for Options and Procedural Hearings. For further discussion of these provisions see Chapter 11 of this book.

[87] r 10.6. *Note:* see also discussion of sheriff's powers and conduct of Options Hearing at para 4.17

[88] r 10.6(1)

[89] r 10.6(2)

[90] rr 10.6(4), 16.2, 33.37 (family actions)

CHAPTER 5

Defended Causes—The Process

Chapters 9 and 11 of the Rules

Process folder

5.1 As mentioned in earlier chapters of this book, the rules relating to processes implement proposals[1] that individual parts of process should be housed in a purpose designed process folder to be supplied by the sheriff clerk's office. The Rules specify that the process folder should be made up following the lodging of a notice of intention to defend. At this stage the folder contains files for the following parts of process which are numbered as follows:

1. Initial writ
2. Notice of intention to defend
3. Interlocutor sheets
4. Duplicate interlocutor sheets
5. Pursuer's production file
6. Defender's production file
7. Motion file.

In addition, an inventory and borrowing inventory of process and files for parts of process to be lodged at later dates are provided.[2]

Parts of process

5.2 Parts of process, such as the initial writ (which must be returned by the pursuer seven days after the period of notice has expired[3]), the defences and the certified copy record for the Options Hearing, are marked up in the inventory of process[4] and given a number of process when lodged. Productions and motions are inserted in the appropriate files and numbered sequentially (*e.g.* the pursuer's productions will be numbered 5/1, 5/2 and so on). All parts of process must be on A4 paper of durable quality and be lodged in flat format without any backing sheet[5] in order that they fit into the files in the process folder.

[1] *Report on Civil Court Processes*, Scottish Courts Administration, 1991

[2] r 9.5

[3] r 9.3

[4] r 11.2(1)

[5] r 11.1

Intimation of parts of process and adjustments

5.3 All parts of process lodged after a case becomes defended (*i.e.* after the defender lodges a notice of intention to defend) and any adjustments must be intimated to every other party who has entered process[6]. Intimation involves sending the other party a copy of the part of process to be lodged or adjustments and, where practicable, copies of any documentary productions.

Methods of intimation

5.4 Intimation may be made using any of the methods of service, citation and intimation which apply to service of initial writs and other court orders[7]. These methods of intimation must be used where intimation is to be made direct to a party.

Intimation to party represented by a solicitor Where a party is represented by a solicitor there are a number of other methods of intimation that may be used where the intimation is to be sent to the solicitor. These are by personal delivery, facsimile transmission, first class ordinary post or delivery to a document exchange[8]. The Rules also define the date at which intimation is deemed to have been given when intimation is made using any of these methods. This is aimed at catering for the situation where, for example, intimation is sent by facsimile transmission in the evening after the solicitor's office has closed for the day. Specifically in this situation it is provided that where intimation is given after 5.00pm it is deemed to have been effected on the day after the fax was sent[9]. However, if the fax was sent before 5.00pm intimation is deemed to have been made on the date of transmission. This provision applies also to intimation by personal delivery.

Intimation sent to a solicitor for a party by ordinary post or by delivery to a document exchange is deemed to have been given on the day after posting or delivery[10].

Intimation made on Saturday, Sunday or public or court holiday Where intimation is made on a Saturday, Sunday or public or court holiday it is deemed to have been given on the next day on which the sheriff clerk's office is open for civil court business[11].

[6] r 11.6(1)
[7] r 11.6(1)
[8] r 11.6(2)
[9] r 11.6(3)(a)
[10] r 11.6(3)(b)
[11] r 11.6(4)

Custody of process and borrowing of parts

5.5 The process folder remains in the custody of the sheriff clerk throughout the currency of the litigation. Parts of the process may, however, be borrowed by a solicitor for a party or the solicitor's authorised clerk[12]. However, the initial writ, interlocutor sheets, borrowing receipts and the process folder may not be borrowed[13], although the sheriff clerk may authorise the borrowing of the initial writ by the pursuer[14] for certain purposes (*e.g.* for re-serve on the defender).

Borrowing of parts of process by party litigant

5.6 A party litigant may only borrow a process, or parts of it, with leave of the sheriff and subject to any conditions the sheriff might impose[15]. Alternatively, a party litigant may inspect the process in the sheriff clerk's office and obtain copies, where practicable, of parts of process from the sheriff clerk[16], on payment of the relevant court fee.

Penalty for failure to return part of process

5.7 The sheriff may impose a fine not exceeding £50 on any solicitor or party litigant who fails to return a borrowed part of process in time for any diet or hearing at which it is required[17]. Such an order is not subject to appeal but may be recalled by the sheriff where cause is shown to explain the failure to return the part of process[18].

Replacement of lost part of process

5.8 Where a part of process is lost or destroyed it may with leave of the sheriff be replaced with a copy (normally a certified copy)[19].

Disposal of parts of process and uplifting of productions

5.9 Chapter 11 of the Rules makes provision for disposal of parts of process and for uplifting of productions from process after a case has been finally determined. These provisions are discussed in Chapter 12 of this book.

[12] r 11.3(1)
[13] r 11.2(2)
[14] r 11.2(3)
[15] r 11.3(3)(a)
[16] r 11.3(3)(b)
[17] r 11.4(1)
[18] r 11.4(2)
[19] r 11.5

CHAPTER 6

Applications by Motion and Minute; Party Minuters

Chapters 13–15 of the Rules

Introduction

6.1 There are a number of different types of application which may be made by minute or motion during the course of a defended action. The procedure for such applications is regulated by Chapters 13–15 of the Ordinary Cause Rules. The motion procedure is the most frequently used of these procedures. Some of the rules that apply to motions also apply to applications made by minute and to party minuter procedure.

Motion procedures

Form of motions

6.2 A wide variety of applications may be made by motion and many of them are discussed throughout this book. Chapter 15 of the Rules regulates the procedure for making an application by motion, which will usually be presented in written form. Any written motion must be lodged in the form prescribed in the Rules[1] with the sheriff clerk together with any document referred to in the motion[2]. A motion may also be made orally if made in the course of any hearing. However, because there are fewer callings under the new Rules, it is likely that most motions will be in written form. It should be noted that a motion may be made orally only with leave of the court[3], presumably on the basis that the other side is entitled to fair notice of any application which may be made by motion.

Lodging, hearing and intimation of motions

6.3 When a written motion is lodged the sheriff clerk enters it in the process motion file. Thereafter, the sheriff clerk fixes a date and time for a hearing and advises the party who has lodged the motion of the details of

[1] Form G6
[2] r 15.1
[3] r 15.1(a)

the hearing[4]. Intimation to other parties is made by the solicitor lodging the motion using the prescribed form of intimation[5]. The period of notice to be given is not less than seven days[6] except where some other period is specified in the Rules (*e.g.* the period of notice for a motion for summary decree or for interim damages is 14 days) or where the sheriff reduces or dispenses with the period of notice on cause shown[7].

Methods of intimation

6.4 Intimation may be made using any of the methods of service which apply generally to the service of initial writs and other court orders. These methods may be used either for intimation to a solicitor for a party or more usually where a party is unrepresented and intimation requires to be made directly to the party. However, where parties are represented by solicitors intimation may instead be made by any of the following methods:

- Personal delivery
- Facsimile transmission
- First class ordinary post
- Delivery to a document exchange[8].

The motion rules also define the date that intimation is deemed to have been given where intimation is made to a solicitor representing a party and where intimation is made on a day when the court is not open for civil court business.

Intimation to solicitor Specifically it is provided that intimation by personal delivery or fax to a solicitor after 5.00pm is deemed to have been made on the day after delivery or transmission, but if delivered or transmitted before 5.00pm intimation it is deemed to have been given on the day of delivery or transmission[9]. Intimation given by ordinary post or through a document exchange is deemed to have been given on the day after posting or delivery[10].

Intimation sent on Saturday, Sunday or holiday Where any intimation is sent on a Saturday, Sunday or public or court holiday the effective date of intimation is the next day on which the sheriff clerk's office is open for civil court business[11].

[4] r 15.1(3)
[5] Form G7
[6] r 15.2(2)
[7] r 15.2(7)
[8] r 15.2(3)(b)
[9] r 15.2(4)(a)
[10] r 15.2(4)(b)
[11] r 15.2(5)

Certificate of intimation

6.5 After intimation of a motion has been given the solicitor who has executed intimation must lodge a certificate of intimation (Form G8) with the sheriff clerk. The certificate provides details of the date and method of intimation and must be lodged not later than two days before the date fixed for hearing the motion[12].

Intimation of opposition to motion

6.6 The party receiving intimation may oppose the motion by completing a notice of opposition (Form G9)[13] and lodging it with the sheriff clerk not later than two days before the date fixed for hearing the motion[14]. The party opposing the motion must also forthwith intimate a copy of the notice of opposition to every other party in the case[15]. The rules for intimation, discussed at para 6.4 apply also in relation to intimating opposition to a motion[16].

Reducing or dispensing with time limits

6.7 The prescribed periods for intimating a motion, lodging a notice of opposition or a certificate of intimation may be dispensed with or reduced where, for example, there is some urgency in having the motion considered and heard by the sheriff[17]. Application, which should be made at the time of lodging the motion, will be considered by the sheriff in chambers.

Hearing of motions

6.8 Where opposition to a motion is intimated and lodged parties must be heard by the sheriff on the date fixed for hearing the motion[18]. After hearing parties the sheriff will normally give his decision from the bench. Thereafter, an interlocutor will be prepared by the clerk of court and be submitted to the sheriff for signing.

An unopposed motion may be determined by the sheriff (or the sheriff clerk) without the attendance of parties in court[19]. If the motion is granted, an interlocutor giving effect to the motion is prepared and signed by the sheriff or, in accordance with the directions of the sheriff principal, the sheriff clerk[20]. The types of unopposed motion which may be determined by a sheriff clerk are prescribed in Practice Notes issued by the Sheriff Principal in each of the sheriffdoms[21]. These provisions give sheriff clerks

12 r 15.2(6)
13 r 15.3(1)(a)
14 r 15.3(1)(c)
15 r 15.3(1)(b)
16 r 15.3(2)
17 r 15.2(7) 15.3(3)
18 r 15.4(5)
19 r 15.4(1)
20 r 15.4(2), 12.1
21 an extract from this Practice Note can be found in the Appendix to this chapter.

similar, but not as extensive, powers as their Court of Session counterparts to consider and determine certain unopposed motions, as follows:

- To authorise re-service of an initial writ (rule 5.9).
- To recall sist and re-enroll for further procedure.
- To close record, under additional procedure, before expiry of adjustment period (rule 10.3(1)).
- To allow a minute of amendment altering the sum sued for (rule 18.1).
- To allow a minute of amendment to be received and answered (rule 18.3(1)(a) and (b)(ii)).
- To order service of a third party notice (rule 20.1(1) and (2)).

Hearing of unopposed motion by sheriff: parties requested to attend

6.9 Although most unopposed motions will be decided without attendance of parties at court, the sheriff has power to direct that a hearing be held in court and that parties be heard on the motion. This might be necessary in the case of a motion seeking an award of access to children where the sheriff requires further information before determining the motion[22]. If a sheriff clerk considers that an unopposed motion, which he has power to deal with, should not be granted he cannot refuse the motion. Instead the motion must be referred to the sheriff[23] who will decide whether it should be granted and also whether parties should attend court for a hearing.

Where a decision is made that there should be an in-court hearing on an unopposed motion the hearing will take place on the date fixed for hearing the motion and the sheriff clerk will advise the solicitor for the party who lodged the motion accordingly[24].

Joint motion or joint minute

6.10 The Rules do not make any specific provision in relation to intimation and hearing of either a joint motion or a motion requesting the court to interpone authority to a joint minute disposing of an action. Accordingly, intimation and hearing of such motions would appear to be necessary unless dispensation from these provisions is sought by parties. It is suggested that this might be sought by incorporating such a request in the joint motion or motion, as the case may be.

22 r 15.4(1)
23 r 15.4(3)
24 r 15.4(4)

Applications made by minute

Application of procedure in Chapter 14

14 prescribes the form of and procedure where an application may be made to the court by minute, which include an application by

6.11 Chapter 14 prescribes the form of and procedure where an application may be made to the court by minute, which include an application by

- The representatives of a party who has died or is under a legal incapacity seeking leave to be sisted as a party to the action (Chapter 25 of the Rules);
- A party to an action seeking transfer to the representatives of a party who has died or is under a legal incapacity (Chapter 25 of the Rules);
- A person who has received intimation of a family action seeking leave to appear as a party (Chapter 33 of the Rules);
- A party seeking variation or recall of an order made in a family action, after final decree (Chapter 33 of the Rules).

The rules in Chapter 14 neither apply to applications where the procedure is prescribed elsewhere (*e.g.* a minute by a connected person in an action of damages[25]), nor to minutes of amendment and abandonment[26]. Nor do the rules apply to a minute of tender or a joint minute disposing of an action as these are not "applications" and, therefore, do not fall within the scope of rule 14.1. (A joint minute must be lodged with a motion seeking an appropriate order.)

Form and content of minute

6.12 Any minute proceeding under the rules in Chapter 14 must include a crave and, where appropriate, a statement of facts supporting the crave and pleas-in-law[27]. Thus, for example, a minute seeking variation of an order for aliment will start with a crave seeking recall of the original order for payment and substitution of a revised payment, followed by a supporting statement detailing the change of circumstances which have prompted the application, and an appropriate plea-in-law. In a minute by a person who has received intimation of a family action (*e.g.* an alleged adulterer) seeking leave to appear as a party it may, however, only be necessary to include a crave to that effect, as in these circumstances the minute will normally be given an opportunity to lodge defences if allowed to appear in the proceedings.

[25] r 36.6(4)
[26] r 14.1(2)
[27] r 14.2

Crave for Options Hearing to be fixed Where the minuter is seeking leave to appear in the proceedings and be sisted as a party to an action or to transfer a cause to the representatives of a party, application may be made in the minute for leave for an Options Hearing to be fixed[28]. This course of action will be necessary in many actions in order to provide the new party with an opportunity to either lodge defences or consider and adopt existing pleadings, and also to provide time for adjustment of the pleadings.

Crave for answers to be lodged In other types of minute (*e.g.* a minute seeking variation or recall of an existing court order) the minuter may seek leave in the minute for an order requiring the other party to lodge answers within a specified period[29].

Intimation and hearing of minute

6.13 The procedure for intimation and hearing of applications made by minute is regulated by the rules which apply to motions. The following rules apply with any necessary modifications:

- Rule 15.2 (intimation of motions)
- Rule 15.3 (opposition to motions), and
- Rule 15.4 (hearing of motions)

Hearing of minute If a notice of opposition is not lodged the minute may be granted by the sheriff in chambers without the attendance of parties. A hearing in court is only necessary with parties in attendance where a notice of opposition is lodged or, in the case of an unopposed minute, where the sheriff directs that he requires to hear parties on the minute. Following the hearing, either in court or in chambers, the sheriff may, if satisfied that the minute should be granted, issue an interlocutor granting the order sought.

In the case of a minute which, for example, seeks variation or recall of an existing court order the sheriff will normally allow a party opposing the application to lodge answers before deciding on the minute. Accordingly, when the minute is first heard it is likely that an interlocutor will be issued ordering answers to be lodged within a specified period and fixing a hearing on the minute and answers for a later date.

Fixing of new Options Hearing Where the order granted by the sheriff is one which sists a person as party to an action or transfers a cause to the representatives of a party, a new Options Hearing will, if sought, be fixed by the sheriff clerk. In calculating the date to be fixed for the hearing, the date

[28] r 14.3(1); see also paras 9.7 and 9.8.

[29] r 14.3(4)

of granting the minute takes the place of the date of expiry of the period of notice for lodging a notice of intention to defend[30]. Thereafter the case will proceed as a defended cause under the Standard Procedure.

Party minuter procedure

Application of procedure

6.14 The application of the procedures in Chapter 13 of the Rules extends only to the circumstances where a person who has not been called as a defender or third party seeks leave to lodge defences or answers and enter process as a party minuter. The person seeking leave must demonstrate a title and interest to enter process.[31]

Form of minute

6.15 Application for leave is made by minute in which there should be specified the minuter's title and interest to be a party to the action and the grounds of the defence thereto[32]. The procedure which applies to an application made by minute under Chapter 13 of the Rules is very similar to that for a minute by a party seeking leave to be sisted as a party to the action under Chapter 14 of the Rules.

Intimation and hearing of minute

6.16 As with other minutes, the rules for motions apply as regards intimation, opposition and hearing. These are, with any necessary modifications:

- Rule 15.2 (intimation of motions)
- Rule 15.3 (opposition to motions), and
- Rule 15.4 (hearing of motions)

Hearing of minute At the hearing of the minute the sheriff, if satisfied that the applicant has a title and interest to enter process, may grant the application and make any order as regards expenses or otherwise as he thinks fit[33]. Where the application is made after the closing of the record, however, the sheriff may only grant leave for the party to enter process if satisfied that there are good reasons why application was not made at an earlier stage in the proceedings[34].

[30] r 14.3(3)
[31] r 13.1
[32] r 13.1(2)
[33] r 13.1(3)
[34] r 13.1(4)

If the application is granted, the sheriff issues an interlocutor allowing the minuter to enter process as a party minuter and to lodge defences or answers within a specific period. When defences or answers are lodged[35] the sheriff clerk fixes a date for an Options Hearing, and the date of lodging becomes the effective date for fixing the hearing.[36] Thereafter the case will proceed as a defended cause under the Standard Procedure, discussed in Chapter 4 of this book.

[35] r 13.2(1) makes reference only to a party minuter lodging *answers*. This presumably is the case if the party minuter is entering process as a third party. However, if party minuter seeks leave to enter process as a defender, clearly he should lodge *defences*.

[36] r 13.2(1)

APPENDIX 6.1

Extract from Practice Note Issued by Sheriffs

1 For the purpose of said rules 12.1 and 15.4(2) "the Sheriff Clerk" shall not include a sheriff clerk below the rank of higher executive officer save that, in any sheriff court within the Sheriffdom where the resident sheriff clerk in charge of a court holds the rank of executive officer, it shall include that sheriff clerk or his temporary replacement provided he is of the same or higher rank.

2 The classes of interlocutor which a sheriff clerk may write and sign, in terms of the said rule 12.1 shall not include any final interlocutor or any interlocutor which the sheriff concerned directs to be written or signed by him or her. Subject to the foregoing, any interlocutor dealing with a motion which has been determined by a sheriff clerk in terms of the said rule 15.4(2) shall be written and signed by that sheriff clerk.

3 The classes of unopposed motion which a sheriff clerk may determine in terms of the said rule 15.4(2) are set out in the Appendix to this direction. However, if the granting of any such motion might also involve any order relating to expenses, it shall be referred to the sheriff who shall deal with it in accordance with rule 15.4(1).

4 This direction shall take effect from 1 January 1994.

APPENDIX

Classes of motion which may be determined by a sheriff clerk in terms of rule 15.4(2):

(a) A motion to authorise re-service of an initial writ in terms of rule 5.9.
(b) A motion to recall a sist and to re-enroll a cause for further procedure.
(c) A motion, made under rule 10.3(1), to close the record before the expiry of the adjustment period provided by rule 10.1(1).
(d) A motion to allow an amendment of a kind specified in rule 18.1.
(e) A motion to allow a minute of amendment to be received and answered within a specified period in terms of rule 18.3(1)(a) and (b)(ii).
(f) A motion for an order for service of a third party notice, made under rule 20.1(1) and (2).

CHAPTER 7

Decrees by Default and Summary Decree

Chapters 16 and 17 of the Rules

Introduction

7.1 "Decree by default" may be obtained where, for example, a party fails to comply with an order of the court or the provisions of a particular rule. "Summary decree" is intended to prevent a party, normally a defender, with no obvious defence delaying decree. The procedures in Chapters 16 and 17 of the Rules apply to all actions except those identified in paras 7.2 and 7.6 of this chapter.

Decree by default

Application of default rules

7.2 The rules in Chapter 16 apply to all actions except family actions (see Chap 13 of this book for default procedures in family actions), actions of multiplepoinding and causes raised under the Presumption of Death (Scotland) Act 1977.[1]

Circumstances leading to default

7.3 A party may be held to be in default as a consequence of a failure to:

- Lodge a production or part of process within a time specified by the sheriff or in the Rules
- Intimate the lodging of a production or part of process
- Implement an order of the sheriff within a specified period, or
- Appear or be represented at any diet.[2]

A diet under this rule includes a proof, proof before answer or debate, and also an Options Hearing or Procedural Hearing[3]. It should be noted that this rule introduces a new default, *i.e.* as a consequence of a failure to intimate to other parties the lodging of a part of process or production[4].

[1] r 16.1
[2] r 16.2(1)
[3] r 16.2(4)
[4] r 16.2(1)(a)

Motion for decree by default

7.4 An application for decree by default may be made by written motion or orally at the bar during any hearing with leave of the court[5].

Sheriff's powers in relation to default

7.5 The sheriff's powers in relation to default include granting decree as craved or decree of absolvitor or dismissal[6]. The sheriff may, however, instead of granting decree prorogate the time for lodging any production or part of process, or implementing an order of court[7]. The sheriff also has power to dismiss an action where no party appears at a diet of court[8].

Summary decree

Application of summary decree rules

7.6 Summary decree procedure is available in any action except a family action, an action of multiplepoinding or a cause raised under the Presumption of Death (Scotland) Act 1977[9], and may be applied for by

- A pursuer on the grounds that the defender has not disclosed a defence to the action, or part of it[10]
- A defender on similar grounds against a pursuer's counterclaim[11], or
- A defender or third party against a claim made by another defender or third party[12].

Motion for summary decree

7.7 Application for summary decree is made by motion and the rules which apply to motions generally apply, subject to the following. First, intimation of the motion must be made by registered post or first class recorded delivery letter, and secondly, the period of notice to be given to other parties is to be not less than 14 days before the date of the hearing[13]. The motion seeking summary decree may move the sheriff to

- grant decree in terms of the crave of the initial writ counterclaim or claim,
- sustain or repel a plea-in-law, or
- dispose of the whole or part of the subject matter of the action, counterclaim or claim.[14]

[5] r 15.1(a)
[6] r 16.2(2)
[7] r 16.3
[8] r 16.2(3); see r 16.2(4) and para 7.3 for definition of "diet".
[9] r 17.1
[10] r 17.2(1)
[11] r 17.3(1)
[12] r 17.3(2)
[13] r 17.2(3)
[14] r 17.2(2)

Hearing of motion and sheriff's powers

7.8 At the hearing of the motion the sheriff may, if satisfied that there is no defence to the action or counterclaim or claim, grant the motion for summary decree in whole or in part. The sheriff also has power to make a number of other orders, including ordering a party, or a partner, director, officer or office bearer of a party, to produce documents or articles or lodge an affidavit in support of any matter of fact asserted in the pleadings or made at the motion hearing[15].

Subsequent motion

7.9 Where the sheriff refuses a motion for summary decree, in whole or in part, a subsequent motion may competently be made provided there has been a change of circumstances[16].

[15] r 17.2(4)

[16] r 17.2(5)

CHAPTER 8

Amendment of Pleadings

Chapter 18 of the Rules

Introduction

8.1 The sheriff has very wide powers to allow amendment. Such amendments fall into the categories discussed in paras 8.2 and 8.3 below. This chapter examines the sheriff's powers to allow amendment and the procedure for seeking an amendment in a defended action. The procedure for amendment of the initial writ in an undefended case is discussed in Chapter 3 of this book[1].

Sheriff's powers

Alteration of sum sued for by pursuer before record closed

8.2 Rule 18.1 provides a simplified procedure to enable the pursuer to alter the sum sued for by amending the crave and intimating the amendment in writing to every other party in the case. This procedure, however, may only be used before the record is closed and where all parties have lodged defences or answers.

Amendment to pleadings and parties in action

8.3 Before final judgment the sheriff may allow amendments to the initial writ[2], the condescendence, defences, answers, and pleas-in-law or other pleadings[3] which are necessary for the determination of the question of controversy between the parties. Amendments to the initial writ may seek to increase or restrict the sum sued for or seek a different remedy from that originally sought[4].

A further type of amendment that a party may seek is one which affects or alters the parties to the action. In particular such an amendment may seek leave to

- Correct or supplement the designation of a party
- Allow a party to sue or be sued in a different capacity

[1] r 7.6; see para 3.10 (procedure in undefended causes)
[2] r 18.2(2)(a)
[3] r 18.2(2)(c)
[4] r 18.2(a)(i) or (ii)

- Add an additional pursuer or person whose concurrence is necessary
- Sist a substitute or additional party where the action had commenced or been presented in the name of the wrong person
- Direct a crave against a third party, or
- Bring in an additional or substitute defender where all parties are not called or the wrong person is called[5]

Procedure for seeking amendment to pleadings

Lodging minute and motion

8.4 An application for amendment to pleadings may be permitted, with leave of the sheriff, at any time before final judgment[6]. Application is made by lodging a minute of amendment and a motion which should move the court to allow the minute of amendment to be received and answered[7]. The procedure that follows intimation of the motion depends largely on whether

- The amendment is opposed
- Answers are lodged, or
- Parties require time to adjust the minute of amendment and any answers lodged

Procedure where answers lodged

8.5 When answers are lodged a further motion may be necessary either to move the sheriff to allow the amendment in terms of the minute and answers or, where parties need to adjust the minute and answers, to fix a period for adjustment. If the sheriff allows a period for adjustment a further date must be fixed to enable parties to be heard on the minute of amendment, answers and adjustments[8].

The need for a further motion may be avoided where the party lodging the minute of amendment anticipates that answers will be lodged and thereafter parties will require time to adjust. This may be achieved if the motion lodged with the minute of amendment covers all these matters. If it does a single interlocutor may be issued: (i) allowing the minute of amendment to be received and answered, (ii) fixing a period for adjustment, and (iii) assigning a diet to hear parties on the minute of amendment and answers, as adjusted.[9]

[5] r 18.2(b), (d)
[6] r 18.2(1), (2)
[7] r 18.3(1)(a), (b)
[8] r 18.3(2)
[9] r 18.3(1) and (2)

Procedure where no answers lodged

8.6 If answers are not lodged following intimation of the motion and minute, and there is no opposition, the motion be granted allowing the pleadings to be amended in terms of the minute of amendment.

Minute to amend to insert an additional or substitute party

8.7 Where the amendment is one which seeks to introduce an additional or substitute party the motion lodged with the minute of amendment should request that the amendment be allowed and an order for service be granted[10]. If the motion is granted the sheriff will issue an interlocutor allowing the amendment and ordering that a copy of the initial writ or record, as amended, is served on the additional or substitute party. In addition the following notices must be served:

- Where party may apply for a time to pay direction
  —Form O3 Notice about time to pay application
  —Form O7 Notice of intention to defend
  —Form O8 Notice to additional/substitute defender
- Any other case
  —Form O7 Notice of intention to defend
  —Form O9 Notice to additional/substitute defender[11]

Following service the action proceeds as if the additional or substitute party had originally been a party to the action. Where a notice of intention to defend is lodged the sheriff clerk is required to fix a date for an Options Hearing[12]. Thereafter the action will proceed as a defended cause and the procedures discussed in Chapter 4 of this book will apply.

Warrant for diligence

8.8 The party seeking the amendment may also apply in the motion lodged with the minute of amendment for a warrant for diligence against the additional or substitute party, *e.g.* warrant to arrest on the dependence[13]. If granted the sheriff clerk will issue a certified copy of the interlocutor as authority for executing diligence[14].

[10] rr 18.3(1)(b)(i), 18.5(1)
[11] r 18.5(1)
[12] r 18.5(2), (3)
[13] r 18.4(1)
[14] r 18.4(2)

Preliminary pleas inserted by amendment

8.9 If there is included in the minute of amendment, answers or adjustments a new preliminary plea, a note setting out the basis of the plea must be lodged with the minute, answers or adjustment. The preliminary plea note will be considered by the sheriff at any Options Hearing, Procedural Hearing or other hearing at which either a proof before answer or debate is sought. Failure to lodge a note setting out the basis of the plea will result in the preliminary plea being repelled by the sheriff.[15]

Expenses and conditions of amendment

8.10 The party seeking the amendment should normally be found liable for the expenses occasioned by the amendment, including the expenses of the answers and any adjustment. Indeed the Rules provide that the sheriff should make such an order for expenses unless it is considered that it would be "just and equitable" to do otherwise. The Rules also provide that the sheriff may attach conditions to the order allowing the amendment. For example, the sheriff might order that payment of the expenses is a condition precedent to the action proceeding.[16]

Effect of amendment on diligence

8.11 An amendment does not validate any diligence used on the dependence prior to amendment which would prejudice creditors. It may, therefore, be necessary to apply for a new warrant to arrest on the dependence of the action[17] if required.

[15] r 18.8; see also paras 4.16 and 4.17 under *Debate* for discussion about procedure relative to preliminary plea notes.

[16] r 18.6

[17] r 18.7

CHAPTER 9

Miscellaneous Procedures and Applications

Chapters 21–27 and 38 of the Rules

Introduction

9.1 This chapter examines the rules for the following procedures:

- Abandonment of cause or counterclaim
- Withdrawal of solicitor for party
- Minutes of sist and transference
- Transfer and remit of causes
- Reference to European Court
- Caution and security.

The procedure for the intimation and hearing of these applications is, with some exception and variations, the motion procedure discussed in Chapter 6 of this book.

Abandonment

9.2 The Rules provide that an action may be abandoned by a pursuer lodging a minute of abandonment at any time before decree of absolvitor or dismissal has been granted. Along with the minute there must be lodged a motion requesting the court to give effect to the minute, and the motion and minute will require to be intimated to all other parties in the action.[1]

Decree of absolvitor sought and expenses

9.3 Where the pursuer is consenting to decree of absolvitor the defender may seek, and will normally be entitled to, the expenses of the action. The question of expenses, however, is a matter for the sheriff's discretion.

[1] r 23.1(1): See also *Walker* v *Walker* (Notes), 1995 SCLR, 389.

Decree of dismissal sought and payment of defender's expenses

9.4 A pursuer seeking leave to abandon his action and obtain decree of dismissal may only do so provided he pays the defender's expenses. In this case the motion lodged with the minute of abandonment must deal with the question of expenses. If the amount of expenses is not agreed, the motion for the pursuer should seek the following orders:

- That the defender lodge an account of expenses within a specified period, and
- That when lodged the defender's account is remitted to the Auditor of Court for taxation

If the pursuer is to obtain decree of dismissal he must pay the defender's full judicial expenses within 28 days of the date of taxation[2]. When the expenses are paid the pursuer may then lodge a further motion (and produce a receipt for payment) requesting the court to dismiss the case. If the pursuer fails to pay the defender's expenses, the defender is entitled to lodge a motion seeking decree of absolvitor with taxed expenses.

Abandonment of counterclaim

9.5 The rules relating to abandonment of an action by a pursuer apply also to abandonment of a counterclaim by a defender[3].

Withdrawal of solicitor for party

9.6 A solicitor who no longer acts for a party must intimate by letter his withdrawal from acting to the sheriff clerk and to the other party or parties in the action[4]. Thereafter, the Rules provide that the party whose solicitor has withdrawn should receive formal notification of his solicitor's withdrawal and be provided with the opportunity of attending court to state whether he intends to continue with his action or defence.

In many courts notification to the defender will be initiated by the court following receipt by the sheriff clerk of the letter intimating withdrawal. The alternative procedure is to await a motion from the other party or parties in the action.[5] In either case the sheriff will issue an interlocutor :

- Ordaining the party whose solicitor has withdrawn to appear at a special hearing, known as a "peremptory diet", to state whether he intends to proceed, and

[2] r 23.1(2)
[3] r 23.2
[4] r 24.1
[5] r 24.2(1)

- Ordering service of a copy of the interlocutor and a notice in Form G10[6].

The peremptory diet is fixed for a date not less than 14 days after the date of the sheriff's interlocutor[7]. After service, the party serving the interlocutor and notice must lodge in process an execution of service[8], in order that the court may be satisfied that service has been effected should it be necessary to consider granting decree. If the party whose solicitor has withdrawn does not appear or is not represented at the peremptory diet the sheriff may grant decree or any other relevant order[9]. In a family action in which evidence must be led before granting decree the sheriff will allow the cause to proceed as undefended and direct that proof be taken by affidavit.

Minutes of sist and transference

Minute of sist

9.7 In an action where a party dies or comes under some legal incapacity, such as a mental disorder or is sequestrated, a representative of the party or his estate may apply for leave to be sisted as a party to the action in place of the original party[10]. The representatives who may seek leave to be sisted may be the executors of a party who has died or any curator bonis or permanent trustee, as the case may be.

Application is made by minute which should include a crave seeking leave for the applicant to be sisted as a party to the action and to appear in the proceedings[11]. There should also be included in the minute a statement supporting the crave, which should include details of the death of the party or the reason for his incapacity and also the representative's title, *e.g.* executor[12]. The minuter may also make application for an Options Hearing to be fixed where, for example, the minuter requires time to consider and adjust the pleadings in the action[13].

The procedure for intimation, opposition and hearing of the minute is regulated by the rules applicable to motions[14]. If the sheriff grants the minute at the hearing and a new Options Hearing has been sought the date of the granting of the minute takes the place of the date of the expiry of the period of notice for the purpose of calculating the date for the Options Hearing[15].

[6] r 24.2(3)
[7] r 24.2(2)
[8] r 24.2(3)
[9] r 24.3
[10] r 25.1
[11] r 14.3(1)
[12] r 14.2
[13] r 14.3(1)
[14] r 14.3(5)
[15] r 14.3(2), (3)

Minute of transference

9.8 If the representatives of a party who has died or is under a legal incapacity do not apply to be sisted, any other party in the action may apply by minute to have the action transferred to such person or persons[16]. The procedure for intimation, opposition and hearing of the minute is the same as that which applies to a minute for sist, except that a copy of the pleadings must be sent with intimation of the minute to the representative[17]. If the crave of the minute is granted the action is transferred to the representative of the party concerned and proceeds thereafter as a defended action. Where it is sought, the sheriff clerk will fix a date for an Options Hearing and intimate this to parties[18].

Transfer and remit of causes

Grounds for transfer to another Sheriff Court

9.9 There are two main grounds for transferring an action to another Sheriff Court. The first is where cause is shown to the sheriff's satisfaction that the action should be remitted to another Sheriff Court. The second is where the sheriff considers that it would be expedient to do so on the grounds of convenience to witnesses and parties.

The power to *remit* an action to another sheriff court "on cause shown"[19] would appear to be supplementary to the more frequently used power to transfer on the grounds of convenience, and it is difficult to envisage circumstances when this power might be used on its own. In any event, where a remit is made under this provision the sheriff must specify the reasons for so doing in the interlocutor remitting the action[20].

An action may be *transferred* on the grounds of convenience in two situations. The first is where there are two or more defenders and the action has been raised in the sheriff court where one of the defenders resides or has a place of business. In this case the sheriff may transfer the action to any other sheriff court which has jurisdiction over one of the other defenders[21]. The second situation is where a plea of no jurisdiction is sustained. Here the sheriff may transfer the action to the court in which, in his opinion, it should have been raised[22]. An action may be transferred under these provisions only on the motion of one of the parties and where

16 r 25.2(1)
17 r 25.2(2)
18 r 14.3(1), (2)
19 r 26.1(1)
20 r 26.1(5)
21 r 26.1(2)
22 r 26.1(3)

the sheriff takes the view that it would be more convenient for the witnesses and parties to have the action proceed in another Sheriff Court[23]. The sheriff must state his reasons for transferring the action in the interlocutor granting the motion[24].

Procedure following receipt of transferred action

9.10 The Sheriff Court receiving the action has no power to decline the case[25]. Following receipt of the process the action proceeds in the court to which it is transferred as if it had originally been raised there[26]. Consideration must be given as to what procedure is appropriate, and this will depend on the stage at which the action had reached prior to transfer. The Rules make no provision as to how proceedings re-commence, and this will largely be at the discretion of the court. If the action is defended it may be that the sheriff clerk will fix a hearing to enable the sheriff to hear parties on the question of further procedure. Alternatively parties might lodge a motion for the action to be enrolled with a view to determining what further procedure is appropriate. In an undefended cause, which has been transferred after discovery that the court where the action was originally raised did not have jurisdiction over the defender, the sheriff may wish to order re-service of the initial writ before granting decree.

Appeal against decision to transfer action

9.11 An appeal against the sheriff's decision to transfer a cause may be made, with leave, to the sheriff principal, but there is no appeal to the Court of Session[27].

Remit to Court of Session

9.12 There are a number of statutory provisions which empower the sheriff or sheriff principal to remit an action to the Court of Session. These include section 37(1)(b) and (2A) of the Sheriff Courts (Scotland) Act 1971 which respectively provide that

- Any action may be remitted on the motion of any party, on the grounds of the importance or difficulty of the case, and
- The sheriff or sheriff principal may of his own accord remit certain types of family actions[28] and an application for adoption of a child.

A remit may also be made under section 1 of the Presumption of Death (Scotland) Act 1977 and in an action against the Crown following

[23] r 26.1(4)
[24] r 26.1(5)
[25] r 26.1(6)
[26] r 26.1(7)
[27] r 26.1(8)
[28] actions of divorce, custody or guardianship of a child

certification by the Lord Advocate under section 44 of the Crown Proceedings Act 1947.

When a remit is made the sheriff clerk sends the process to the Deputy Principal Clerk of Session within four days of the remit, and also sends written notification to each party in the case[29]. Before sending the process to the Court of Session, the sheriff clerk endorses a certificate on the interlocutor sheet that he has sent such written notification to parties[30].

Remit from the Court of Session

9.13 Section 14 of the Law Reform (Miscellaneous Provisions) (Scotland) Act 1985 provides that the Court of Session may remit any action to the Sheriff Court if it considers that:

- The action could have been brought in the Sheriff Court
- The nature of the action makes it appropriate to do so.

Following receipt of a process remitted under this provision the sheriff clerk records the date of receipt on the interlocutor sheet, fixes a date for a hearing to decide what further procedure is appropriate, and sends written notice of the date of the hearing to all parties in the case[31]. The hearing is fixed for the first suitable court day occurring not earlier than 14 days from the date of receipt of the process[32].

Reference to European Court

Sheriff's powers

9.14 The sheriff has a discretion to refer a case to the Court of Justice of the European Communities (the European Court) for a preliminary ruling where a decision on a question of EC law is necessary to enable the issue in the action to be decided. However, where a question or issue in connection with EC law arises and there is no remedy or right of appeal at a later stage of the proceedings against the decision, the sheriff does not have a discretion and in these circumstances reference to the European Court is mandatory.

Application for and form of reference

9.15 A reference, which may be made by the sheriff of his own motion or on the motion of any party[33], is in the form of a request to the court and includes a statement of the case for the European Court and the

29 r 26.2(1), (2)
30 r 26.2(2)
31 r 26.3
32 r 26.3(b)
33 r 38.2

question(s) on which a preliminary ruling is sought. The form of reference must be in the form prescribed in the Rules (Form E1).

Procedure following decision to make reference

9.16 If the sheriff decides that a reference should be made the action is continued. Within four weeks after the date of the continuation the sheriff must prepare a draft reference, a copy of which is sent by the sheriff clerk to parties[34]. Thereafter, parties have four weeks within which to lodge a note of any adjustments to the draft reference[35]. Any adjustments lodged are considered by the sheriff who must within 14 days of the last date for lodging adjustments make and sign the reference[36]. Thereafter, the sheriff clerk intimates the making of the reference to parties[37] and sends a certified copy of the reference to the Registrar of the European Court (except where an appeal against the making of the reference has been marked and is pending[38]).

Sist of action pending ruling of European Court

9.17 The action will normally be sisted pending the decision of the European Court. The sheriff may, however, recall the sist for the purpose of considering an application for an interim order[39].

Caution and security

Application of the Rules

9.18 There are a number of situations where the sheriff may order a party to lodge caution or security in an action before the court. These include caution:

- For recall of an arrestment used on the dependence
- For expenses as a condition precedent to the action proceeding
- To be found by a party litigant in relation to witness expenses
- In place of sisting a mandatory, on behalf of a party who is abroad.

The rules in Chapter 27 apply in any action where the sheriff has power to order caution or security and in relation to expenses ordered to be given in an election petition under section 136(2)(i) of the Representation of the People Act 1983.[39a]

[34] r 38.3(1), (2)
[35] r 38.3(3)
[36] r 38.3(4)
[37] r 38.3(5)
[38] r 38.5
[39] r 38.4
[39a] r See s 726(2) of the Companies Act 1985 in relation to an order for caution against a company which has raised an action.

Motion seeking order to find caution or give security

9.19 Application for an order against a party to find caution or give security is made by motion, and the motion should set out the grounds for seeking the order[40]. If the sheriff grants the motion an interlocutor will be issued which should specify both the amount and method of finding caution and also the period of time within which it is to be found[41].

Methods of finding caution or giving security

9.20 A person ordered to find caution must do so by bond of caution. Instead of a bond of caution the court may, however, order the person to consign a sum of money with the sheriff clerk who will place it on deposit receipt. Security may also be given by any other method approved by the sheriff including a combination of two or more methods of security (*e.g.* by guarantee, by consignation or by deposit receipt in the joint names of agents for parties).[42]

Any document used to satisfy the finding or caution or giving of security must be lodged in process.[43] However, in the case of a deposit receipt in the joint names of agents for parties a copy may be lodged.[44] Any bond of caution or other document lodged in process may not be borrowed.[45] When lodged, the sheriff clerk is required to satisfy himself that the bond of caution or document is in proper form.[46]

Caution or security by authorised insurance company

9.21 An insurance company providing caution or security must be authorised under section 3 or 4 of the Insurance Companies Act 1982 to carry on insurance business of class 15(b) in Schedule 2 of that Act, and a statement to that effect must be included in the bond of caution or security document[47]. The Rules also provide that the bond of caution must specify the obligations of the cautioner and the party, and their heirs and executors, under the bond[48].

Failure to find caution or give security

9.22 Where a party fails to find caution or give security any other party may apply by motion for decree by default or any other relevant order[49].

40 r 27.2
41 r 27.3
42 r 27.4(1), (2)
43 r 27.4(3)
44 r 27.4(4)
45 r 27.4(5)
46 r 27.7(1)
47 rr 27.5, 27.6(2)
48 r 27.6(1)
49 r 27.9

Other orders relating to caution or security

9.23 Any party who is dissatisfied with sufficiency or form of caution or security may apply by motion for the matter either to be resolved by the court or for decree by default[50]. Where a cautioner becomes insolvent or dies the party entitled to benefit from the caution may apply by motion for a new order for caution or security[51].

[50] r 27.7(2), 27.9
[51] r 27.8

CHAPTER 10

Recovery of Evidence

Chapter 28 of the Rules

Introduction

10.1 This chapter examines the rules regulating the following procedures for recovery of evidence:

- Recovery of documents using either a commission and diligence or the optional procedure
- Orders under section 1 of the Administration of Justice (Scotland) Act 1972
- Production of public records
- Commission for examination of witnesses
- Letters of request.

Recovery of documents

Form of application

10.2 An application for a commission and diligence for recovery of documents is made by motion. Along with the motion there must be lodged a part of process known as a "specification of documents" which contains details of the documents sought to be recovered from the "haver"[1]. The haver is the person who has or is believed to have the documents in question, and may either be a party to the action or have no connection with it. In the latter situation the haver is referred to as a third party haver.

Intimation and hearing of motion

10.3 The motion, together with a copy of the specification, is intimated to the other parties in the action and also to any third party haver. The rules relating to intimation and hearing of motions apply[2]. Where the documents sought are held by a Crown Department or a Health Service hospital intimation is made to the Lord Advocate[3]. When granting a motion for

[1] r 28.2(1), (2)
[2] see Chap 6 of this book (Motions)
[3] r 28.2(3)

recovery of documents the sheriff has power to order the party seeking the order to find caution or give security[4]. There are two available methods for recovery of documents:

- The optional procedure
- Execution of a commission and diligence by a commissioner appointed by the court.

Optional procedure

10.4 In many cases the party who has obtained the order for recovery will, in the first instance, use the simplified optional procedure. Under this procedure the party seeking recovery of the documents serves on the haver an order requiring the haver to produce the documents sought to the sheriff clerk within seven days of the date of service[5].

Production of the documents is made by the haver lodging or sending the documents to the sheriff clerk. At the same time the haver must return the order together with a certificate stating that all the documents sought have been produced or information about the location of any documents which are not in the possession of the haver[6].

The sheriff clerk must intimate to parties not later than the day after receipt that the documents have been received[7]. The party who has sought recovery of the documents has seven days from the date of intimation to uplift the documents; no other party may uplift the documents within this period. If the documents are not so uplifted the sheriff clerk is required to intimate this to the other parties in the case[8] who then have the opportunity, if they so wish, to uplift the documents. If the documents are not uplifted by any of the parties the sheriff clerk must return them to the haver[9].

If the party who has uplifted the documents subsequently decides not to lodge them in process as productions the documents must be returned to the sheriff clerk[10]. Following return of the documents the sheriff clerk intimates this fact to the other parties in the action, who may uplift the documents should they wish to lodge them as productions. If no party uplifts the documents within 14 days from the date of intimation the sheriff clerk is required to return them to the haver[11].

[4] r 28.2(4); see Chap 9 of this book (Caution and Security)
[5] r 28.3(1), (2); Form G11
[6] r 28.3(2); Form G11
[7] r 28.3(3)
[8] r 28.3(4), (5)
[9] r 28.3(6)
[10] r 28.3(7)
[11] r 28.3(7)(a), (b)

Where the document produced by the haver is an extract from a book the sheriff has power, on the motion of the person seeking recovery of the book, to order that the book is inspected and that copies are taken[12]. If a question of confidentiality arises in connection with a book the sheriff may direct that it is inspected at the sight of a commissioner[13]. The sheriff also has power to order production of any book (not being a banker's book or book of public record) containing entries falling within the specification of documents[14].

If the party seeking recovery of the documents is not satisfied that there has been full compliance with the order for recovery or that adequate reasons for non-compliance have been given, he may execute the commission and diligence using the procedures discussed below.[15]

Execution of commission and diligence

10.5 *Procedure for appointing and instructing commissioner* Where the party seeking recovery of the documents requires to execute a commission and diligence the appointment of a commissioner should be sought in the motion for commission and diligence. The motion should include the name and address of at least one proposed commissioner for approval and appointment by the sheriff.

The party seeking recovery of the documents is responsible for instructing and providing the commissioner with copies of the specification and pleadings and a certified copy of the interlocutor appointing him[16]. This party is also responsible for instructing a clerk and shorthand writer for the commission[17] and for payment of the fees of the commissioner, clerk and shorthand writer[18]. Although provision is made for the appointment of a clerk and a shorthand writer, in practice usually only a shorthand writer is employed.

Intimation of diet for execution of commission The commissioner, in consultation with parties, fixes a date, time and place for executing the commission and cites the haver to appear by serving a citation in Form G13 together with a copy of the specification of documents and, where it is thought necessary, a copy of the pleadings[19].

Procedure at and report of commission At the commission the parties and the haver may be represented by a solicitor or advocate[20]. The

[12] r 28.3(9)
[13] r 28.3(10)
[14] r 28.3(11)
[15] rr 28.3(8), 28.4
[16] r 28.4(1)(a)
[17] r 28.4(1)(b)
[18] r 28.4(1)(c)
[19] r 28.4(2)–(4)
[20] r 28.4(5)

shorthand writer and haver are put on oath by the commissioner[21], and the haver is then examined by the solicitor for the party executing the commission. Thereafter any party present or represented at the commission may put questions to the haver.

After the commission has been executed a report[22] is prepared by the commissioner and submitted to the sheriff clerk together with the documents recovered and an inventory thereof. The sheriff clerk, not later than the day after receipt of the report, documents and inventory, sends intimation to parties that these have been received[23]. The procedure thereafter as regards the uplifting, lodging and returning of documents which are not uplifted is the same as that which applies to documents recovered under the optional procedure[24] discussed in para 10.4 above.

Orders under section 1 of the Administration of Justice (Scotland) Act 1972

10.6 Section 1 of the 1972 Act makes provision for the recovery of documents and other property and for the granting of orders in relation to

- production or recovery of documents or other property
- inspection, photographing, taking samples or carrying out experiments on documents or other property
- preservation, custody and detention of documents or other property
- obtaining information as to the identity of a person who might be a witness or a defender[25]:

An order under section 1 may be applied for both before and after proceedings have been raised. Where made prior to an action being raised the application must be made by summary application in terms of the Act of Sederunt (Sheriff Court Summary Application Rules) 1993. The following paragraphs examine the procedure which applies where an order is sought after proceedings have commenced by ordinary action.

An application for an order under section 1 is made by motion. A specification of the document or property for which the order is sought must be lodged with the motion[26]. The rules for intimation, opposition and hearing of motions apply.

21 r 28.4(6)
22 r 28.4(7)
23 r 28.4(8)
24 r 28.4(9)–(12)
25 rr 28.5–28.7; ss 1(1) and 1A of the 1972 Act
26 r 28.2(1), (2)

Execution of orders under section 1(1)

10.7 *Recovery of documents or other property* Execution of an order for recovery of documents or other property granted under section 1(1) may be made using either the optional procedure or the procedure for executing a commission and diligence[27] as outlined in paras 10.4 and 10.5 above.

Inspection etc of documents or other property Rule 28.6 makes provision for the execution of an order for inspection or photographing of a document or property and for taking samples or carrying out an experiment on the samples or property. The order granted appoints a person to carry out such procedures[28], and a certified copy of the interlocutor granting the order is sufficient authority for the order to be carried out[29].

Apart from prescribing that the party who has obtained the order must serve a copy of the interlocutor, specification and pleadings on the haver[30], the Rules do not provide for the procedure for execution of the order. Certain aspects of the procedure applicable to the execution of a commission and diligence for recovery of documents may, it is suggested, be applied. In particular, it would be appropriate for the party who has obtained the order to instruct the person appointed to carry out the inspection, etc and provide this person with the relevant papers and be responsible for payment of any fees. As regards the time and place for execution of the order this might be arranged by the person appointed to carry out the inspection, etc, in consultation with parties. Following the execution of the order a report should be prepared and submitted to the court.

Preservation etc of documents or other property Where an order is granted in relation to the preservation, custody and detention of documents or property, it will be necessary to appoint a commissioner to execute a commission and diligence to recover the documents or property with a view to these being placed in the custody of a person other than the haver[31]. The party who has obtained the order is responsible for providing the commissioner with copies of the specification and pleadings, a certified copy of the interlocutor appointing the commissioner, and also for serving a copy of the order on the haver and paying the commissioner's fees[32]. Thereafter, the procedure for executing the order follows that which applies to any other commission and diligence. After execution of the

[27] rr 28.3, 28.4 apply to orders granted under r 28.5
[28] r 28.6(1)
[29] r 28.6(2)
[30] r 28.6(3)
[31] r 28.7(1)
[32] r 28.7(2)

commission a report is prepared by the commissioner and lodged with the sheriff clerk. The documents or property taken by the commissioner, and an inventory thereof, are also lodged pending the further orders of the sheriff on the future custody and detention of the documents or property[33].

Execution of an order under section 1A of 1972 Act

10.8 There is no rule regulating the procedure for execution of an order granted under section 1A for disclosure of information of the identity of a person who might be a witness or defender. In terms of section 1A the sheriff has power to order any person to disclose such information, and it may be that the sheriff's interlocutor is sufficient for the purposes of recovery of such information. If not it may be that a commissioner will require to be appointed to examine the person concerned.

Procedure where confidentiality claimed

10.9 A haver may claim confidentiality for documents or other property recovered by a commission and diligence or by order under the 1972 Act. Where such a claim is made the commissioner (or the haver where the optional procedure is used) must place the documents or property, so far as practicable, in a sealed envelope or packet[34] and mark it "*confidential*".

If any party wishes to have the sealed packet opened up, a motion to that effect must be lodged[35]. The motion may be lodged by the party who obtained the order for recovery at any time. However, other parties may only apply after they have received intimation from the sheriff clerk that the party seeking recovery has failed to uplift the documents. A motion seeking the opening of a confidential envelope or packet must be intimated in the usual way to all other parties. Intimation must also be made to any haver who is not a party to the action by first class recorded delivery post[36], in order to provide the haver with the opportunity to oppose the motion[37].

Warrant for production of original documents from public records

10.10 An extract of a document registered and in the custody of the keeper of a public record (*e.g.* a deed registered in the Books of Council and Session) is usually sufficient for the purposes of civil court

[33] r 28.7(3)
[34] r 28.8(1)
[35] r 28.8(2)
[36] r 28.8(3)
[37] r 28.8(4)

proceedings. However, if a party considers it is necessary to have the original document produced, application may be made by motion[38] to the court to certify that the document is required for the purposes of the action or proceedings. It should be noted that intimation of a motion under this provision must be given to the keeper at least seven days before lodging the motion[39].

Authorisation from Court of Session

10.11 In the case of a public record kept by the Keeper of the Registers of Scotland or the Keeper of the Records of Scotland, the sheriff on consideration of a motion may issue an interlocutor certifying that the original record should be produced, but only if satisfied that this is necessary for "the ends of justice"[40]. If the sheriff issues an interlocutor in these terms the party seeking production of the record is required to write to the Deputy Principal Clerk of Session, enclosing a copy of the sheriff's interlocutor, requesting authorisation from the Court of Session for the keeper to exhibit the original record to the sheriff[41].

On receipt of a letter under this provision the Deputy Principal Clerk of Session must submit it to a Lord Ordinary who may grant warrant for production of the original record[42]. If authority is granted the party seeking production of the record must serve a certified copy of the warrant on the keeper[43].

Commission to examine witnesses

10.12 Evidence of witnesses is normally given orally at a proof, except in the following situations where evidence may be taken on commission where:

- A witness is resident outwith the jurisdiction of the court or, if resident within the court's jurisdiction, resides at a place remote from the court[44]
- A witness is unable to attend court because of age, infirmity or sickness[45]
- The evidence of a witness is in danger of being lost, for example where the witness is in danger of dying or is about to go abroad, and the evidence needs to be preserved (to lie *in retentis*)[46].

38 r 28.9(1)
39 r 28.9(2)
40 r 28.9(3)
41 r 28.9(3)
42 r 28.9(4)
43 r 28.9(5)
44 r 28.10(1)(a)(i), (ii)
45 r 28.10(1)(a)(iii)
46 r 28.10(1)(b)

Application to take evidence on commission is made by motion which must specify the name and address of at least one proposed commissioner[47]. If the sheriff grants the motion an interlocutor will be issued approving the appointment of the commissioner. This interlocutor is sufficient authority for citing witnesses to appear at the commission[48].

Commission without interrogatories—"open commission"

10.13 In the Sheriff Court, unless cause is shown to the contrary, a commission is granted without interrogatories[49]. A commission without interrogatories is described as an "open commission". The arrangements for executing the commission are the responsibility of the party who has obtained the commission. This involves providing the commissioner with a copy of the pleadings, a certified copy of the interlocutor appointing the commissioner and making all the arrangements for taking the evidence of the witness including instructing a shorthand writer and paying the fees of the commissioner and shorthand writer[50].

At the commission all parties are entitled to be present and represented[51]. The evidence is usually recorded in shorthand and the oath *de fideli administratione* is administered to the shorthand writer by the commissioner[52]. The commissioner also administers an oath or affirmation to the witness[53]. The procedure for taking the examination of a witness at a commission is much the same as the examination of a witness in court at a proof, with the commissioner performing a role similar to that of the sheriff.

After the commission a report is prepared which will include the extended shorthand notes of evidence. The report is lodged with the sheriff clerk together with any documents produced by a witness and an inventory of the documents[54]. On receipt of the report and other documents the sheriff clerk intimates receipt to parties[55]. The onus, however, for lodging the report in process lies with the party who has obtained the commission[56].

Commission on interrogatories

10.14 Interrogatories are written questions which are put to a witness whose evidence is taken by commission. The interrogatories are drafted by the party who has obtained the commission and are lodged in process

47 r 28.10(2)
48 r 28.10(3)
49 r 28.10(5)
50 r 28.12(1)
51 r 28.12(2)
52 r 28.10(4)(a)
53 r 28.10(4)(b)
54 r 28.12(3)
55 r 28.12(4)
56 r 28.12(5)

when prepared. Any other party in the action may in response to the interrogatories draft and lodge cross-interrogatories[57]. After parties have had the opportunity to adjust and consider the interrogatories and cross-interrogatories they are extended and returned to the sheriff clerk who submits them to the sheriff for approval or settlement of any dispute[58]. The process of approval involves ensuring that the questions are relevant and relate to matters on record; a hearing may be necessary if there is a dispute about the content or relevancy of any of the questions.

When approved, the party who has obtained the commission is responsible for making arrangements for the commission to be executed. This includes providing the commissioner with the interrogatories and cross-interrogatories, a copy of the pleadings and a certified copy of the interlocutor containing the commissioner's appointment[59], and also instructing a clerk to the commissioner and paying, in the first instance, the fees of the commissioner and any clerk[60]. The commissioner, however, is required to fix the date for executing the commission, in consultation with parties[61].

The conduct of the commission is much the same as that for an open commission, except that the questions put to the witness are those in the interrogatories and cross-interrogatories. The commissioner may, however, ask supplementary questions to clarify any answer given.

The procedure for lodging the executed interrogatories and any documents produced is the same as that for an open commission[62].

Use of evidence taken on commission at proof

10.15 Evidence taken on commission may be used as evidence at a proof, subject to any objections by parties[63]. It should also be noted that evidence taken on commission cannot be used if a witness subsequently becomes available to attend the proof[64]. The party wishing to use the report of the commission or the executed interrogatories should formally intimate at the proof that it is to form part of his case. If the party who obtained the commission does not use the evidence, it may be used by any other party[65]. Any objections to the use of evidence taken on commission will be dealt with by the sheriff[66] at the proof.

[57] r 28.11(1), (2)
[58] r 28.11(3)
[59] r 28.11(4)(a)
[60] r 28.11(4)(b), (c)
[61] r 28.11(5)
[62] r 28.11(6–8); see also para 10.13
[63] r 28.13(1) and (2)
[64] r 28.13(3)
[65] r 28.13(4)
[66] r 28.13(2)

Letters of request

10.16 Where a witness resides outside Scotland the party seeking to obtain the evidence may apply to have it taken by means of a letter of request to a court or tribunal outside Scotland[67]. This procedure also applies to other matters such as the recovery, inspection and preservation of documents or other property[68]. Letters of request may be used in the United Kingdom, in a Hague convention country[69] or in any other country which will assist in obtaining the evidence sought.

An application for a letter of request is made by minute[70] with which there should be lodged the proposed letter of request in the form prescribed in the Rules[71]. When lodged, the sheriff clerk fixes a date for the sheriff to hear parties on the minute. The minute must then be intimated and heard in the same manner as any other minute[72].

Conditions which apply before request may be granted

10.17 It is a condition of the granting of a letter of request that the solicitor for the applicant is personally liable for the whole expenses of the procedure. This includes the expenses of the court or tribunal requested to obtain the evidence and of the witness who is to be examined. On granting an application the sheriff must fix a sum of money to be consigned by the solicitor for the applicant to cover these expenses[73]. If the evidence is to be taken by interrogatories and cross-interrogatories it would appear to be appropriate for these to be lodged, adjusted and approved[74] before the letter of request is issued. A translation of the letter of request and any interrogatories and cross-interrogatories may also be necessary in any country where the official language is not English[75].

Transmission of letter of request

10.18 When the conditions referred to in para 10.17 have been complied with, the sheriff clerk will forward the letter of request together with any interrogatories and cross-interrogatories and translations to the Foreign and Commonwealth Office for onward transmission or direct to the court or tribunal, as appropriate[76].

[67] r 28.14(1)
[68] r 28.14(2)
[69] The Hague Convention on the Taking of Evidence Abroad in Civil or Commercial Matters (Cmnd. 6727(1977))
[70] r 28.14 (3) and Form G16
[71] Forms G16, G17
[72] see Chap 6 of this book
[73] r 28.14(4)
[74] r 28.11; see also para 10.14
[75] r 28.14(5)
[76] r 28.14(6)

CHAPTER ELEVEN

Proof

Chapter 29 of the Rules

Introduction

11.1 The procedures examined in this chapter relate to matters preliminary to proof such as fixing or limiting the mode of proof, citing witnesses, lodging productions[1] and arranging for a shorthand writer. Also considered are the rules which make provision for the conduct of proofs and for proof to be established by means other than the calling of witnesses (*i.e.* by reference to oath, by remit to a person of skill and by affidavits).

Orders in relation to fixing proof

11.2 In Chapter 4 of this book the rules which make provision at an Options Hearing or a Procedural Hearing for the fixing of a proof, proof before answer or debate are examined. There are, however, other rules which need to be considered in relation to the fixing of a proof or debate and which provide, in particular, for

- The renouncing of probation (a procedure which is rarely used)
- Limiting the mode of proof, and
- Fixing of separate proofs on the merits and quantum.

These rules may be applied at either an Options or Procedural Hearing or some other stage in the proceedings, for example after a hearing on a motion to amend the pleadings.

Renouncing probation

11.3 At the time of closing the record or later, parties may by joint minute renounce probation[2], if they are agreed on the facts and are willing to dispense with the hearing of oral evidence. When renouncing probation parties must lodge a joint minute which may include a statement of the facts and productions which are admitted. Thereafter, the sheriff may fix a debate[3] or may issue judgment in the action on the basis of the averments and supporting documents.

[1] see para 4.15 for the procedure for lodging of documents founded on in pleadings.

[2] r 29.4(1)

[3] r 29.4(2)

Limiting mode of proof and separate parts of proof

11.4 When fixing proof or proof before answer the sheriff may limit the mode of proof[4], for example to proof by writ or oath. In actions with a monetary crave the sheriff may order parts of proof on liability and quantum to be heard separately[5].

Preliminary procedures

Witnesses

11.5 Witnesses are cited to a proof, on a period of seven days' notice[6], by the solicitor representing the party in the action. The seven-day period is, of course, the minimum period of notice and in practice a much longer period of notice is desirable. The rules provide for citation to be made either by registered post or first class delivery letter[7]. If citation cannot be effected by post a sheriff officer may be employed to cite the witness using any of the methods which a sheriff officer may use to serve an initial writ[8]. The form of citation[9] informs the witness of the name of the case, the date when he or she is required to attend court to give evidence and the penalty which may be imposed for failing to attend court. The solicitor who cites the witness is personally responsible for the fees and expenses of witnesses[10].

The solicitor or sheriff officer, after citation has been effected, completes a certificate of citation in the prescribed form[11]. Rule 29.7 stipulates that the certificate should be lodged[12]. However, in practice this is rarely done unless it is necessary to establish that citation has been effected in connection with a motion for warrant to arrest a witness who has failed to attend court (see below).

A party litigant who requires to have witnesses cited to attend court to give evidence must, not later than four weeks before the proof, lodge a motion requesting the sheriff to fix caution to cover the expenses of the witnesses[13]. The purpose of this provision is to ensure that funds are available to pay the witnesses' expenses for attending court and the sheriff officer's fees for citing the witnesses. The sheriff in granting such a motion must fix an amount of caution to be found, specify the method of finding caution (usually by consignation in court) and the period of time within

[4] r 29.5
[5] r 29.6
[6] r 29.74
[7] r 29.7(1)(a)
[8] r 29.7(1)(b)
[9] Form G13
[10] r 29.7(5)
[11] Form G13
[12] r 29.7(4)
[13] r 29.8(1)(a)

which it is to be found[14]. Before instructing a sheriff officer to cite witnesses the party litigant must have complied with the sheriff's order in relation to finding caution[15].

Where, after fixing caution to cover the expenses of the party litigant's witnesses, the party litigant decides not to cite all of the witnesses on his original list, application may be made to the sheriff by motion to reduce the amount of caution fixed[16].

Warrant for second diligence If there is good reason to believe that a witness who has been cited will not attend the proof diet, an application may be made to the sheriff by motion for what is known as "second diligence" to compel the witness to attend[17]. If a motion in these terms is granted the witness may be arrested by a sheriff officer and be conveyed to prison to be detained there until caution for his attendance at the proof is found. As the witness may be detained until caution is found this points to the desirability of fixing caution when granting the motion for second diligence, rather than leaving it to the witness to apply after he or she has been arrested. A warrant for second diligence is effective without endorsement by the sheriff clerk or sheriff in any sheriffdom. The witness may be found liable for the expense of the motion for second diligence and the execution of the warrant and decree may be granted for such expenses.[18]

Warrant to apprehend In practice the second diligence procedure, which is available prior to proof, is not much used, probably on the basis that in many cases it will not be known whether a witness will attend court until the proof diet. In circumstances where a witness does not attend in answer to a citation the Rules make provision for the party who has cited the witness to apply for a warrant to apprehend to bring the witness to court[19]. Before granting such a motion the sheriff must be satisfied, on production of a certificate of citation, that the witness was duly cited.

Penalty for failure to attend The maximum penalty which a sheriff may impose on a witness who fails to attend court after having been duly cited is £250. The sheriff before imposing such a penalty must be satisfied that

- The witness has been properly cited
- If the witness has demanded payment of travelling expenses these have been paid, and
- The witness does not have a reasonable excuse for failing to attend court[20].

[14] see Chap 7 of the Rules for other methods of finding caution
[15] r 29.8(1)(b)
[16] r 29.8(2)
[17] r 29.9(1)
[18] r 29.9(2)
[19] r 29.10(1)
[20] r 29.10(2)

Where a penalty is imposed the sheriff may grant decree against the witness for payment of the penalty to the party on whose behalf the witness was cited[21]. The witness may also be found liable for the expense of both the motion for warrant to apprehend and the arrangements for the witnesses' apprehension[22].

Productions

11.6 The time for lodging any productions which are to be used at proof is 14 days before the date when the proof is to commence[23]. If not lodged within this period productions may not be put in evidence unless the other parties consent or the sheriff grants leave[24]. Where the sheriff grants leave for the late lodging of productions he may find the party concerned liable in any expenses occasioned as a consequence[25].

Parties must lodge, not later than 48 hours before the proof, a full copy of all their productions for the sheriff's use at the proof. The copies must be numbered according to the number of process of the principal productions and where a production consists of more than one page the pages should be securely fastened together[26].

Any productions or parts of process which have been borrowed should be returned to process before 12.30pm on the day before the proof[27].

Notices to admit and notices of non-admission

11.7 Rule 29.14 provides a method by which proof in relation to documentary productions and averments made in the pleadings may be reduced where such matters, although subject to a general denial in the pleadings, are not in fact in dispute. The procedure puts the onus on the party on whom the notice is served to admit the facts specified in the notice or bear the consequences referred to below. This procedure may be invoked at any time after proof has been allowed by intimating to other parties a notice calling on them to admit facts relating to issues averred in the pleadings or other matters such as the authenticity of documents lodged as productions[28]. The party serving the notice to admit must, after service, lodge a copy in process[29].

A party who does not admit any facts or does not admit or seek to challenge the authenticity of any document specified in a notice intimated under rule 29.14 must in response intimate a notice of non-admission within 21 days after the date of intimation of the notice[30]. A copy of the notice of non-admission must be lodged in process after service[31].

[21] r 29.10(2)(b)
[22] r 29.10(1)
[23] r 29.11(1)
[24] r 29.11(2)
[25] r 29.11(2)(b)
[26] r 29.12
[27] r 29.13
[28] r 29.14(1)
[29] r 29.14(5)
[30] r 29.14(2)
[31] r 29.14(5)

Failure to lodge a notice of non-admission will result in the party being deemed to have admitted the matters specified in the notice and the documents or facts can be used in evidence at a proof on this basis[32], if otherwise admissible. A party failing to respond to a notice to admit within 14 days of intimation of the notice may be penalised by being found liable for the expenses of proving the facts or documents specified in the notice[33]. A deemed admission in terms of this rule applies only to the particular action in which the notice is given and cannot be used against the party concerned for any other purpose[34].

Instruction and payment of shorthand writer

11.8 The pursuer is responsibile for instructing a shorthand writer where it is necessary to record the evidence at a proof[35]. However, payment of the shorthand writer's fees are in the first instance paid by parties equally[36].

Procedure at proof

11.9 Proof is taken continuously so far as possible, although the sheriff has power to adjourn the diet[37] where, for example, proof cannot be completed in one day. Witnesses are examined on oath or following administration of an affirmation[38].

Recording of evidence

11.10 The record of evidence at the proof includes any objection to a question put to a witness or to the line of evidence, any submissions made to an objection and the court's ruling[39]. Evidence in ordinary actions is normally recorded by a shorthand writer[40]. The Rules, however, also make provision, subject to the court's approval, for recording evidence by tape recording or other mechanical means[41]. Tape recording equipment is, at the time of writing, available in all courts in the sheriffdoms of Tayside, Central and Fife and Grampian, Highlands and Islands for recording proceedings in criminal jury trials and fatal accident inquiries. It is understood that for this reason the equipment is not generally available for recording evidence in civil cases, except in exceptional circumstances where, for example, a shorthand writer is not available.

[32] r 29.14(3)
[33] r 29.14(4)
[34] r 29.14(6)
[35] r 29.15
[36] r 29.18(2)
[37] r 29.17
[38] r 29.16
[39] r 29.18(5)
[40] r 29.18(1)(a)
[41] r 29.18(1)(b)

Procedure where recording of evidence dispensed with

11.11 Although rarely used there is provision in the Rules for parties to dispense with the recording of evidence, provided they are in agreement and obtain the sheriff's approval[42]. Where the recording of evidence has been dispensed with the sheriff may, at the request of parties, be required to note the terms of any objection to the admissibility of evidence on the grounds of confidentiality or to the production of a document and the decision on the objection[43]. In the case of any other objection the sheriff can be asked to record, in the note to the interlocutor disposing of the merits of the case, the terms of the objection and the decision thereon[44].

Appeal on question of confidentiality of evidence or productions

11.12 Provision is made in rule 29.19 for application to be made in the course of a proof for leave to appeal to the sheriff principal where a party is dissatisfied with the sheriff's ruling on an objection to the admissibility of evidence on the ground of confidentiality or to the production of a document on any ground. The party must "express immediately his formal dissatisfaction"[45]. If leave is granted the proof may continue in relation to matters not dependent on the ruling appealed against[46]. However, the appeal must clearly be determined before the proof can be concluded. The rule also provides that the sheriff principal should dispose of the appeal "with the least possible delay"[47].

The matters which may be appealed under rule 29.19 (a provision which is not much used) are the only issues which may be appealed during the course of a proof[48]. Other issues must await the sheriff's interlocutor disposing of the merits of the case before an appeal can be marked.

Close of proof and issue of judgment

11.13 At the close of the proof the sheriff hears parties on the evidence[49]. In most cases the sheriff will make avizandum and issue a written judgment at later date. The sheriff is directed, by rule 29.20, to issue his judgment "with the least possible delay" after having heard parties at the close of proof.

[42] r 29.18(1)
[43] r 29.18(12)(a)
[44] r 29.18(12)(b)
[45] r 29.19(1)
[46] r 29.19(4)
[47] r 29.19(2)
[48] r 29.19(3)
[49] r 29.20

Transcript of record of evidence

11.14 A transcript of the record of evidence is not as a general rule requested. It may, however, be ordered by direction of the sheriff[50], for example to assist at a hearing on evidence in a lengthy proof where evidence has been heard over a period of time. The cost of obtaining a transcript in a defended action is in the first instance paid for by the solicitors for parties in equal proportions. In an undefended case the solicitor for the pursuer is responsible for payment of the transcript.[51]

The transcript of the evidence (which is certified by the shorthand writer who recorded the evidence or by the person who has transcribed the tape recorded evidence[52]) is sent to the sheriff clerk who lodges it in process. The original transcript may not be borrowed from process except with leave of the sheriff or by a party who is considering an appeal[53]. However, where a transcript has been ordered for the use of the sheriff, any party wishing a copy may obtain one from the shorthand writer on payment of the appropriate fee[54]. It may be that when the sheriff or parties have considered the transcript it is thought that some alterations are necessary. In these circumstances alterations may be made and be authenticated by the sheriff after having heard parties thereon[55].

In an action where the sheriff has not directed that the evidence should be transcribed and an appeal is marked the appellant may request a transcript from the shorthand writer for the purposes of the appeal. In this case the solicitor for the appellant will be responsible in the first instance for the cost of transcribing the evidence and for lodging the transcript when prepared in process[56].

Other modes of proof

11.15 In addition to the rules which apply where evidence is given orally by witnesses at a proof, there are rules (including those for commission to take evidence: see Chap 10 of this book) which provide for evidence to be taken by other means, *i.e.* by reference to oath, remit to a person of skill and by affidavit or statement. Reference to oath and remit to a person of skill are procedures which are rarely used in modern practice.

Reference to oath

11.16 Reference to oath is a procedure whereby a party may apply by motion to refer either the whole case or part of it to the oath of his

50 r 29.18(6)
51 r 29.18(6)(a), (b)
52 r 29.18(7)
53 r 29.18(10)
54 r 29.18(9)
55 r 29.18(8)
56 r 29.18(11)

opponent[57]. This is done on the basis that the opponent's deposition will determine the issue or issues between the parties which are subject to the reference. Where a reference has been made and the party fails to appear at the diet for taking the deposition, the sheriff may hold that party as confessed and grant decree[58].

Remit to person of skill

11.17 Application for a remit to a person of skill is made by motion[59]. Where the motion is made jointly or of consent of all parties the report of the person of skill is final and conclusive in relation to the matters contained in the remit[60]. The expense of the remit is, in the first instance, shared equally between parties[61]. A remit made on the motion of one party only does not have the same status as a joint remit. In particular, it is not final or conclusive with regard to the matters remitted to the person of skill. The expense of such a remit must be borne, in the first instance, by the party moving for the remit[62].

Affidavit evidence

11.18 Application may be made by motion to allow the evidence of any witness to be received by way of affidavit[63]. Similar provisions apply where a party wishes a statement or document to be admitted in evidence without calling as a witness the maker of the statement or document[64]. The affidavit, statement or document must be lodged with the motion as these must be considered by the sheriff before the motion may be granted[65].

57 r 29.1(1)
58 r 29.1(2)
59 r 29.2(1)
60 r 29.2(2)
61 r 29.2(3)(b)
62 r 29.2(3)(a)
63 r 29.3(1)
64 r 29.3(2); such evidence is admissible under s 2(1)(b) of the Civil Evidence (Scotland) Act 1988.
65 r 29.3

CHAPTER 12

Decree, Interlocutors, Extract and Appeal

Chapters 30–31 of the Rules

12.1 This chapter examines decrees, interlocutors in relation to final judgments, extracts, appeals and expenses. The rules relating to these matters do not affect or repeal the provisions of the substantive law, other than to the extent provided by Schedule 2 of the Rules which contains repeals to repealed sections 4–6 and 11 and the Schedule to the Sheriff Courts (Scotland) Extracts Act 1892. These provisions, which related to extracts issued by the Sheriff Court, have been re-enacted in the ordinary cause rules in more modern form.

Decree

12.2 Chapter 30 of the Rules deals with decrees, extracts and execution of the decree, The term "decree" in this Chapter is a general term, and applies to any judgment, deliverance, interlocutor, act, order, finding or authority which may be extracted.[1]

Decrees for payment of foreign currency

12.3 In circumstances where a decree has been craved in foreign currency or its equivalent, a certificate in Form G18 of the Rules must be produced before an extract can be obtained.[2] This certificate must be obtained either from the Bank of England or a clearing bank and should certify the rate of exchange prevailing either on the date of decree, the date on which extract is ordered, or the date or within three days before the date on which extract is ordered. The certificate which must also state the sterling equivalent of the sum sued for,[3] is lodged with the minute craving decree. The minute craving decree must also state the relevant rate of exchange and the sterling equivalent.

Taxes on money under the control of the court

12.4 There are several circumstances where a sum of money may be

[1] r 30.1
[2] r 30.3(2)
[3] r 30.3(1)

ordered to be consigned with the court. One example is the fund *in medio* in a multiplepoinding. Where the court has ordered money to be consigned, then before granting decree the court has to be satisfied that all taxes and duties which may be due to the Inland Revenue have been paid. This is achieved by the production of a certificate signed by an authorised officer of the Inland Revenue stating that all taxes and duties have been paid.[4] This provision does not apply in an action of multiplepoinding in relation to the payment of taxes or duties on the estate of a deceased claimant. In such a case decree, warrant or order for payment may be granted albeit that taxes or duties payable have not been paid or satisfied.[5]

Interlocutors

12.5 The interlocutor of a sheriff contains details of the decree or order granted. The date of any interlocutor will normally be the date that the order was pronounced. However, where the sheriff has reserved his decision and it is given at a later date, the date of the interlocutor is the date it is received by the sheriff clerk.[6] On receipt of the sheriff's decision the sheriff clerk will date the interlocutor and send a copy of it to each party.[7] This date is important because it is the date from which the days of appeal will be calculated.[8]

Any clerical error in an interlocutor may be corrected by the sheriff at any time before extract.[9]

Issue of extract of decree

12.6 Following the issue of an interlocutor by the sheriff containing a decree or other extractable order, an extract may be issued by the sheriff clerk to the successful party. In most courts the extract requires to be requested by the party, except in an action of divorce where an extract of the decree is issued to both parties as a matter of course. When a decree may be extracted depends on the nature of the decree:

- A decree in absence may be extracted after 14 days have expired from the date decree was granted.[10] The 14 days are calculated from the day after decree so that the extract is issued on the fifteenth day.

4 r 30.2(1)
5 r 30.2(2)
6 r 12.2(5)(a)
7 r 12.2(5)(b)
8 r 31.1
9 r 12.2(2)
10 r 30.4(1)(a)

- Where final decree has been granted in a defended action the extract can be issued after the expiry of the period within which an appeal can be marked if no appeal is marked, *i.e.* 14 days from the date of decree.[11]
- Where a decree has been granted and leave to appeal the order is required, the decree cannot be extracted until the time limit for requesting leave to appeal has passed, *i.e.* seven days from the date of decree.[12]
- If leave to appeal is applied for and refused the decree can be extracted on the day after the application is refused.[13]
- If an appeal has been marked the decree cannot be extracted until the day after the date of final disposal of the appeal.[14] This means that where an appeal is taken to the sheriff principal and his judgment is subsequently appealed to the Court of Session, no extract can be issued until the Court of Session has disposed of the appeal.

	Earliest date for issue of extract
Undefended action	extract 14 days after decree
Defended action	extract 14 days after decree if not appealed
Leave to appeal required but no application	extract 7 days after decree
Leave to appeal refused	extract after date of refusal
Leave to appeal granted but no appeal marked	extract 7 days after leave granted
Appeal marked	extract on date of final disposal of appeal*

*if appeal is marked from sheriff principal to the Court of Session the date of disposal by the Court of Session will be the final disposal

It should be noted that if the sheriff has reserved the question of expenses when pronouncing decree, no extract can be issued until 14 days after the question of expenses has been decided. The sheriff does, however, have a discretion to direct otherwise.[15]

11 r 30.4(1)(b)(iii)
12 r 30.4(1)(b)(ii)
13 r 30.4(1)(b)(iii)
14 r 30.4(1)(b)(iv)
15 r 30.4(1)(c)

There is provision in the Rules for an extract to be issued earlier than the periods stated above.[16] However in the case of a defended action, or where the question of expenses has been reserved, a motion for early extract will only be granted if made in the presence of parties, or if the sheriff is satisfied that the parties have received intimation of the motion.[17]

An extract of an award of custody, access or aliment may be issued even when an appeal has been marked, except where an order excusing obedience to or implement of the original order has been made[18] (see para 12.12).

Form of extract

12.7 Appendix 2 to the Rules provides styles of extract.[19] These styles however provide only the framework for extract decrees. The general principle of extracting is that the extract should accurately reflect the terms of the decree granted. The extract forms contained in the appendix should be used "with such variation as circumstances may require"[20]. Where there is no prescribed form a style of extract is used which is closest in style to the order granted.[21] It is suggested that the terms of any extract should be checked to ascertain that it is in accordance with the terms of the decree.

Any extract issued contains the words "this extract is warrant for all lawful execution hereon".[22] What constitutes lawful execution is contained in section 7(1) of the Sheriff Courts (Extracts) Act 1892 as amended by section 87 of the Debtors (Scotland) Act 1987.

Where on appeal the sheriff principal adheres to the decision of the sheriff the date of the decree to be extracted will be the date of the decision of the sheriff principal and not the original date of decree.[23]

Service of charge where address of defender is unknown

12.8 Rule 30.9 provides that a charge may be served on a defender whose address is not known by serving the charge on the sheriff clerk of the Sheriff Court district where the defender's known address is located. The sheriff clerk displays the charge on the walls of court for the period of the charge. The days of charge are calculated from the date it was first displayed, and when the days of charge have expired the sheriff clerk will endorse on the charge a certificate that it has been displayed in accordance with the rule.[24]

16 r 30.4(2)
17 r 30.4(3)
18 r 30.5
19 r 30.6(1)
20 r 1.4
21 r 30.6(2)
22 r 30.7
23 r 30.8(1)
24 r 30.9

Appeals

Time limits

12.9 Any interlocutor which may be appealed against may be appealed within 14 days of the date of the interlocutor, unless a different time limit is provided in any statute. This period does not apply if an early extract has been issued following a motion under rule 30.4(2).[25]

Sections 27 and 28 of the Sheriff Courts (Scotland) Act 1907 specify those interlocutors which can be appealed without leave to the sheriff principal and to the Court of Session respectively. Any interlocutors other than those listed in these sections require leave to appeal. This is applied for by motion which may be made orally at the time the sheriff makes the order against which it is sought to appeal, or it may be applied for by written motion, which must be lodged within seven days of the date of the interlocutor in respect of which leave is sought.[26]

If leave to appeal is granted, the appeal must be marked within seven days of the date on which leave is granted.[27]

Form of appeal

12.10 An appeal can be marked by writing a note of appeal:

- On the interlocutor sheet, or
- On a separate sheet to be lodged with the Sheriff Clerk.

The appeal is marked in the following form: "The pursuer/applicant/claimant/defender/respondent or other party, as the case may be, appeals to the sheriff principal/Court of Session".[28] In marking the appeal, it is advisable to consider whether a note from the sheriff is required. In any final interlocutor on the merits, other than an undefended divorce, the sheriff must write a note, and it is therefore not necessary to request one.[29] If a note is considered necessary in an interlocutor in which there is no requirement for the sheriff to write a note, this may be requested when marking the appeal by adding the words "and requests the sheriff to write a note." If a note is requested by the party marking the appeal the sheriff is required by the Rules of Procedure to provide one.[30]

The applicant dates and signs the note of appeal, and where the appeal is to the Court of Session the name and address of the solicitor or agent who will be acting in the appeal should be specified in the note.[31]

[25] r 31.1
[26] r 31.2
[27] r 31.2(2)
[28] r 31.3(1)
[29] r 12.2(3)
[30] r 12.2(4)
[31] r 31.3(2)

Notice of appeal

12.11 The sheriff clerk will intimate the marking of the appeal to the other parties in the action. This is done within four days of the appeal being marked, and the sheriff clerk will certify on the interlocutor sheets that he has done so. The process is then transmitted by the sheriff clerk to the sheriff principal or the Court of Session, as appropriate, also within four days.[32]

Appeals in connection with custody, access and aliment

12.12 Where an appeal is marked against an award of custody, access or aliment the appellant can ask the sheriff, sheriff principal or Court of Session to suspend obedience to or implement of the interlocutor pending the outcome of the appeal. If this is not done the marking of the appeal does not suspend obedience to the interlocutor.[33]

Interim possession pending appeal

12.13 The general rule is that on an appeal being marked the sheriff is "functus" pending the outcome of the appeal, and can make no further order in the case. There is however an exception to this in relation to the making of orders for interim possession, preservation of property, preservation of evidence, and any other interim order which the interests of justice may require. The party requiring an interim order should lodge a motion specifying what order is sought. The appellate court has power to review an interim order granted under this provision. This review can be requested before the appeal hearing if that is considered to be necessary.[34]

Abandonment of appeal

12.14 An appeal cannot be abandoned after marking unless all parties consent, or the sheriff principal grants leave to abandon the appeal[35].

Taxation of expenses

12.15 Any expenses allowed, unless modified at a fixed amount, must be taxed by the auditor of court before decree is granted.[36] In an undefended action, however, if the pursuer's solicitor elects to charge the inclusive fees as provided in the Act of Sederunt (Fees of Solicitors in the Sheriff Court) 1993, taxation is not necessary. The procedure for taxation of accounts is

32 r 31.3(3)
33 r 31.5
34 r 31.6
35 r 31.7
36 r 32.1

set out in rule 32.3. On receipt of intimation of a diet of taxation from the sheriff clerk the party who has lodged the account must intimate the date to all other parties and send them a copy of the account. If the other parties do not appear at the taxation diet the auditor will require proof of intimation. The production of a recorded delivery receipt or a copy letter intimated by fax or document exchange will usually be sufficient proof.

At the taxation diet the auditor will hear parties and tax the account in accordance with the Act of Sederunt mentioned above. After taxation the auditor will append a certificate to the account certifying the amount at which the account has been taxed. If consideration of the account is reserved, the auditor will intimate his decision in writing to the parties who attended the diet of taxation. A party who has attended a diet of taxation may lodge a note of objections with the sheriff clerk within seven days of the taxation or the decision on the taxation.[37] If no objections are lodged the sheriff may approve the Auditor of Court's report and grant decree for the taxed expenses. If there are objections the sheriff is empowered to dispose of these in a summary manner.

A solicitor who conducted the cause may ask the court to grant decree for expenses in his name rather than in the name of the party in whose favour they were awarded.[38] This provision is seldom used, but would probably be appropriate if a solicitor was concerned about receiving payment of his fees from his client.

Retention and disposal of process

12.16 After final disposal of a case the process is weeded out by the sheriff clerk so that only certain parts of process are retained.[39] Any productions lodged in the process should be uplifted from the sheriff clerk within 14 days of the final determination of the cause, or any appeal. If productions are not uplifted within this period the sheriff clerk will intimate to the party who lodged the production that it must be uplifted within 28 days of the notice, otherwise the sheriff will be asked to direct how it should be disposed of.[40]

37 r 32.4
38 r 32.2
39 r 11.7
40 r 11.8

CHAPTER 13

Family Actions

Chapter 33 of the Rules

Introduction

13.1 In drafting the new ordinary cause rules the opportunity was taken to bring together under one chapter all of the rules particular to family actions which had previously been scattered throughout the Rules. Unless otherwise stated in the Rules the provisions of the other chapters also apply to family actions, and in particular the procedure in Chapters 9 (Standard procedure) and 10 (Additional procedure) apply to defended family actions. There is however one important difference in the Options Hearing provisions for family actions, *i.e.* the parties must, except on cause shown, appear personally at the hearing. This provision was introduced following suggestions received by the Rules Council in response to their consultation exercise which preceded the drafting of the new Rules. The intention behind the provision was that the presence of parties would help to focus the issues at the Options Hearing and lead to earlier settlement of the action. It was initially regarded with considerable scepticism, but the view has recently been expressed that it does in some cases lead to earlier settlement of family actions, although not necessarily at the Options Hearing itself.

Chapter 33 of the Rules sets out those procedures which are distinct to family actions. The scope of the chapter is wide because of the considerable diverse body of legislation dealing with matters between spouses, parents and their children. It is not the intention of this work to examine the law relating to family matters; the reader must consult the relevant legislation and other works for this information. The provisions of the primary legislation are referred to and explained only to the extent that this is necessary for the understanding of the rule. It has to be emphasised that these rules cannot and do not repeal or amend any of the primary legislation relating to family actions as defined in the Rules. Their purpose is to provide procedures to enable the provisions of the primary legislation to be operated in court proceedings. In drafting the Rules in Chapter 33 the opportunity was taken to harmonise Sheriff Court and Court of Session procedures in relation to family actions.

Definition of family action

13.2 Family action is defined in rule 33.1 as meaning:

"(a) an action of divorce;
(b) an action of separation;
(c) an action of declarator of legitimacy;
(d) an action of declarator of illegitimacy;
(e) an action of declarator of parentage;
(f) an action of declarator of non-parentage;
(g) an action of declarator of legitimation;
(h) an action or application for any parental rights;
(i) an action of affiliation and aliment;
(j) an action of, or application for or in respect of, aliment;
(k) an action or application for financial provision after a divorce or annulment in an overseas country within the meaning of Part IV of the Matrimonial and Family Proceedings Act 1984;
(l) an action or application for an order under the [Matrimonial Homes (Family Protection) (Scotland) Act 1981];
(m) an application for the variation or recall of an order mentioned in section 8(1) of the Law Reform (Miscellaneous Provisions) (Scotland) Act 1966."

Rule 33.1(2) and (3) identifies the primary legislation which is referred to in the chapter, and also provides definitions for a number of terms used in the chapter.

Averments

13.3 The Rules make provision for various averments which must be included in the pleadings of particular types of family action. These averments generally have their foundation in the relevant primary legislation, and are required in order to comply with the substantive law provisions.

Divorce or separation

13.4 In an action of divorce or separation averments must be made in the condescendence about the following matters:

- Whether there are any proceedings continuing in Scotland or in any other country in respect of the marriage or which are capable of affecting its validity or subsistence
- Where proceedings are continuing the following details must be included in the averments in the writ:
  —the court, tribunal or authority before whom the proceedings have commenced

—the date of commencement
—the names of the parties
—the date or expected date of proof in the proceedings
—any other facts relevant to whether the action being raised should be sisted under Schedule 3 to the Domicile and Matrimonial Proceedings Act 1973.[1]

This information is required to enable compliance with Schedule 3 to the 1973 Act. Paragraph 8 of the Schedule requires that where averments are made that proceedings are continuing elsewhere, the court must sist the action before it. Where there are no other proceedings it is necessary to state this in the initial writ by including an averment that there are no other proceedings pending in respect of the marriage or which are capable of affecting its validity or subsistence.

In a defended action where proceedings are continuing before another court and the initial writ does not contain details about those other proceedings, or the details in the initial writ are incomplete or incorrect, the defender and any minuter are obliged by virtue of the provisions in rule 33.2(3) to provide the appropriate information in the defences or minute.[2]

Custody

13.5 Where in an action of divorce or separation an order for custody of a child is sought the party seeking custody must include averments giving particulars of any other proceedings which relate to the child in respect of whom the order is sought. In other family actions there must also be an averment giving particulars of any other action pending which relates to the marriage of the parents of that child.[3] This provision applies not only to proceedings which are continuing, but also to proceedings relating to custody which have been concluded.[4] The definition of "child" in this context includes a child who has been accepted into the family as defined in section 42(4) of the Family Law Act 1986. Where there are no other proceedings it is necessary to state this in the initial writ by including an averment that there are no other proceedings pending in respect of the marriage or which are capable of affecting its validity or subsistence.

Where the particulars required are incomplete or where there are no such averments in the writ, but there are proceedings known to the defender or any minuter, a similar requirement should be included in the defences or minute.[5]

[1] r 33.2
[2] r 33.2(3)(c)
[3] r 33.3(1)(a), (b)
[4] r 33.3(1)(a), (2)
[5] r 33.3(2)

Maintenance orders

13.6 In any family action where aliment or periodical allowance is sought, or is sought to be varied or recalled, the pleadings of the party seeking the order must contain an averment about any maintenance order granted either in favour of, or against, that party or any other person in respect of whom the order is sought.[6]

Aliment

13.7 Rule 33.6 is included as a consequence of the Child Support Act 1991 and includes requirements for averments in relation to what the Rules refer to as "top up maintenance orders".

The court retains jurisdiction to make such orders:

- Where a child is, will be or would be receiving education or training and the order is made solely for the purposes of meeting some or all of the expenses,
- To meet some or all of the expenses incurred by a child's disability, or
- To make an order against the person who has care of the child.[7]

Where a "top up" order is applied for the initial writ must include the following averments:

- That a maintenance assessment under section 11 of the Child Support Act 1991 is in force
- The date of the maintenance assessment
- The amount and frequency of periodical payments of child support maintenance fixed by the maintenance assessment, and
- The grounds on which the sheriff retains jurisdiction under section 8(6)–(8) or (10) of the 1991 Act.[8]

When making such an application a copy of any document issued by the Child Support Agency must be produced with the initial writ, although on cause shown the sheriff may dispense with this provision.[9]

If aliment is sought, other than under section 8(6)-(8) or (10) of the 1991 Act, averments must be inserted to establish the ground on which the court retains jurisdiction (*e.g.* that the habitual residence of the absent parent is outwith the UK, or that the child is not a child within the meaning of section 55 of the Act).[10]

A summary of the averments required in craves for divorce, parental rights and aliment can be found at Appendix 13.1 to this chapter.

[6] r 33.5; see also s 106 of the Debtors (Scotland) Act 1987

[7] Child Support Act 1991

[8] r 33.6(2)

[9] r 33.6(2)(b)

[10] r 33.6(3)

Actions of declarator of non-parentage or illegitimacy

13.8 Where an action for declarator of non-parentage or illegitimacy is raised by a person who has previously been named as a parent in an application for a maintenance assessment (under section 4, 6, or 7 of the 1991 Act) there must be included in the initial writ averments relating to that application. Where in such an application an allegation of paternity has been made against the pursuer the Secretary of State may have an interest under the 1991 Act, in which case the Secretary of State must be named as a defender, receive service of the initial writ and is entitled to defend the action.[11]

Other averments in relation to proceedings under the Child Support Act 1991

13.9 In any family action which involves parties in respect of whom a decision has been made in any application, review or appeal under the 1991 Act relating to a child of the parties the initial writ must include an averment stating that such a decision has been made and giving details of the decision. The document issued by the Child Suport Agency giving details of the decision should also be produced, unless the sheriff directs otherwise.[12]

Application for warrant for intimation

Procedure

13.10 Rule 33.7 provides for intimation to be made on any persons who may have an interest in relation to the types of action specified in each of the sub-paragraphs. The rule also makes provision for various prescribed forms to be served on such persons. These forms of intimation advise the individuals concerned of how to respond to the intimation. With the exception of Form F7 (form of intimation where custody of a child is sought), the appropriate response by a person wishing to appear in the proceedings is to lodge a minute in the proceedings. The provisions of Chapter 14 of the Rules (minute procedure) apply to any such minute lodged (see Chap 6 of this book). A summary of the craves for intimation which may be sought in actions for divorce, custody and aliment is at Appendix 13.1 to this chapter.

[11] r 33.6(4)

[12] r 33.6(5)

Crave for intimation

13.11 Where intimation is necessary, the pursuer must include in the initial writ a crave for intimation.[13] It should be noted that Rule 33.7 provides only that a crave must be included in appropriate cases. It does not provide that a warrant for intimation if craved must be granted. The view is taken by some sheriffs that they do not have a discretion to refuse to grant a warrant for intimation where one is requested. There is however an alternative view that rule 33.15(1) provides a discretion in so far as it provides that "the sheriff may order intimation to such person as he thinks fit". It is suggested that it would be prudent to ascertain the procedure to be followed in the court where a warrant is to be sought.

Intimation where address of defender not known (Form F1)

13.12 Where the address of the defender is not known and cannot reasonably be ascertained, warrant should be craved to intimate to every child of the marriage who has reached the age of 16, and also to one of the defender's next of kin who has reached that age. The form advises the recipient to inform the sheriff clerk if the address of the defender is known.

Where the address or identity of any of the defender's children or the next of kin is not known a crave for a warrant to intimate is not required. Where this is the case the initial writ must contain an averment of that fact and also averments relating to the steps which have been taken to ascertain that information.[14] Note that these provisions relate to intimation to the children and next of kin, and are additional to service of the action on a person whose whereabouts are unknown the procedure for which is provided in rule 5.6.

Adultery (Form F2)

13.13 In an action in which adultery is alleged a warrant to intimate on the person named in the writ as the person with whom adultery is alleged to have been committed is required. It should be noted that this provision is not restricted to those actions where the crave for divorce is based on the grounds of adultery. The terms of the rule apply to any family action in which adultery is alleged[15]. This provision does not apply, however, if the person is not named in the writ and the writ contains an averment that the identity of the person is not known and cannot reasonably be ascertained, or if the pursuer alleges that the defender has been guilty of rape or incest with the named person.[16] In the case of incest, rule 33.8 will apply (see para 13.24)

[13] r 33.7(1)
[14] r 33.7(1)(a), 33.4; see also para 13.23
[15] r 33.7(1)(b)
[16] r 33.7(1)(b)(i), (ii)

Mental disorder (Form F3)

13.14 Where the defender is suffering from mental disorder intimation is made to every child of the marriage who has reached the age of 16 and to one of the next of kin who has reached that age. If the defender has a *curator bonis*, intimation should also be made on that person.[17] It is to be noted that these intimations are additional to service of the action on the defender (see para 13.30).

Polygamous marriage (Form F4)

13.15 Section 2(2) of the Matrimonial Proceedings (Polygamous Marriages) Act 1972 allows the court to consider a number of applications, in so far as the Sheriff Court is concerned the relevant applications are an application for a decree for divorce, judicial separation, aliment, in respect of a marriage entered into under a law which permits polygamy. In such a case intimation must be made to any additional spouse of either party.[18]

Orders for parental rights (Form F5 or F6)

13.16 In an action of divorce or separation where the sheriff may make an order for parental rights in respect of a child (defined in section 8 of the Law Reform (Parent and Child) (Scotland) Act 1986 as guardianship, custody or access) intimation must be made

- To any local authority who has care of the child using Form F5[19]
- If the child has been accepted as a child of the marriage and is liable to be maintained by a third party, to the third party using Form F5[20], or
- Where a third party exercises *de facto* parental rights, to that third party using Form F6[21].

Custody where parent or guardian is not a party to the action

13.17 In a family action where custody of a child is craved intimation must be made to any parent or guardian who is not a party to the action.[22] Section 47 of the Children Act 1975 provides that custody will not be granted to a person who is not a parent or guardian of the child unless any of the following apply:

- The applicant is a relative or step-parent, has the consent of a parent or guardian and has had care and possession of the child for at least three months before the application is made

[17] r 33.7(1)(c)
[18] r 33.7(1)(d)
[19] r 33.7(1)(e)(i)
[20] r 33.7(1)(e)(ii)
[21] r 33.7(1)(e)(iii)
[22] r 33.7(1)(f)

- If the applicant is not a relative or step-parent he or she must have the consent of the parent or guardian and must have had care and possession of the child for a period or periods amounting to at least 12 months of which three months must have been immediately preceding the application
- If the applicant does not have the consent of the parent or guardian he or she must have had care and possession of the child for periods amounting to at least three years of which three months must have been immediately preceding the application

Where none of the above apply the court still has discretion to grant an application for custody on cause shown. The procedure in this type of action is discussed further at para 13.34.

Form of notice to local authority under section 49(1) of the Children Act 1975 (Form F8)

13.18 Intimation in an action where the pursuer seeks custody of a chlid must be made to a local authority in the following situations:

- Where the pursuer is not a parent of the child and is resident in Scotland to the local authority within which area the pursuer resides[23]; or
- Where the pursuer is not resident in Scotland to "such local authority as the sheriff thinks fit".[24]

The object of this intimation is to require the local authority to prepare a report for the court on "all the circumstances of the child and on the proposed arrangements for the care and upbringing of the child" as required by section 49(1) of the Act.

Intimation to a child (Form F9)

13.19 In any family action affecting a child intimation is to be made to the child, if the child is not a party to the action.[25] This provision has been the subject of some controversy. It was introduced to enable the court to give effect to article 12 of the UN Convention on the Rights of the Child. This article provides that a child who is capable of forming a view has a right to express that view in any action which affects him, and also provides that the court is to give any view expressed due weight in accordance with the age and maturity of the child. The rule, however, places no restriction on the age at which intimation would be appropriate. It is understood that most sheriffs take the view that intimation should not be made to a child who is not capable of expressing a view, and that discretion should be exercised in deciding whether to grant a crave for intimation in the case of very young children.

[23] r 33.7(1)(g)
[24] r 33.7(4)
[25] r 33.7(1)(h)

The practice in some courts is to require the pursuer to crave the court to dispense with intimation and to include an averment in the initial writ showing why intimation should be dispensed with. Other courts take the view that rule 33.15 allows the sheriff to dispense with intimation where it is considered that it would not be appropriate even where no crave to dispense with intimation is made. Practices in relation to the granting of craves for intimation to children do vary throughout the courts, and it would be advisable to seek confirmation of the procedures in the particular court from which warrant is to be sought before lodging an action for warranting.

Transfer of property (Form F10)

13.20 In terms of section 8(1)(aa) of the Family Law (Scotland) Act 1985 either party may apply for an order for the transfer of property. Where the property in question is subject to a security, or requires the consent of a third party to transfer the property, intimation must be made to the creditor or third party.[26]

Avoidance transaction (Form F11)

13.21 Where an application for an avoidance transaction in respect of property is made under section 18 of the Family Law (Scotland) Act intimation must be made on any third party involved in the transaction or any party having an interest in the transaction.[27]

Orders under the Matrimonial Homes (Family Protection) Act 1981 (Form F12)

13.22 If the pursuer in an action makes an application for an order under the 1981 Act, and he is a non-entitled partner, and the entitled partner has a spouse, intimation is to be made to that spouse.[28] Moreover, where the entitled spouse or partner is a tenant or occupies the matrimonial home by permission of a third party, intimation is to be made to the landlord or third party if the application is under section 2(1)(e), 2(4)(a), 3(1), 3(2), 4, 7, 13 or 18 of the 1981 Act.[29]

Period of notice for intimation and intimation on person whose address is unknown

13.23 Any intimation made in terms of rule 33.7(1) is made on a period of notice of 21 days. There is, however, provision for the sheriff to reduce the period of notice, but not to less than two days.[30]

[26] r 33.7(1)(i)
[27] r 33.7(1)(j)
[28] r 33.7(1)(k)(i)
[29] r 33.7(1)(k)(ii)
[30] r 33.7(3)

If the address of the person on whom intimation is required is not known and cannot reasonably be ascertained the pursuer must include a crave in the initial writ to dispense with intimation.[31] Although this rule does not require it, it is suggested that the writ should also include averments as to what steps have been taken to ascertain the address of the person. This is required by rule 3.1(6) for actions where the address of the defender is unknown and an explanation of the steps taken would assist the sheriff in considering whether to dispense with intimation.

If the identity or address of a person to whom intimation is required subsequently becomes known a motion should be lodged for intimation to be made, or to dispense with intimation on that person.[32]

Improper association (Form F13)

13.24 The provision for intimation where an improper association is alleged differs from the provisions discussed in the foregoing paragraphs. Warrant for intimation is not granted at the time of raising the action. Instead a motion for intimation or to dispense with intimation must be made after the expiry of the period of notice.[33] An "improper association" is defined as sodomy, incest or a homosexual relationship.[34]

The motion, which must be lodged immediately after the expiry of the period of notice, should either seek an order for intimation on the named person or to dispense with intimation.[35] If the sheriff grants a motion to dispense with intimation he may also order the name of the person to be deleted from the condescendence.[36]

Intimation to the local authority

13.25 Section 10 of the Matrimonial Proceedings (Children) Act 1958 allows the court in certain circumstances in an action of divorce or separation to commit a child to the care of the local authority. Section 12 of that Act provides that the court can place a child under the supervision of the local authority. Where the court is considering making an order under either section 10 or 12 intimation must be made on the Chief Executive of the local authority. The sheriff will order one of the parties to make such intimation on Form F28, which intimation must be accompanied by a copy of the pleadings and a copy of any relevant motion.[37]

31 r 33.7(5)
32 r 33.7(6)
33 r 33.8(1)
34 r 33.8(4)
35 r 33.8(1)
36 r 33.8(2)(c)
37 r 33.40

Citation service and intimation

Form of warrant of citation and intimation

13.26 The form of warrant of citation in a family action differs from that used in other ordinary actions under rule 5.2. Citation is in Form F14[38] which invites the defender to lodge a notice of intention to defend should he or she wish to respond to the initial writ. It should be noted that the responses available to a defender in a family action are wider than those in other ordinary actions (see para 13.46). Where warrant to intimate is granted or dispensed with the terms of the sheriff's order are added to the warrant of citation.

Productions

13.27 Before a warrant to cite may be issued in an action of divorce the extract marriage certificate must be produced, and in any action where the sheriff may make an order for custody of a child the extract birth certificate must be produced.[39] A photocopy or an abbreviated extract is not sufficient, what is required is a full extract issued by the Registrar of Births Deaths and Marriages. It should be noted that it is a very common error in drafting a writ in a family action that the dates referred to in the condescendence as the date of marriage and the date of birth of the child differ from those in the certificates. This is a matter which should be checked prior to presentation of the writ.

Form of citation and notice of intention to defend

13.28 Different forms of citation, certificate of citation and notice of intention to defend are used in family actions. Form F15 is the form of citation, and it takes account of the provisions of rule 33.34 and advises the defender of the situations when a notice of intention to defend should be lodged (see para 13.46). Form F26 (notice of intention to defend) is also served with the writ[40] and following citation Form F16 (certificate of citation) is completed by the person effecting service and returned to court with the writ.[41]

Service or intimation (local authority)

13.29 Where service or intimation is to be made on a local authority under rule 33.7(1)(g), 33.7(4) or 33.15(2) it must be effected within seven days of the date of granting the warrant to cite or the order for intimation. If a local

[38] r 33.10
[39] r 33.9
[40] r 33.11(1)
[41] r 33.11(2)

authority is named as a defender in a writ Form F8 must be attached to a copy of the writ served on the defender.[42] The purpose of Form F8 is to advise the local authority of its obligation to provide a report in terms of section 49(2) of the Children Act 1975.

Specifically the situations in which service or intimation must be made are as follows:

- Rule 33.7(1)(g) (where pursuer not a parent of the child and resident in Scotland)
- Rule 33.7(4) (where pursuer craves custody and is not resident in Scotland)
- Rule 33.15(2) (where a party makes an application or averment in a family action which would have required intimation under rule 33.7 if it had been made in an initial writ)[42]

Forms to be served with copy initial writ and warrant	
Divorce	Form F15
	Form F26
2 years with consent	Form F19
	Form F20
5 years	Form F23
Separation	Form F15
	Form F26
2 years with consent	Form F21
	Form F22
5 years	Form F24
Custody	Form F15
	Form F26
if consent required	Form F7
	Form F25
if local authority defender	Form F8
Whereabouts unknown	Form F15
	Form F26
	Form F17
	Form F18
if divorce 2 years with consent	Form F19 and F20
if 5 years	Form F23

[42] r 33.12

Service in action where the defender suffers from mental disorder

13.30 Rule 33.7(1)(c) provides for intimation on the defender's children over 16 and next of kin where the defender suffers from a mental disorder. This, however, does not constitute service. Where the defender is resident in a hospital or similar institution he or she is cited by serving the following documents on the medical officer in charge of the hospital by registered or first class post along with the copy initial writ:

- A citation (Form F15)
- Notice under rule 33.14(1) (notice advising of effect of decree of divorce or separation and form of consent if appropriate)
- Forms F17 (request to medical officer) and F18 (certificate)

The medical officer in Form F17 is requested to give a copy of the writ to the defender and explain the contents provided he or she is satisfied that to do so will not cause any danger to the health of the defender.[43]

The medical officer is required to certify, in Form F18, whether he has given the defender the copy initial writ and other forms. If he is of the view that the defender should not be given these documents because it would be dangerous to his health he must certify this on the form.[44] After completing the form the medical officer is required to return it to the pursuer or his solicitor.[45] In a situation where the initial writ has not been given to the defender the sheriff may, at any time before decree, order further medical enquiry or further service or intimation as he thinks fit.

General provisions relating to family actions

Appointment of curator *ad litem* to a person suffering from mental disorder

13.31 In an action of divorce or separation where it appears to the court that the defender is suffering from mental disorder the sheriff must appoint a curator *ad litem*.[46] The rule does not specify at what stage this intimation is to be made, but it is thought that it should be done as soon as the sheriff becomes aware of the situation. It may be that the first point at which it is brought to the sheriff's attention is when the initial writ is presented for warranting. However, the defender's condition may not be apparent until a later stage, for example in the pursuer's affidavits in an undefended action or in the defences in a defended case.

[43] r 33.13(a)–(c)
[44] r 33.13(d)
[45] r 33.13(2)
[46] r 33.16(2)(a)

Within seven days after the appointment of a curator *ad litem* the pursuer must send the curator a copy of the writ and any defences lodged, including any adjustments and amendments. Where an Options Hearing has been fixed a copy of the Form G5 (intimation of Options Hearing) should be sent to the curator by the sheriff clerk.[47]

In all actions for divorce or separation, except those which are based on two years' separation with consent (see para 13.32), within 21 days of his appointment the curator must consider what further action to take on behalf of the defender.[48] This will depend on the stage which the action has reached. In particular the curator must decide whether to lodge

- A notice of intention to defend
- Defences
- A minute adopting defences already lodged, or
- A minute stating he does not intend to lodge defences.[49]

If the curator intimates at this stage that he does not intend to lodge defences he may still appear at a later stage of the action to protect the interests of the defender.[50] If the curator feels at any stage that the defender is not suffering from a mental disorder he should report this to the court and seek his discharge.[51]

The pursuer is responsible in the first instance for the fees incurred by the curator *ad litem* up to the point where he lodges defences, adopts defences already lodged, decides not to lodge defences or is discharged.[52] The question of which party ultimately pays for the curator's fees will be determined when the sheriff deals with the question of expenses in the action.

Intimation to the Mental Welfare Commission

13.32 In addition to appointing a curator *ad litem* where a defender who suffers from a mental disorder is being sued for divorce on the ground of two years' separation with consent the sheriff must make an order for intimation of the ground of the action to the Mental Welfare Commission for Scotland.[53] It should be noted that there is no requirement for the pursuer to include a crave for this intimation. The order for intimation includes a requirement that the Commission is to report on whether the defender is capable of deciding whether to give his consent[54]. This report is lodged with the sheriff clerk who puts it in process, and intimates that this has been done to the solicitor for the pursuer, the solicitor for the defender and the curator *ad litem*.[55] In cases where the Mental Welfare Commission

[47] r 33.16(3)
[48] r 33.16(5)(b)
[49] r 33.16(6)
[50] r 33.16(7)
[51] r 33.16(8)
[52] r 33.16(9)
[53] r 33.16(2)(b)(i)
[54] r 33.16(2)(b)(ii)
[55] r 33.16(4)

has lodged a report the curator has 14 days from the date of lodging the report to decide on what response is appropriate and in particular which of the writs referred to in para 13.31 above should be lodged.[56]

Applications for sist

13.33 An application for a sist under Schedule 3 to the Domicile and Matrimonial Proceedings Act 1973 where there are other proceedings pending before another court is made by written motion.[57] The provisions of Chapter 15 of the Rules (Motion procedure) will apply to such an application (see Chap 6 of this book).

Consents to custody of child

13.34 Section 47(2) of the Children Act 1975, which provides that an applicant for custody requires to obtain the consent of the parents of the child, is discussed at para 13.17. In most cases the person whose consent is required will either be a defender to the action or require to be given intimation in terms of rule 33.7. In these circumstances Form F7 (form of notice to parent or guardian) and Form F25 (form of consent) need to be served with the initial writ or intimation.[58] The certificate of service or intimation to be completed by the pursuer's solicitor after service must state that these forms have been served.

If the parent or guardian wishes to consent he completes and signs Form F25. The signature must be witnessed and thereafter the form is sent to the sheriff clerk. No time limit is prescribed for the return of this form, but it is suggested that this should be done, if possible, before the expiry of the period of notice.[59] The person giving consent can withdraw it by letter sent to the sheriff clerk.[60] On receipt of such a letter the sheriff clerk intimates the terms of the letter to every party to the action.[61]

Reports on children where an order for custody or access is sought

13.35 Rules 33.20 and 33.21 make provision for a report on the circumstances of the child and the proposed arrangements for the care and upbringing of the child to be submitted to the court in relation to certain custody or access applications. In para 13.29 above reference is made to the requirement to intimate the raising of certain custody actions to a local authority under section 49(2) of the Children Act 1975 with a view to the

[56] r 33.16(5)(a), (6)
[57] r 33.17
[58] r 33.19(1)
[59] r 33.19(2)
[60] r 33.19(3)
[61] r 33.19(4)

local authority submitting a report. In addition to this mandatory provision the sheriff may, at any stage of a family action, call for a report on a child from either a local authority under section 11(1) of the Matrimonial Proceedings (Children) Act 1958 or section 12(2)(a) of the Guardianship Act 1973 or a reporter (*e.g.* a solicitor). When a report is required under section 49 of the 1975 Act the form of intimation (F8) advises the local authority of the requirement under the Act to provide a report. In other cases the sheriff will direct that the party seeking the report instruct the reporter, except where the report is ordered by the sheriff in which case the pursuer or minuter will be responsible for instructing the report.[62] Rules 33.20 and 33.21 also make provision for payment of the fees and expenses of the local authority or the reporter.

On completion the report is sent to the sheriff clerk by the local authority or the reporter together with a copy for each party.[63] The sheriff clerk will send a copy to each party.[64] Where a report has been called for decree cannot be granted until the report has been lodged.[65]

Referral to a family mediation and conciliation service

13.36 The sheriff may where he thinks it is appropriate refer any dispute relating to custody or access to a specified family mediation and conciliation service.[66] This could be done on the motion of either or both parties or *ex proprio motu* by the sheriff. The mediation or conciliation service must be specified in the interlocutor.

Joint minutes

13.37 Where parties have reached an agreement relating to parental rights, aliment for a child or an order for financial provision, a joint minute may be entered into in respect of the matters agreed. The sheriff may grant decree in respect of matters in the joint minute which may include matters which were not craved either in the writ or in any claim in the defences.[67]

Undefended family actions

13.38 The procedure for decree in an undefended family action in which no notice of intention to defend has been lodged varies according to the nature of action. In some actions a decree in absence may be granted on the basis of the averments in the writ without any further enquiry (see

62 r 33.21(2)
63 rr 33.20(1), 33.21(4)
64 rr 33.20(2), 33.21(5)
65 rr 33.20(3), 33.21(6)
66 r 33.22
67 r 33.26

Chap 3 of this book and para 13.43). In the actions referred to in the next paragraph, however, decree may only be granted after evidence has been considered by the court. This evidence is usually given in the form of affidavits.

Affidavit evidence

13.39 Affidavit evidence is required in an undefended action for

- Divorce
- Separation
- Declarator of legitimacy
- Declarator of illegitimacy
- Declarator of parentage
- Declarator of non-parentage
- Declarator of legitimation
- The variation or recall of an order mentioned in section 8(1) of the Law Reform (Miscellaneous Provisions) Act 1966 (application for the variation or recall of a court of session decree)

Affidavit evidence will also be required in any of the above actions which are initially defended but subsequently proceed as undefended. If an action is defended on an ancillary matter, but not on the merits, the sheriff may direct that affidavit evidence may be given in relation to the merits.[68]

In addition to the provisions listed above there are some general provisions which extend the use of affidavit evidence in relation to both defended and undefended actions. These are:

- Rule 29.3(1) which allows a motion to be lodged in any ordinary action requesting that evidence of a witness be given by affidavit, and
- Rule 33.27 which provides that affidavit evidence may be accepted in a family action for any hearing for an order or interim order

Provisions relating to evidence generally are discussed further in Chapter 11 of this book.

Decree in absence where affidavit evidence required

13.40 To obtain a decree in absence where affidavit evidence is required the pursuer lodges a minute for decree (Form F27)[69]. This minute is lodged along with the affidavits[70], which must be prepared in accordance

[68] r 33.28
[69] r 33.29(1)(b)
[70] r 33.29(1)(a)

with the Practice Notes issued by the sheriffs principal. Each sheriffdom has a Practice Note in similar terms relative to the completion of affidavits. In practice, the sheriff clerk returns many affidavits before they even reach the sheriff because of minor errors which could easily be avoided. Solicitors when preparing affidavits should ensure that the content complies with the appropriate Practice Note and should also check that the following points of detail are in order:

- The names in any certificates referred to in the affidavit are stated in exactly the same terms
- All dates referred to as dates of birth, marriage etc are correct in accordance with the appropriate certificate

The Practice Notes issued by the sheriffs principal are summarised below.

The minute for decree must dispose of all of the craves in the initial writ. If craves are to be dismissed this should be minuted for and if decree is sought in terms other than as craved in the initial writ the terms in which decree is sought should be clearly specified.

Summary of main points of Practice Notes

Affidavits to be	on A4 paper
	unbacked and unfolded
	stapled
	headed up "at __________ on the (day) of (month) Nineteen Hundred and __________ Compeared __________ who being solemnly sworn depones as follows"
	given the full name, age address and occupation of the deponent
	written in the first person
	in numbered paragraphs which follow step by step the averments in the writ to the extent that they are within the knowledge of the witness
	signed on each page by the witness and the person before whom the affadavit is sworn
	ended with the words "all of which is truth as the deponent shall answer to God."
or	"all of which is affirmed to be true." where witness has not sworn, but has affirmed

Other matters relating to affidavits

productions must	be referred to by their number in process
	be docketed and signed by the witness and the notary
photographs	any photographs lodged must be docketed and signed by the witness and the notary
pursuer's affidavit	relative to defender's financial position must state as precisely as possible the date at which information relating to the defender's financial position was valid
	speak to own financial position as at date of affidavit
	where there is a crave for capital allowance, periodical allowance, aliment for child or children, or expenses in the initial writ, but no decree is sought in respect of these, narrate the reasons why decree is not sought.
	where the consent of the defender has been lodged, refer to that consent which must be docketed and signed by the pursuer and the person before whom the affidavit is sworn

Affidavits—welfare of child

13.41 Where evidence relating to the welfare of a child is required at least one of the affidavits giving such evidence must be given by a person who is not a parent or party to the action.[71]

Granting decree and extract

13.42 If, after having considered the initial writ, minute and productions, the sheriff is satisfied with the evidence contained in the affidavits he will grant decree. The sheriff, however, has power to order any further procedure he thinks fit before granting decree (*e.g.* he may call for further affidavits, or require parole evidence to be led). The decree may be extracted after 14 days, and where a decree for divorce is granted a copy of the extract is sent automatically by the sheriff clerk to each party in the action.[72] The sheriff clerk also sends a copy of the extract to the Registrar of Births, Deaths and Marriages so that their records can be amended.

71 r 33.28(3)

72 rr 33.29(2), 33.30

Decree in absence: affidavit evidence not required

13.43 The family actions in which affidavit evidence is not required before decree in absence can be granted are

- Actions for parental rights
- Actions or applications for aliment
- Actions of affiliation and aliment
- Actions for financial provision after an overseas divorce or anulment
- Actions or applications for an order under the Matrimonial Homes (Family Protection) (Scotland) Act 1981[73]

With the exception of an action for parental rights, in actions where affidavit evidence is not required decree in absence may be applied for in terms of rule 7.2 (see paras 3.2–3.6)

In an undefended action for parental rights in which affidavit evidence is not required the sheriff is directed to make such enquiry as he thinks fit before pronouncing decree.[74] The question of what enquiry may be made is a matter for the sheriff. In some instances he may call for a report to assist him in meeting his obligation to have regard to the welfare of the child, and in some instances he is in fact required to have a report before he can grant decree (see para 13.35). In other cases the sheriff may be satisfied on the basis of the pleadings or after having heard the solicitor for the pursuer.

In an undefended action for aliment, when the minute for decree is lodged the pursuer must also lodge all documentary evidence of the means of parties which is available to him[75]. The sheriff may fix a hearing if he requires further information before granting decree.[76]

Motions in undefended actions

13.44 It should be noted that the motion procedure (Chapter 15 of the Rules) does not apply to undefended family actions[77]. The effect of this is that the sheriff has a discretion to deal with a motion in an undefended action in any manner which he considers appropriate including making an order for intimation, having regard to the nature of the motion.

Defended actions

13.45 The provisions of Chapter 9 (Standard procedure) apply to all defended family actions except where they would be inconsistent with any

[73] r 33.28(1)(a)
[74] r 33.31(2)
[75] r 33.57(1)
[76] r 33.57(2)
[77] r 33.33

of the provisions of Chapter 33 or where they are specifically excluded. There are however some special rules in Chapter 33 relating to defended family actions. See also Chapter 4 of this book for the procedure which applies generally to defended actions.

Notice of intention to defend

13.46 A notice of intention to defend is lodged in a family action when the defender wishes

- To challenge the jurisdiction of the court
- To oppose any crave in the writ
- To make a claim for
  —aliment
  —an order for financial provision
  —an order for parental rights (as defined in s 8(3) of Family Law (Scotland) Act 1985)
  —an order under section 16(1)(b) or (3) of the Family Law (Scotland) Act 1985 (an order setting aside or varying an agreement as to financial provision)
  —an order under section 18 of the Family Law (Scotland) Act 1985 (an order relating to an avoidance transaction)
  —an order under the Matrimonial Homes (Family Protection) (Scotland) Act 1981[78]

To lodge a notice of intention to defend the defender completes Form F26 and lodges it with the sheriff clerk before the expiry of the period of notice[79]. A court fee is payable on lodging the notice of intention to defend, and this must be inserted in Form F26 by the pursuer prior to service of the initial writ.

On receipt of a notice of intention to defend rule 9.2 comes into play and the sheriff clerk fixes and intimates a date for the Options Hearing, the last date for adjustment and the last date for lodging defences. Further details of procedure under Chapter 9 of the Rules can be found in Chapter 4 of this book.

Defences

13.47 Where the defender wishes to make a claim or seek any order the defences must contain a crave and averments in support of the claim or order sought.[80] It is suggested that defences in a family action including a claim or seeking any order should be set out in a similar fashion to defences containing a counterclaim in an ordinary action. See para 4.8 of this book.

[78] r 33.34(1)
[79] r 33.34(2)
[80] r 33.34(2)(b)

Attendance of parties at the Options Hearing

13.48 One important provision which applies only in family actions is that the parties must, unless cause is shown, attend in person at the Options Hearing.[81] The intention behind this provision is that parties should be brought together as early as possible in the proceedings in order to encourage early resolution of the matters in dispute.

Abandonment of action

13.49 Where the pursuer abandons a family action the defender may continue to pursue any claim made in the defences as if it was a separate cause.[82] This provision is the equivalent of the counterclaim provision for other types of ordinary actions (see para 4.8).

Decree by default

13.50 The provisions of Chapter 16 of the Rules (Decree by default) do not apply to family actions. Rule 33.37 however contains appropriate default provisions for family actions. This rule provides that a party is in default if he or she fails

- To lodge or intimate the lodging of any part of process
- To implement an order of the sheriff within a specified period
- To appear or be represented at any diet[38].

If no party appears at any diet in a family action the sheriff may dismiss the action.[84] There is no definition of the word "diet" in this rule as there is in Chapter 16. However rules 9.12(7) and 10.6(4) define the Options Hearing and the Procedural Hearing respectively as a diet for the purposes of rule 33.37.

There is a question as to whether the failure of a party to appear personally at the Options Hearing would create a default situation. It may be considered that the reference to "party" includes the person representing the party. However there is an alternative view that this particular provision means that a default situation is created by the failure of the party to attend "personally", even if represented. In one case, the sheriff principal held on appeal that it was sufficient for a party to be represented at the Options Hearing, and that failure to appear personally did not constitute a default.[85]

Where a party is in default in an action in which decree may *not* be

[81] r 33.36; see also para 13.50 re failure of party to attend the Options Hearing
[82] r 33.35
[83] r 33.37(1)
[84] r 33.7(3)
[85] *Grimes* v *Grimes*, 1995 SCLR 268

granted without evidence the sheriff may allow the action to proceed as undefended[86] and order that affidavits be lodged.

Where the default has occurred in an action in which if it is undefended decree may be granted *without* evidence the sheriff may

- Grant decree as craved
- Grant a decree of absolvitor
- Dismiss the action or any claim made or order sought[87]

In all of the above circumstances expenses may be awarded[88]

The sheriff may, on cause shown, prorogate the time for lodging any production or part of process or for intimating or implementing any order.[89]

Applications and Orders relating to certain family actions

13.51 Parts IV-XIII of Chapter 33 include further rules which apply to certain types of family actions. It should be noted in particular that in relation to applications for parental rights different Parts apply depending on whether the application is made in an action of divorce or separation or some other family action (*i.e.* Parts IV or IX).

Part IV—Applications and orders relating to children in actions of divorce or separation (rr 33.38–46)

13.52 This Part deals with applications and orders for parental rights and aliment relating to children in actions of divorce and separation. Where an application for custody is being made by a party to such an action it is made by a crave in the writ or the defences as appropriate.[90] A person who is not a party to the action may make an application for an order relating to a child by minute in the process.[91] Where this is the case minute procedure will apply (see Chap 6 of this book and Chapter 14 of the Rules).

Any application for an order for interim aliment, interim custody, interim access, or for variation of an order under section 10(1) or 12(1) of the Matrimonial Proceedings (Children) Act 1958 is made by motion in the process in a pending action.[92] Applications made after decree for any of these orders are made by minute in the original process. On a minute

86 r 33.37(2)(a)
87 r 33.37(2)(b)–(d)
88 r 33.37(2)(e)
89 r 33.37(4)
90 r 33.39(1)(a)
91 r 33.39(1)(b)
92 r 33.43

being lodged a motion is required for any interim order sought in relation to the minute proceedings.[93]

Where after decree a person over 18 years of age is seeking aliment application is made by minute in the process of the action in which the order for aliment was made when the person was under the age of 18 years.[94] This procedure is also used for any application for variation of aliment granted on favour of a person over 18 years of age. Any interim application pending determination of the minute is made by motion.

Part V—Orders relating to financial provision (rules 33.47–52)

13.53 Orders

- For financial provision
- Under the Family Law Act 1985 setting aside or varying agreement as to financial provision
- Relating to avoidance transactions, and
- Under the Matrimonial Homes (Family Protection) (Scotland) Act 1981,

If sought by the pursuer or defender in a divorce action, are craved in the initial writ or defences.[95]

Any application made after decree is made by minute in the original process.[96] If a person who is not a party to the action wishes to make an application this is done by minute in the action,[97] and in relation to interim aliment is made by motion.[98]

An application for an incidental order can be made by motion in a depending action,[99] but the sheriff may consider that the application should properly be made in the writ or the defences.[100] In these circumstances a minute of amendment would be required to amend the writ or defences to include an appropriate crave and averments. Any application for financial provision which may be made after decree in terms of the Family Law (Scotland) Act 1985 is made by minute in the process.[101] Any application for an interim order in relation thereto is made by motion.

Parts VI and VII

13.54 Part VI of the Rules (rule 33.53) is a repetition of previous rules relating to avoidance transactions (see para 13.53). Part VII deals with the manner in which an application for financial provision in an overseas divorce or annulment is made.

93 r 33.44
94 r 33.46
95 r 33.48(a)
96 r 33.52
97 r 33.48(b)
98 r 33.50
99 r 33.49(a), (b)
100 r 33.49(2)
101 r 33.51

Part VIII—Actions of aliment (rr 33.56–59)

13.55 Rule 33.58 contains similar provisions to those already discussed at para 13.52 in providing that applications in pending actions are made by motion and any application after decree is made by minute in the original process.

Variation of an agreement for aliment Section 7(2) of the Family Law (Scotland) Act 1985 allows an agreement which has been entered into in respect of aliment to be varied or terminated by the court on a material change of circumstances. An application of this nature is to be by summary application unless there is a pending family action before the court.[102] Any application made in terms of this provision would be subject to the summary application rules.[103]

Part IX—Actions relating to parental rights (rr 33.60–65)

13.56 The rules in this part apply to all family actions where there is an application for parental rights except actions of divorce or separation. Applications for parental rights may be made in three ways, *i.e.* by

- An action for parental rights (*i.e.* custody, guardianship, access)
- A crave in any family action
- Minute in an action to which the applicant is not a party[104]

Applications for variation of parental rights after decree are made by minute in the original process.[105]

In an application for parental rights the pursuer must call one of the following as a defender:

- The parents or other parent of the child
- Any guardian of the child
- Any person who has accepted the child into his family
- Any person having *de facto* custody of the child
- Any local authority in whose care or custody the child is kept
- The Lord Advocate where there is no other person in the above list who can be called upon.[106]

The Lord Advocate is named to represent the public interest where there is no contradictor to the action.

It must also be remembered that in appropriate cases the child should receive intimation.[107] The local authority in whose area the child is resident may also have received intimation.[108]

[102] r 33.59
[103] Act of Sederunt (Sheriff Court Summary Applications Rules) 1993
[104] r 33.61
[105] r 33.65(1)
[106] r 33.62
[107] r 33.7(1)(h)
[108] r 33.7(1)(g), (4); see para 13.18

Section 11(1) of the Guardianship Act 1973 provides that in exceptional circumstances the sheriff may make an order committing a child to the care of a local authority, or may order a child to be under the supervision of a local authority. If the sheriff is considering making such an order he must ordain one of the parties to intimate to the appropriate local authority, if not a party to the action:

- A copy of the pleadings
- A copy of any relevant motion
- Form F28[109].

If the sheriff makes an order the sheriff clerk must intimate the making of the order to the local authority together with a copy of the interlocutor containing the order.[110]

Rule 33.65 provides that any application relating to parental rights made after decree is made by minute in the original process.

Part X—Actions under the Matrimonial Homes (Family Protection) (Scotland) Act 1981 (rr 33.66–72)

13.57 Applications under this Act can be made by

- An action for such an order
- Crave in the initial writ or defences in any family action
- Minute in the action where the applicant is not a party.[111]

Any application dispensing with the consent of the non-entitled spouse to a dealing (s 7(1)) or in relation to a poinding (s 11), if not made in a pending action, is made by summary application. Where this is the case the procedure in the summary applications rules will apply.[112]

Persons to be called as defenders If the applicant is a spouse seeking an order against the other spouse, that spouse must be called as a defender.[113] If the applicant is a third party making an application under section 7(1) (dispensing with the consent of a non-entitled spouse to a dealing) section 8(1) (an order requiring the non-entitled spouse to make any payment due by the entitled spouse in respect of a loan) both spouses must be called as defenders.[114] Where the application is in respect of the occupancy rights of co-habiting couples the other partner must be called as a defender.[115]

109 r 33.64(1)
110 r 33.64(2)
111 r 33.67(1)
112 r 33.67(2)
113 r 33.68(a)
114 r 33.68(b)
115 r 33.68(c)

Procedure Some applications made under the 1981 Act are permitted by the Rules to be by motion and others by minute. In general those to be made by motion are made whilst the action is pending[116], while those to be made by minute relate to the variation or recall of orders made by the court[117].

An application to sist an action to enforce occupancy rights will only apply to that part of the action relating to the enforcement of those rights, although there is provision for the sheriff to direct otherwise.[118]

Section 15(4) and (5) of the 1981 Act provides that intimation is to be made to the Chief Constable where a power of arrest is attached to a matrimonial interdict, or where such a power is varied or recalled after intimation has been made. Form F30 (certificate of delivery) must be lodged in process after intimation to the Chief Constable.[119] The requirement to intimate any variation or recall of a power of arrest is often ignored, as is the requirement to intimate to the Chief Constable the granting of decree of divorce. (When decree is granted the power of arrest falls.) Failure to intimate could have serious consequences for the defender, as an arrest might be made on the basis of a power of arrest which was no longer in force.

Part XI—Simplified divorce applications

13.58 The rules provide for a simplified form of divorce application sometimes known as a "do-it-yourself divorce" in certain restricted circumstances. The intention behind this provision is, as the rules suggest, to provide a simple procedure for obtaining a divorce where the following apply:

- The grounds for divorce are non-cohabitation for two years with consent of the defender or non-cohabitation for five years
- No children of the marriage are under 16
- No financial provision is being sought
- Neither party suffers from mental disorder
- No other proceedings are pending in any court which could bring the marriage to an end[120].

116 r 33.69
117 r 33.70
118 r 33.71
119 r 33.72(1)
120 r 33.73(1)

Form of application and service

13.59 A simplified divorce is applied for by completing an application form which can be obtained from the sheriff clerk's office—Form F31 for two years with consent[121] and Form F33 for five years[122]. All of the averments necessary and the form of consent, if appropriate, are included in the application form which also contains instructions for completion. The affidavit which is required to be sworn by the pursuer is also part of the form; only one affidavit is necessary. The marriage certificate should be lodged along with the form.

Simplified divorce procedure was introduced to enable parties to make application without the need for legal representation, and for this reason the application must be signed by the applicant. Where a consent is required this must be obtained before submitting the application to the sheriff clerk. The sheriff clerk, and only the sheriff clerk, is responsible for the service of a simplified divorce application.[123] Citation may be effected by registered post or by first class recorded delivery post. The latter is usually used. If it is necessary to instruct a sheriff officer to reserve the action, in the event of postal service being ineffective, the sheriff clerk will advise the applicant accordingly. An additional fee has to be paid to the sheriff clerk by the applicant before a sheriff officer will be instructed.[124]

In any case where divorce is sought on the grounds of five years' non-cohabitation and the defender's address is not known, citation is executed by displaying the application form and Form F36 on the walls of court for 21 days and by intimating a copy of the application and Form F37 to every child of the marriage over 16 and to one of the defender's next of kin over 16.[125]

Opposition

13.60 Opposition to an application is made by letter to the sheriff clerk on the grounds that the person responding challenges the jurisdiction of the court or opposes the grant of the application. When such notice is received the application for simplified divorce must be dismissed and an ordinary action for divorce initiated. The only exception will be if the sheriff considers the objection to be frivolous.[126]

Evidence and decree

13.61 Parole evidence is not permitted in a simplified divorce application.[127] If the sheriff is satisfied as regards service and if the

[121] r 33.74(1)
[122] r 33.74(2)
[123] r 33.76(2)
[124] r 33.76(4)
[125] r 33.77
[126] r 33.78
[127] r 33.79

application form including the affidavit has been properly completed, decree will normally be granted on the expiry of the period of notice. An extract of the decree will be issued to both parties by the sheriff clerk not sooner that 14 days after decree.[128] Any application for an order which could be made in an action of divorce, after decree, must be made by minute.[129]

Appeal

13.62 Appeal against a decree in a simplified divorce must be made within 14 days of decree[130] and may be made by letter giving the reasons for the appeal.

Part XII—Variation of Court of Session decrees

Application and intimation to Court of Session

13.63 Section 8 of the Law Reform (Miscellaneous Provisions) (Scotland) Act 1966 allows a party to apply to the sheriff for variation of certain Court of Session decrees. Application is made by initial writ[131], and a copy of the interlocutor which is sought to be varied is lodged with the writ. The copy interlocutor is certified by a clerk of the Court of Session.[132] A copy of the initial writ must be lodged with the Court of Session before the writ is lodged in the sheriff court, and a certificate is attached to the initial writ certifying that this has been done.[133]

Remit of application to Court of Session

13.64 If a motion is lodged in terms of section 8(3) of the 1966 Act requesting that the application is remitted to the Court of Session, the sheriff must grant the motion and order the cause to be transmitted to the Court of Session. The process in this situation is to be transmitted within four days of the order.

Procedure for hearing and disposing of application when defended

13.65 Where the defender following service lodges a notice of intention to defend, and if no motion to remit is made, the pursuer must within 14 days lodge the following documents, or copies of them, from the Court of Session process.

[128] r 33.80; Form F38
[129] r 33.81
[130] r 33.82
[131] r 33.84(1)
[132] r 33.84(2)
[133] r 33.84(3)

- The pleadings
- Interlocutor sheets
- Any opinion of the court
- Any productions on which he seeks to found.[134]

As regards further procedure the sheriff may on joint motion made after the lodging of the above documents

- Dispense with proof on cause shown; or
- Hear parties, whether or not defences have been lodged, and thereafter grant decree or otherwise dispose of the cause as he thinks fit.[135]

In the absence of a joint motion it is suggested that the procedures under Chapters 9 and 10 of the Rules will apply. After the disposal of the case and the expiry of the days of appeal, or after any appeal marked has been disposed of, the process is transmitted by the sheriff clerk to the Court of Session.[136]

In an undefended cause where no notice of intention to defend has been lodged decree may be granted only following affidavit evidence.[137]

Part XIII—Child Support Act 1991

13.66 Part XIII introduces a number of rules as a consequence of the provisions of the 1991 Act on court proceedings and existing court orders. Rule 33.89 makes provision for expenses in an action where the Secretary of State (for Social Security) is named in an action for declarator of non-parentage or illegitimacy, for his interest in connection with an application for a maintenance assessment in relation to the child and the parties to the application. In particular, the rule provides that no expenses may be awarded against the Secretary of State where he does not defend the action.[138]

Rules 33.90 and 33.91 make provision for interlocutors and extract decrees where a maintenance assessment made by the Child Support Agency supersedes a court order for maintenance of a child. On the making of a maintenance assessment the court order ceases to have effect in so far as it relates to aliment for the child, and the sheriff clerk is required to endorse on the relevant interlocutor, and any extract decree issued thereafter, a certificate in terms provided in Form F39 and rule 33.91(1). When the sheriff clerk is subsequently advised by the Child Support Agency that the maintenance assessment is cancelled or ceases to have effect a certificate in terms of Form F40 and rule 33.91(2) is endorsed on the interlocutor and any extract decree to record that the court order again has effect.[139]

134 r 33.85(1)
135 r 33.85(2)
136 r 33.86
137 r 33.28
138 r 33.89
139 rr 33.90, 33.91

APPENDIX 13.1

Crave for divorce (or separation)

	Averments
Rule 3.1(5)(a)	Grounds of jurisdiction
Rule 3.1(5)(b)	Facts on which jurisdiction based
Rule 33.2	Details of any other proceedings
Rule 3.1(6)	Steps taken to trace defender whose whereabouts are unknown
Rule 33.4	Steps taken to trace person on whom intimation is required whose whereabouts are unknown
Rule 33.5	Whether maintenance order granted (if periodical allowance craved)
	Craves for intimation
Rule 33.7(1)(a) and (c)(i)	Child and next of kin (whereabouts unknown or mental disorder)
Rule 33.7(1)(b)	Adultery (where averred)
Rule 33.7(1)(c)(ii)	Any *curator bonis*

Crave for parental rights

	Averments
Rule 3.1(5)(a)	Ground of jurisdiction
Rule 3.1(5)(b)	Facts on which jurisdiction based
Rule 33.3(1)(b)(i)	Any other proceedings
Rule 33.3(1)(b)(ii)	Proceedings relating to parent's marriage (if not ancillary to divorce)
Rule 3.1(6)	Steps taken to trace defender whose whereabouts are unknown
Rule 33.4	Steps taken to trace person on whom intimation is required whose whereabouts are unknown

	Intimation
Rule 33.7(1)(a) and (c)(i)	Child and next of kin (whereabouts unknown or mental disorder)
Rule 33.7(1)(f)	Any parent or guardian not a party
Rule 33.7(1)(g) and (4)	Local authority (if applicant not parent or resident in Scotland)
Rule 33.7(1)(h)	Child

Crave for aliment

	Averments
Rule 33.5	Whether order under section 106 of Debtors (Scotland) Act 1987 granted
	When and by whom such order granted
Rule 3.1(5)(a)	Grounds of jurisdiction
Rule 3.1(5)(b)	Facts on which jurisdiction based
	If for "top up"
Rule 33.6(2)	Date and details of maintenance assessment
Rule 33.6(2)(a)(iv)	Grounds of jurisdiction
	If not "top up"
Rule 33.6(3)	Grounds of jurisdiction
	or
	Child not a child within the meaning of section 55 of the Child Support Act 1991
	or
	Habitual residence of person with care or absent parent or child outwith the UK
	Intimation
Rule 33.7(1)(h)	Child

CHAPTER 14

Miscellaneous Actions

Chapters 34–37 of the Rules

Actions relating to heritable property

14.1 Chapter 34 of the Rules makes provision for the following:

- Actions for sequestration for rent
- Actions of removing
- Applications under Part II of the Conveyancing and Feudal Reform (Scotland) Act 1970.

The focus of consideration here is on the procedural rules which apply to these actions. More detailed explanations of the actions and the circumstances in which they are competent are dealt with in other works. It should be noted that the rules in Chapter 34 do not stand alone but require to be applied along with those other rules which apply to ordinary actions generally.

Sequestration for rent

14.2 In an action for sequestration and sale for non-payment or recovery of rent due or in security of rent to become due the landlord may include in the initial writ a crave for payment. Where decree is granted for payment an extract decree may be issued in "common form", *i.e.* in the same manner as a decree in an action for payment of money. The Rules also make provision for service of a Form of Notice advising the defender of the right to apply for certain orders under the Debtors (Scotland) Act 1987 (*e.g.* release of articles sequestrated).[1]

The warrant to cite (or first deliverance) in an action of sequestration for rent includes an order to sequestrate an inventory and secure the effects of the tenant. This warrant, which is added to the normal warrant to cite, must include authority to open, shut and lockfast places.[2]

Where the effects of the tenant have been sequestrated and the rent remains unpaid, the sheriff may on the motion of the pursuer grant warrant to sell the sequestrated effects[3] to satisfy the rent claimed together with any

[1] r 34.1; Form H1
[2] r 34.2; Form O1
[3] r 34.3(1)

interest and expenses. If a sale takes place it must be reported to the sheriff clerk within 14 days after the date of the sale, and there must be lodged at the same time the "roup rolls" (an inventory of the items in the sale) and a statement of the debt[4]. Thereafter, the sheriff may issue an interlocutor approving the report of sale and granting decree against the defender for payment of any balance of rent due[5].

At any stage in an action for sequestration and sale the sheriff may appoint a person to take charge of the tenant's sequestrated effects or may order the tenant to find caution[6].

Removings

14.3 Sections 34–38A of the Sheriff Courts (Scotland) Act 1907 and rules 34.5–34.9 make provision for actions of removing, the periods within which certain actions may be raised, the forms of notice to be given and the methods of giving notice. Such actions are very rare in modern times.

Applications under Part II of the Conveyancing and Feudal Reform (Scotland) Act 1970

14.4 Rule 34.10 regulates the form of action to be initiated where the pursuer wishes to combine a crave under Part II of the 1970 Act with a crave for some other remedy (*e.g.* ejection or interdict). In these circumstances, it is provided that the action must be made by initial writ under the ordinary cause rules. Application is made by summary application where the action seeks no other remedy than that provided in Part II of the 1970 Act. The rule also restates the provisions in the 1970 Act relating to appeal, *i.e.* the sheriff's decision in respect of a decree granted in terms of Part II of the 1970 Act is final[7]. This, however, does not effect a party's right to appeal a decision made in relation to any other crave[8].

Actions of multiplepoinding

14.5 A multiplepoinding is an action which is raised where there are two or more claims over a fund or property (referred to as the fund *in medio*) held by a third party (the holder of the fund). The purpose of raising the action is to seek from the court a determination as to which party is entitled to the fund *in medio* or, where there is more than one party who may be entitled to a share in the fund, a decision as to how the fund should be divided.

[4] r 34.3(2)
[5] r 34.3(3)
[6] r 34.4
[7] r 34.10(2)
[8] ss 27, 28 of the Sheriff Courts (Scotland) Act 1907

The action may be raised in the sheriff court having jurisdiction over the fund or in which one of the defenders is domiciled[9]. The procedures which apply are very different to those for other ordinary actions. In particular, the timetable for defended actions is different and, with the exception of the undernoted rules, the Standard and Additional Procedures do not apply.

Rules of Standard Procedure which apply to actions of multiplepoinding

- Rule 9.3 return of initial writ
- Rule 9.5 process folder
- Rule 9.6 defences
- Rule 9.7 implied admissions
- Rule 9.13 inspection and recovery of documents
- Rule 9.14 exchange of list of witnesses

Raising the action

14.6 The action may be raised either by the person who holds the fund or by any other person having an interest or wishing to make a claim on the fund[10]. In an action raised by the holder of the fund, the pursuer must call as defenders all persons known to have an interest in the fund. Where the action is raised by a claimant the pursuer must call as a defender the holder of the fund[11].

Condescendence of fund

14.7 A detailed condescendence of the fund must be included in the condescendence of the initial writ by the pursuer where the pursuer is the holder of the fund[12]. If the pursuer is *not* the holder of the fund a separate condescendence must be lodged by the holder of the fund following service of the initial writ[13] together with a list of all persons known to have an interest in the fund[14]. Both these documents when lodged must be intimated to all other parties prior to the expiry of the period of notice[15].

[9] rr 2(9), (15)(a) of Sched 8 to the Civil Jurisdiction and Judgments Act 1982
[10] r 35.3(1)
[11] r 35.3(2)
[12] r 35.4(1)
[13] r 35.4(2)(a)(i)
[14] r 35.4(2)(a)(ii)
[15] r 35.4(2)

Warrant to cite

14.8 When the initial writ is lodged the sheriff clerk will issue a warrant to cite the defenders[16]. This warrant, which is different in form to that used in other ordinary actions, provides that a defender who wishes to respond to the initial writ by, for example, making a claim on the fund must first lodge a notice of appearance and not a notice of intention to defend. Moreover, the warrant also provides for the situation where the holder of the fund is a defender and, as discussed above, is required to lodge a condescendence of the fund with a list of parties known to have an interest in the fund.

Methods of service and forms

14.9 The methods of service are the same as those which apply to other actions[17]. There is, however, a different form of citation to be served with the copy initial writ and, as mentioned above, a notice of appearance is sent to the defender instead of a notice of intention to defend.[18] After service, a certificate detailing the method(s) of service used is completed and signed by the solicitor or sheriff officer who has effected service[19].

Advertisement

14.10 In addition to obtaining a warrant to cite the defenders the pursuer may make an application to the sheriff for an order for advertisement[20]. Such an order will, of course, be necessary where the address of any of the defenders is not known. However, it may be that there are potential claimants whose identity is not known, in which case advertisement may be the only way of reaching all potential claimants. Advertisement may be ordered either at the time of issuing a warrant to cite or at a later stage on the motion of any of the parties or by the sheriff *ex proprio motu*[21].

Lodging of notice of appearance and fixing date for first hearing

14.11 Where a notice of appearance, or a condescendence of the fund, is lodged the sheriff clerk fixes a date for what is referred to in the Rules as the "first hearing" and intimates the date to all parties[22]. The date to be assigned for the first hearing is the "first suitable court day" occurring not sooner than four weeks after the expiry of the period of notice[23].

[16] r 35.5; Form M1
[17] see paras 2.11–2.15
[18] r 35.6(1); Forms M2, M4
[19] r 35.6(2); Form M3
[20] r 35.7; Form M5
[21] r 35.16
[22] r 35.9; Form M5
[23] r 35.9(9)

Conduct of first hearing

14.12 The rules regulating the conduct of the first hearing are in many respects similar to those for Options and Procedural Hearings. In particular, the sheriff is directed to conduct the hearing, and any subsequent hearing, "with a view to securing the expeditious progress of the cause by ascertaining from parties the matters in dispute"[24]. This may involve finding out from parties whether they wish to challenge either the jurisdiction of the court or the competency of the action, or to object to the condecendence or make a claim. Depending on the response the sheriff will fix a period of time within which parties may lodge defences, objections or claims. Where the holder of the fund has lodged a list containing the names of persons who have an interest in the fund, but who have not been called as defenders, the sheriff may allow amendment of the initial writ to add such persons as defenders and order service on them of the initial writ, as amended[25]. At the conclusion of the first hearing the sheriff is required to fix a date for a second hearing[26].

Lodging and form of defences, objections and claims

14.13 The defender's response must be contained and be lodged in a single document under separate headings detailing the defence, objection to the fund or the claim, as the case may be[27]. This document must be lodged with the sheriff clerk within the time allowed at the first hearing together with any documents founded on[28]. The procedure which follows thereafter depends on whether the defender has lodged defences, objections, a claim or a combination of these. In particular, the Rules provide for these matters to be dealt with in the following sequence:

- Defences
- Objections, and
- Claims.

Procedures where defences or objections lodged

14.14 Defences are lodged when a party wishes to challenge the jurisdiction of the court or the competence of the action, and as mentioned above these issues must be heard and be disposed of[29] before the action can proceed as regards any objections or claims. When defences are lodged the sheriff may allow parties a period within which to adjust the initial writ and defences. At the end of the adjustment period the sheriff will close the record[30] and fix a debate on the question of jurisdiction or competency. If

[24] r 35.10(1)
[25] r 35.10(4)
[26] r 35.10(3)
[27] r 35.11(1)
[28] r 35.11(2)
[29] r 35.12(2)
[30] r 35.12(1)

the defences are sustained that will be the end of the action. However, if repelled the action will proceed to consideration of any objections to the fund or any claims.

A party who wishes to object to the condescendence of the fund (for example on the basis that property or money has been wrongly included in the fund) must lodge defences, and these must be disposed of before the action can proceed as regards claims. When lodged the sheriff may allow a period for adjustment and thereafter close the record and fix a proof or debate on the objections as appropriate[31].

Approval of fund *in medio*

14.15 When any objections lodged have been disposed of, or if there are no objections, the sheriff may on the motion of the holder of the fund (without ordering intimation to other parties) approve of the condescendence of the fund and find the holder liable only in one single payment[32]. The sheriff may also issue an order for consignation of the fund by the holder (where the fund is a sum of money) or for sale of the whole or part of the fund and for the proceeds thereof to be consigned[33]. After consignation, the holder of the fund may apply by motion for exoneration and discharge, and for expenses which will be payable out of the fund[34].

Procedure in relation to claims

14.16 Where claims have been lodged, and there is competition, the action proceeds by the sheriff allowing a period for adjustment, following which the record will be closed[35]. The Rules enable the sheriff thereafter to regulate further procedure as appropriate. This may involve fixing a debate to hear parties on their claims or a proof where there is a dispute about facts. If there is no competition, or when the competition has been decided following proof or debate, the sheriff may rank and prefer the claims and grant decree accordingly[36]. The sheriff also has power, where there are a number of claims, to remit these to a reporter to prepare a scheme of division. The expenses of the remit, when approved by the sheriff, are a charge on the fund to be deducted before division of the fund amongst the claimants[37].

Preliminary pleas

14.17 The procedure relating to preliminary pleas in actions of multiplepoinding is similar to that which applies to other actions. Provision

[31] r 35.13(1)
[32] r 35.13(2)
[33] r 35.15(1)
[34] r 35.15(2), (3)
[35] r 35.17(2)
[36] r 35.17(1)
[37] r 35.18

is made for any party insisting on a preliminary plea to lodge a note of the basis of the plea not later than three days before any hearing fixed to determine further procedure following the lodging of defences, objections or claims[38]. This will normally be the second hearing referred to in para 14.12 above. A party failing to lodge a note will be deemed to be no longer insisting on the plea and the sheriff must repel the plea[39].

Before fixing a debate on a preliminary plea the sheriff must be satisfied that there is a preliminary matter of law which "justifies" a debate[40].

Actions of damages

14.18 Chapter 36 of the Rules contains special rules which apply to actions for damages.[41] These rules are supplementary to those other rules which apply generally to ordinary actions. Chapter 36 is in five parts dealing with the following procedural matters:

Part I: averments and intimation in relation to connected persons in actions for damages following the death of a person from personal injuries;

Part II: interim payment in actions for damages for personal injuries or the death of a person from personal injuries;

Part III: provisional damages in actions for personal injuries:

Part IV: management of damages payable to a person under a legal disability; and

Part V: actions in which a claim for damages is made under the Sex Discrimination Act 1975.

Part I—Averments and Intimation in relation to connected persons

14.19 *Averments* In an action for damages raised by a relative or executor of a person who has died from personal injuries, the pursuer must include averments in the condescendence of the initial writ in relation to the following matters, as the case may be:

- That there are no other persons (*i.e.* connected persons) with a title to sue who are not parties to the action
- That there are connected persons, as specified in the crave of the initial writ
- That there are connected persons on whom intimation should be dispensed with on the grounds that

[38] r 35.14(1)
[39] r 35.14(2)
[40] r 35.14(3)
[41] r 36.1

—their names and whereabouts are not known or cannot reasonably be ascertained or
—they are unlikely to be awarded more than £200 each.[42]

Warrant to intimate or to dispense with intimation on connected persons Application for a warrant to intimate or to dispense with intimation on any connected person is made by crave in the initial writ.[43] In considering a motion to dispense with intimation on either of the grounds mentioned above the sheriff should consider the desirability of avoiding a multiplicity of actions and the difficulty and expense of tracing any connected person.[44] If not satisfied that intimation should be dispensed with, the sheriff may, where the connected person's name and whereabouts is known, order intimation. Where the name or whereabouts of the person is not known, the sheriff may order the pursuer to take further steps to ascertain the identity or address of the person or may order advertisement.[45] Where such information about a person, on whom intimation has been dispensed with, subsequently comes to light a motion must be lodged seeking warrant to intimate.[46]

Where application is made to dispense with intimation on the grounds that the person's identity or whereabouts is not known, it is suggested that averments should be included in the initial writ detailing the steps taken to ascertain the identity or whereabouts of the person.

Minute by connected person to enter process Any connected person receiving intimation may apply by minute to become an additional pursuer to the action and for leave to adopt the existing grounds of the action and to amend the craves, condescendence and pleas-in-law[47]. The procedure for intimation, opposition and hearing the minute is as provided in rule 14.3(5), and the period for lodging answers is 14 days from the date of intimation of the minute.[48]

Failure to enter process If a connected person on whom intimation has been made does not apply to be sisted as an additional pursuer and subsequently raises a separate action, the expenses of that action will not be awarded to the connected person, except on cause shown[49].

Part II—Interim payment of damages

14.20 *Application by motion* The pursuer in an action of damages for personal injuries or the death of a person from personal injuries may, at any time after defences have been lodged, apply by motion for an order for

[42] r 36.2
[43] rr 36.3, 36.4
[44] r 36.4(2)
[45] r 36.4(3)
[46] r 36.5
[47] r 36.6(1), (2)
[48] r 36.6(3), (4). *Note:* the provisions of r 14.3(1)–(4) (procedure in minutes) do not apply
[49] r 36.7

interim payment of damages. The motion procedures apply to such a motion, except for the period of notice which is 14 days.[50] An application for interim payment of damages may be made in the same way in a counterclaim for damages for personal injuries[51].

Sheriff's powers on hearing motion Before granting a motion for interim payment of damages the sheriff must be satisfied either that the defender has admitted liability, or the pursuer, if the action proceeds to proof, is likely to succeed and obtain decree without any substantial finding as to contributory negligence[52]. Moreover, no order may be made against a defender unless the sheriff is satisfied that the defender is

- Insured in respect of the claim
- A public authority, or
- A person whose means and resources are such as to enable him to make an interim payment.[53]

If a motion for an interim payment is granted the sheriff ordains the defender to make payment of a sum "not exceeding a reasonable proportion of the damages which, in the opinion of the sheriff, are likely to be recovered by the pursuer."[54] A subsequent motion for an interim payment may be made where there has been a change of circumstances[55].

Adjustment on final decree On final decree, the sheriff may, where an interim payment has been made, order repayment of part of the interim payment where it exceeds the amount awarded[56].

Part III—Provisional damages: application for provisional and for further damages

14.21 Application may be made under section 12(2)(a) of the Administration of Justice Act 1982 for an award of provisional damages by crave in the initial writ. In addition to the crave the pursuer must include in the initial writ an appropriate plea-in-law and supporting averments, including averments that

- There is a risk that the pursuer might in the future develop some serious disease or suffer serious deterioration as a result of the act or omission which gave rise to the action, and
- The defender was at the time of the act or omission which gave rise to the action a public authority or corporation or insured or otherwise indemnified[57].

[50] r 36.9(1), (2)
[51] r 36.9(3)
[52] r 36.9(3)(a), (b)
[53] r 36.9(5)
[54] r 36.9(3)
[55] r 36.9(6)
[56] r 36.10
[57] r 36.12

In the event of the pursuer developing the disease or suffering a deterioration an application for a further award of damages may be made by minute in the process of the action to which it relates[58]. The minute, which must include a crave for further damages, supporting averments and pleas-in-law[59], should be lodged with a motion for warrant for service on the other parties in the action and on any insurer or indemnifier of a party, if known to the pursuer[60]. Answers may be lodged in response to the minute within 28 days after service of the minute and warrant[61]. Following the lodging of answers the sheriff may, on the motion of any party, determine what further procedure is appropriate[62].

Part IV—Management of damages payable to a person under a legal disability

14.22 In an action for damages where an award is made to, or there has been an extra-judicial settlement in favour of, a person under a legal disability (*e.g.* to a child or a person suffering from a mental disorder), the sheriff must make an order regarding payment or management of the award[63]. In particular, the sheriff may order that management of the award for the benefit of the person under a legal disability is undertaken by either of the following:

- A judicial factor
- The Accountant of Court
- The guardian of the person
- The sheriff clerk (under the direction of the sheriff) of the Sheriff Court district where the person resides[64]

The sheriff may also order the payment of damages to be made direct to the person under a legal disability[65]. This might be ordered where, for example, a small sum of damages is to be paid to a child.

Part V—Sex Discrimination Act 1975

14.23 *Appointment of assessor* Rule 36.18 makes provision for the appointment of an assessor in an action raised in respect of a claim for discrimination under section 66(1) of the Sex Discrimination Act 1975. The appointment of an assessor may be made either by the sheriff of his own motion or on the motion of any party to the action[66]. The person to be

58 r 36.13
59 r 36.13(1)
60 r 36.13(2)
61 r 36.13(3)
62 r 36.13(4)
63 r 36.14
64 r 36.15(a)–(c)
65 r 36.15(d)
66 r 36.18(1)

appointed must be someone who the sheriff considers has special qualifications in relation to the subject matter of the action[67].

Intimation of action to Equal Opportunities Commission Rule 36.18(3) requires the pursuer in an action raised under section 66(1) of the 1975 Act to notify the Equal Opportunities Commission by sending them a copy of the initial writ by first class recorded delivery[68]. This provision is in addition to the requirement in the Act that notice of the intention to institute proceedings should be given to the Secretary of State[69].

Causes under the Presumption of Death (Scotland) Act 1977

Action of declarator

14.24 Section 1(1) of the 1977 Act provides that an action for declarator of the death of a person who is thought to have died or has been missing for at least seven years may be raised by any person having an interest. This will usually be the spouse or a beneficiary, although the Lord Advocate may raise an action in the public interest[70].

Jurisdiction

14.25 An action may be raised either in the Court of Session or in the Sheriff Court. The action may be raised in the Sheriff Court, however, only where

- The missing person was domiciled in Scotland on the date when last known to be alive or was habitually resident there throughout the year ending with that date and the missing person's last known residence in Scotland was within the sheriffdom, or
- The pursuer in the action is the spouse and is domiciled in Scotland at the date of raising the action or was habitually resident there throughout the year ending with that date and was resident in the sheriffdom for a period of not less than 40 days before the date of raising the action.

The particular Sheriff Court in which the action may be raised depends on either the missing person's last known place of residence, or the pursuer's residence in the sheriffdom.

67 r 36.18(2)
68 r 36.18(3)
69 s 66(5) of the Sex Discrimination Act 1975
70 s 1(4) of the 1977 Act

Initial writ and parties to action

14.26 In the initial writ the missing person is named as a defender[71]. There must also be included in the initial writ a crave for warrant to intimate to the missing person's spouse and children or his nearest known relative if he has no children, any person with an interest, including any insurance company, and the Lord Advocate[72]. The Rules permit the sheriff on the motion of the pursuer to dispense with intimation on any of these persons, other than the Lord Advocate[73].

Service on missing person

14.27 Service on the missing person is usually effected by advertisement, although service by notice on the walls of court is not incompetent[74]. The advertisement, the form of which is prescribed, should be published in a newspaper circulating in the area of the missing person's last known address. The advertisement invites any person wishing to defend the action to lodge a minute seeking leave to be sisted as a party to the action[75].

Intimation

14.28 Intimation is made to those parties listed in the crave of the initial writ (see para 14.26) by serving on them the prescribed form of intimation[76] along with a copy of the initial writ. The intimation advises recipients of the procedure should they wish to appear in the action and make an application in terms of section 1(5) of the 1977 Act.

Procedure when minute lodged

14.29 Any person with an interest in the action who wishes to appear in the action must lodge a minute seeking leave to be sisted as a party to the action. An application may also be made under section 1(5) of the Act for any determination or appointment not sought by the pursuer, for example, a determination of the missing person's domicile or the appointment of a judicial factor on the estate[77]. The Rules provide that a minute under section 1(5) should contain a crave, averments supporting the crave and appropriate pleas-in-law[78]. The procedure in an action in which a minute is lodged as prescribed in Chapter 14 of the Rules (Applications by minute)[79].

[71] r 37.2(1)
[72] r 37.2(3)
[73] r 37.2(5)
[74] rr 37.2(1), 5.6; see also para 2.15
[75] r 37.2(2); Form P1
[76] r 37.2(4); Form P2
[77] s 2 of the 1977 Act
[78] r 37.2(6)
[79] r 14.3; see paras 6.11–13

Procedure when no minute lodged

14.30 Where no person lodges a minute indicating a knowledge of the missing person's whereabouts the sheriff may order further advertisement[80]. After any further advertisement ordered, the pursuer may, if no minute has been lodged, apply by motion for an order for proof[81] which will be by affidavit evidence unless the sheriff otherwise orders[82].

Application for variation or recall of decree

14.31 Section 4(1) of the Act makes provision for application to be made to vary or recall a decree granted in an action of declarator by any person having an interest. The procedure is by minute lodged in the process of the action to which it relates[83]. On the lodging of such a minute the sheriff will issue an order for service on the missing person, if his whereabouts are known, and intimation on those persons who would have been entitled to receive intimation of the original action[84]. The interlocutor ordering service and intimation will also fix a period within which parties receiving service or intimation of the minute must lodge answers[85].

Answers to minute of variation

14.32 Answers to a minute for variation or recall may be lodged including a crave under section 4(3) of the Act for a determination or appointment not sought in the minute[86]. When making an application under section 4(3) a copy of the answers must be sent by registered post or by first class recorded delivery to the minuter and to those persons who have received service or intimation of the minute[87]. Proof of posting must be lodged in process[88].

Appointment of judicial factor

14.33 Section 2(2) of the Act makes provision for the appointment of a judicial factor on the estate of a missing person. The procedure to be adopted in relation to such an application is that which applies generally to the appointment of judicial factors, *i.e.* the Act of Sederunt (Judicial Factors Rules) 1992[89]. Where a judicial factor is appointed any subsequent application to vary or recall the appointment is made by note in the petition appointing the judicial factor[90].

[80] r 37.3
[81] r 37.4(1)
[82] r 37.4(2)
[83] r 37.5(1)
[84] rr 37.5(2)(a), (b), 37.2(3)
[85] r 37.5(2)(c)
[86] r 37.5(3); s 2 and 4 of the 1977 Act
[87] r 37.5(4)(a)
[88] r 37.5(4)(b)
[89] r 37.6(1)
[90] r 37.6(2)

APPENDIX

Act of Sederunt (Sheriff Court Ordinary Cause Rules) 1993 (SI No 1956)

Note: The forms which appear in the appendices to these Rules are not reproduced in this work.

Initiation and progress of causes

Chapter 1 Citation, interpretation, representation and forms

Citation

1.1 These Rules may be cited as the Ordinary Causes Rules 1993.

Interpretation

1.2—(1) In these Rules, unless the context otherwise requires—

"document" has the meaning assigned to it in section 9 of the Civil Evidence (Scotland) Act 1988; "period of notice" means the period determined under rule 3.6 (period of notice after citation).

(2) For the purposes of these Rules—

(a) "affidavit" includes an affirmation and a statutory or other declaration; and

(b) an affidavit shall be sworn or affirmed before a notary public or any other competent authority.

(3) Where a provision in these Rules requires a party to intimate or send a document to another party, it shall be sufficient compliance with that provision if the document is intimated or sent to the solicitor acting in the cause for that party.

(4) Unless the context otherwise requires, anything done or required to be done under a provision in these Rules by a party may be done by the agent for that party acting on his behalf.

(5) Unless the context otherwise requires, a reference to a specific Chapter, Part, rule or form, is a reference to the Chapter, Part, rule or form in Appendix 1, so specified in these Rules; and a reference to a specified paragraph, sub-paragraph or head is a reference to that paragraph of the rule or form, that sub-paragraph of that paragraph or that head of that sub-paragraph, in which the reference occurs.

Representation

1.3—(1) Subject to paragraph (2), a party to any proceedings arising solely under the provisions of the Debtors (Scotland) Act 1987 shall be entitled to be represented by a person other than a solicitor or an advocate provided that the sheriff is satisfied that such person is a suitable representative and is duly authorised to represent that party.

(2) Paragraph (1) shall not apply to an appeal to the sheriff principal.

Forms

1.4 Where there is a reference to the use of a form in these Rules, that form in Appendix 1 or Appendix 2, as the case may be, to these Rules, or a form substantially to the same effect, shall be used with such variation as circumstances may require.

Chapter 2 Relief from compliance with Rules

Relief from failure to comply with rules

2.1—(1) The sheriff may relieve a party from the consequences of failure to comply with a provision in these rules which is shown to be due to mistake, oversight or other excusable, cause, on such conditions as he thinks fit.

(2) Where the sheriff relieves a party from the consequences of a failure to comply with a provision in these Rules under paragraph (1), he may make such order as he thinks fit to enable the cause to proceed as if the failure to comply with the provision had not occurred.

Chapter 3 Commencement of causes

Form of initial writ

3.1—(1) An ordinary cause shall be commenced by initial writ in Form G1.

(2) The initial writ shall be written, typed or printed on A4 size paper of durable quality and shall not be backed or folded.

(3) Where the pursuer has reason to believe that an agreement exists prorogating jurisdiction over the subject-matter of the cause to another court, the initial writ shall contain details of that agreement.

(4) Where the pursuer has reason to believe that proceedings are pending before another court involving the same cause of action and between the same parties as those named in the instance of the initial writ, the initial writ shall contain details of those proceedings.

(5) An article of condescendence shall be included in the initial writ averring—

(a) the ground of jurisdiction; and

(b) the facts upon which the ground of jurisdiction is based.

(6) Where the residence, registered office or place of business, as the case may be, of the defender is not known and cannot reasonably be ascertained, the pursuer shall set out in the instance that the whereabouts of the defender are not

known and aver in the condescendence what steps have been taken to ascertain his present whereabouts.

(7) The initial writ shall be signed by the pursuer or his solicitor (if any) and the name and address of that solicitor shall be stated on the back of every service copy of that writ.

Actions relating to heritable property

3.2—(1) In an action relating to heritable property, it shall not be necessary to call as a defender any person by reason only of any interest he may have as the holder of a heritable security over the heritable property.

(2) Intimation of such an action shall be made to the holder of the heritable security referred to in paragraph (1)—

(a) where action relates to any heritable right or title; and

(b) in any other case, where the sheriff so orders.

Warrants of citation

3.3—(1) The warrant of citation in any cause other than—

(a) a family action within the meaning of rule 33.1(1),

(b) an action of multiplepoinding,

(c) an action in which a time to pay direction under the Debtors (Scotland) Act 1987 may be applied for by the defender,

shall be in Form O1.

(2) In a cause in which a time to pay direction under the Debtors (Scotland) Act 1987 may be applied for the defender, the warrant of citation shall be in Form O2.

(3) In a cause in which a warrant of citation in accordance with Form O2 is appropriate, there shall be served on the defender (with the initial writ and warrant) a notice in Form O3.

Warrants for arrestment to found jurisdiction

3.4—(1) Where an application for a warrant for arrestment to found jurisdiction may be made, it shall be made in the crave of the initial writ.

(2) Averments to justify the granting of such a warrant shall be included in the condescendence.

Warrants and precepts for arrestment on dependence

3.5—(1) A copy of—

(a) an initial writ with warrant to cite which includes a warrant to arrest on the dependence,

(b) defences which include, or a minute of amendment which includes, a counterclaim with warrant granted to arrest on the dependence endorsed on that writ,

certified as a true copy by the pursuer or defender, as the case may be, or his solicitor, shall be sufficient warrant to arrest on the dependence if it is otherwise competent to do so.

(2) A precept of arrestment may be issued by the sheriff clerk on production to him of—

(a) an initial writ containing a crave for payment of money on which a warrant of citation has been issued;
(b) defences which include, or a minute of amendment which includes, a counterclaim containing a crave for payment of money; or
(c) a document of liquid debt.

Period of notice after citation

3.6—(1) Subject to rule 5.6(1) (service where address of person is not known) and to paragraph (2) of this rule, a cause shall proceed after one of the following periods of notice has been given to the defender:—

(a) where the defender is resident or has a place of business within Europe, 21 days after the date of execution of service; or
(b) where the defender is resident or has a place of business outside Europe, 42 days after the date of execution of service.

(2) Subject to paragraph (3), the sheriff may, on cause shown, shorten or extend the period of notice on such conditions as to the method or manner of service as he thinks fit.

(3) A period of notice may not be reduced to a period of less than 2 days.

(4) Where a period of notice expires on a Saturday, Sunday, or public or court holiday, the period of notice shall be deemed to expire on the next day on which the sheriff clerk's office is open for civil court business.

Chapter 4 Caveats

Orders against which caveats may be lodged

4.1 A person may lodge a caveat against—

(a) an interim interdict sought in an action before he has lodged a notice of intention to defend; or
(b) an interim order (other than an order under section 1 of the Administration of Justice (Scotland) Act 1972 (orders for inspection of documents and other property, etc.)) sought before the expiry of the period within which he could lodge a notice of intention to defend.

Form, lodging and renewal of caveats

4.2—(1) A caveat shall be in Form G2 and shall be lodged with the sheriff clerk.

(2) A caveat shall remain in force for a period of one year from the date on which it was lodged and may be renewed on its expiry for a further period of one year and yearly thereafter.

(3) Where a caveat has been lodged and has not expired, no order in respect of which the caveat was lodged may be pronounced unless the sheriff is satisfied that all reasonable steps have been taken to afford the person lodging the caveat an opportunity of being heard; and the sheriff may continue the hearing on such an order until he is satisfied that such steps have been taken.

Chapter 5 Citation, service and intimation

Signature of warrants

5.1—(1) Subject to paragraph (2), a warrant for citation, intimation or arrestment on the dependence may be signed by the sheriff or sheriff clerk.

(2) The following warrants shall be signed by the sheriff:

(a) a warrant containing an order shortening or extending the period of notice or any other order other than a warrant which the sheriff clerk may sign;

(b) a warrant for arrestment on the dependence in a family action within the meaning of rule 33.1(1) in respect of a claim to which section 19 of the Family Law (Scotland) Act 1985 (arrestment in action for aliment or claim for financial provision) applies; and

(c) a warrant for intimation ordered under rule 33.8 (intimation where improper association).

(3) Where the sheriff clerk refuses to sign a warrant which he may sign, the party presenting the initial writ may apply to the sheriff for the warrant.

Form of citation and certificate

5.2—(1) Subject to rule 5.6 (service where address of person is not known), in any cause other than—

(a) a family action within the meaning of rule 33.1(1),

(b) an action of multiplepoinding, or

(c) an action in which a time to pay direction under the Debtors (Scotland) Act 1987 may be applied for by the defender,

citation by any person shall be in Form O4 which shall be attached to a copy of the initial writ and warrant of citation and shall have appended to it a notice of intention to defend in Form O7.

(2) In a cause in which a time to pay direction under the Debtors (Scotland) Act 1987 may be applied for by the defender, citation shall be in Form O5 which shall be attached to a copy of the initial writ and warrant of citation and shall have appended to it a notice of intention to defend in Form O7.

(3) The certificate of citation in any cause other than a family action within the meaning of rule 33.1(1) or an action of multiplepoinding shall be in Form O6 which shall be attached to the initial writ.

(4) Where citation is by a sheriff officer, one witness shall be sufficient for the execution of citation.

(5) Where citation is by a sheriff officer, the certificate of citation shall be signed by the sheriff officer and the witness and shall state—

(a) the method of citation; and

(b) where the method of citation was other than personal or postal citation, the full name and designation of any person to whom the citation was delivered.

(6) Where citation is executed under paragraph 3 of rule 5.4 (depositing or affixing by sheriff officer), the certificate shall include a statement—

(a) of the method of service previously attempted;

(b) of the circumstances which prevented such service being executed; and

(c) that a copy was sent in accordance with the provisions of paragraph (4) of that rule.

Postal service or intimation

5.3—(1) In any cause in which service or intimation of any document or citation of any person may be by recorded delivery, such service, intimation or citation shall be by the first class recorded delivery service.

(2) Notwithstanding the terms of section 4(2) of the Citation Amendment (Scotland) Act 1982 (time from which period of notice reckoned), where service or intimation is by post, the period of notice shall run from the beginning of the day after the date of posting.

(3) On the face of the envelope used for postal service or intimation under this rule there shall be written or printed the following notice:—

"This envelope contains a citation to or intimation from (*specify the court*). If delivery cannot be made at the address shown it is to be returned immediately to:– The Sheriff Clerk (*insert address of sheriff clerk's office*).".

(4) The certificate of citation or intimation in the case of postal service shall have attached to it any relevant postal receipts.

Service within Scotland by sheriff officer

5.4—(1) An initial writ, decree, charge, warrant or any other order or writ following upon such initial writ or decree served by a sheriff officer on any person shall be served—

(a) personally; or

(b) by being left in the hands of a resident at the person's dwelling place or an employee at his place of business.

(2) Where service is executed under paragraph (1)(b), the certificate of citation or service shall contain the full name and designation of any person in whose hands the initial writ, decree, charge, warrant or other order or writ, as the case may be, was left.

(3) Where a sheriff officer has been unsuccessful in executing service in accordance with paragraph (1), he may, after making diligent enquiries, serve the document in question—

(a) by depositing it in that person's dwelling place or place of business; or

(b) by affixing it to the door of that person's dwelling place or place of business.

(4) Subject to rule 6.1 (service of schedule of arrestment), where service is executed under paragraph (3), the sheriff officer shall, as soon as possible after such service, send a letter containing a copy of the document by ordinary first class post to the address at which he thinks it most likely that the person on whom service has been executed may be found.

Service on persons furth of Scotland

5.5—(1) Subject to the following provisions of this rule, an initial writ, decree, charge, warrant or any other order or writ following upon such initial writ or decree served on a person furth of Scotland shall be served—

(a) at a known residence or place of business in England, Wales, Northern

Ireland, the Isle of Man, the Channel Islands or any country with which the United Kingdom does not have a convention providing for service of writs in that country—

(i) in accordance with the rules for personal service under the domestic law of the place in which service is to be executed; or

(ii) by posting in Scotland a copy of the document in question in a registered letter addressed to the person at his residence or place of business;

(b) in a country which is a party to the Hague Convention on the Service Abroad of Judicial and Extra-Judicial Documents in Civil or Commercial Matters dated 15th November 1965 or the Convention in Schedule 1 or 3C to the Civil Jurisdiction and Judgments Act 1982—

(i) by a method prescribed by the internal law of the country where service is to be executed for the service of documents in domestic actions upon persons who are within its territory;

(ii) by or through the central, or other appropriate, authority in the country where service is to be executed at the request of the Foreign Office;

(iii) by or through a British Consular Office in the country where service is to be executed at the request of the Foreign Office;

(iv) where the law of the country in which the person resides permits, by posting in Scotland a copy of the document in a registered letter addressed to the person at his residence; or

(v) where the law of the country in which service is to be executed permits, service by an *huissier*, other judicial officer or competent official of the country where service is to be executed; or

(c) in a country with which the United Kingdom has a convention on the service of writs in that country other than the conventions mentioned in sub-paragraph (b), by one of the methods approved in the relevant convention.

(2) Any document which requires to be posted in Scotland for the purposes of this rule shall be posted by a solicitor or a sheriff officer; and on the face of the envelope there shall be written or printed the notice set out in rule 5.3(3).

(3) In the case of service by a method referred to in paragraph (1)(b)(ii) and (iii), the pursuer shall—

(a) send a copy of the writ and warrant of service with citation attached, or other document, as the case may be, with a request for service by the method indicated in the request to the Secretary of State for Foreign and Commonwealth Affairs; and

(b) lodge in process a certificate signed by the authority which executed service stating that it has been, and the manner in which it was, served.

(4) In the case of service by a method referred to in paragraph (1)(b)(v), the pursuer to the sheriff officer, shall—

(a) send a copy of the writ and warrant for service with citation attached, or other document, as the case may be, with a request for service by the method indicated in the request to the official in the country in which service is to be executed; and

(b) lodge in process a certificate of the official who executed service stating that it has been, and the manner in which is was, served.

(5) Where service is executed in accordance with paragraph (1)(a)(i) or (1)(b)(i) other than on another party in the United Kingdom, the Isle of Man or the Channel Islands, the party executing service shall lodge a certificate by a person who is conversant with the law of the country concerned and who practises or has practised law in that country or is a duly accredited representative of the Government of that country, stating that the method of service employed is in accordance with the law of the place where service was executed.

(6) Every writ, document, citation or notice on the face of the envelope mentioned in rule 5.3(3) shall be accompanied by a translation in an official language of the country in which service is to be executed unless English is an official language of that country.

(7) A translation referred to in paragraph (6) shall be certified as correct by the person making it; and the certificate shall—

(a) include his full name, address and qualifications; and
(b) be lodged with the execution of citation or service.

Service where address of person is not known

5.6—(1) Where the address of a person to be cited or served with a document is not known and cannot reasonably be ascertained, the sheriff shall grant warrant for citation or service upon that person—

(a) by the publication of an advertisement in Form G3 in a specified newspaper circulating in the area of the last known address of that person, or
(b) by displaying on the walls of court a copy of the instance and crave of the initial writ, the warrant of citation and a notice in Form G4;

and the period of notice fixed by the sheriff shall run from the date of publication of the advertisement or display on the walls of court, as the case may be.

(2) Where service requires to be executed under paragraph (1), the pursuer shall lodge a service copy of the initial writ and a copy of any warrant of citation with the sheriff clerk from whom they may be uplifted by the person for whom they are intended.

(3) Where a person has been cited or served in accordance with paragraph (1) and, after the cause has commenced, his address becomes known, the sheriff may allow the initial writ to be amended subject to such conditions as to re-service, intimation, expenses or transfer of the cause as he thinks fit.

(4) Where advertisement in a newspaper is required for the purpose of citation or service under this rule, a copy of the newspaper containing the advertisement shall be lodged with the sheriff clerk by the pursuer.

(5) Where display on the walls of court is required under paragraph (1)(b), the pursuer shall supply to the sheriff clerk for that purpose a certified copy of the instance and crave of the initial writ and any warrant of citation.

Persons carrying on business under trading or descriptive name

5.7—(1) A person carrying on a business under a trading or descriptive name may sue or be sued in such trading or descriptive name alone; and an extract—

(a) of a decree pronounced in the sheriff court, or
(b) of a decree proceeding upon any deed, decree arbitral, bond, protest of a bill, promissory note or banker's note or upon any other obligation or document on which execution may proceed, recorded in the sheriff court books against such person under such trading or descriptive name,

shall be a valid warrant for diligence against such person.

(2) An initial writ, decree, charge, warrant or any other order or writ following upon such initial writ or decree in a cause in which a person carrying on business under a trading or descriptive name sues or is sued in that name shall be served—

(a) at any place of business or office at which such business is carried on within the sheriffdom of the sheriff court in which the cause is brought; or
(b) where there is no place of business within that sheriffdom, at any place where such business is carried on (including the place of business or office of the clerk or secretary of any company, corporation or association or firm).

Endorsation unnecessary

5.8 An initial writ, decree, charge, warrant or any other order or writ following upon such initial writ or decree may be served, enforced or otherwise lawfully executed anywhere in Scotland without endorsation by a sheriff clerk; and, if executed by a sheriff officer, may be so executed by a sheriff officer of the court which granted it or by a sheriff officer of the sheriff court district in which it is to be executed.

Re-service

5.9 Where it appears to the sheriff that there has been any failure or irregularity in citation or service on a person, he may order the pursuer to re-serve the initial writ on such conditions as he thinks fit.

No objection to regularity of citation, service or intimation

5.10—(1) A person who appears in a cause shall not be entitled to state any objection to the regularity of the execution of citation, service or intimation on him; and his appearance shall remedy any defect in such citation, service or intimation.

(2) Nothing in paragraph (1) shall preclude a party from pleading that the court has no jurisdiction.

Chapter 6 Arrestment

Service of schedule of arrestment

6.1 If a schedule of arrestment has not been personally served on an arrestee, the arrestment shall have effect only if a copy of the schedule is also sent by registered post or the first class recorded delivery service to—

(a) the last known place of residence of the arrestee, or

(b) if such place of residence is not known, or if the arrestee is a firm or corporation, to the arrestee's principal place of business if known, or, if not known, to any known place of business of the arrestee;

and the sheriff officer shall, on the certificate of execution, certify that this has been done and specify the address to which the copy of the schedule was sent.

Arrestment on dependence before service

6.2—(1) An arrestment on the dependence of a cause used before service shall cease to have effect unless—

(a) the initial writ is served within 20 days from the date of arrestment; and

(b) in the case of an undefended cause, decree in absence has been pronounced within 20 days after the expiry of the period of notice.

(2) After such an arrestment has been executed, the party who executed it shall forthwith report the execution to the sheriff clerk.

Movement of arrested property

6.3—(1) Any person having an interest may apply by motion for a warrant authorising the movement of a vessel or cargo which is the subject of an arrestment to found jurisdiction or on the dependence of a cause.

(2) Where the court grants a warrant sought under paragraph (1), it may make such further order as it thinks fit to give effect to that warrant.

Chapter 7 Undefended causes

Application of this Chapter

7.1 This Chapter applies to any cause other than an action in which the sheriff may not grant decree without evidence.

Minute for granting of decree without attendance

7.2—(1) Subject to the following paragraphs, where the defender—

(a) does not lodge a notice of intention to defend,

(b) does not lodge an application for a time to pay direction under the Debtors (Scotland) Act 1987,

(c) has lodged such an application for a time to pay direction and the pursuer does not object to the application or to any recall or restriction of an arrestment sought in the application,

the sheriff may, on the pursuer endorsing a minute for decree on the initial writ, at any time after the expiry of the period for lodging that notice or application, grant decree in absence or other order in terms of the minute so endorsed without requiring the attendance of the pursuer in court.

(2) The sheriff shall not grant decree under paragraph (1)—

(a) unless it appears *ex facie* of the initial writ that a ground of jurisdiction exists under the Civil Jurisdiction and Judgments Act 1982 where that Act applies, and

(b) the cause is not a cause—

(i) in which decree may not be granted without evidence;
(ii) to which paragraph (4) applies; or
(iii) to which rule 33.31 (procedure in undefended family action for parental rights) applies.

(3) Where a defender is domiciled in another part of the United Kingdom or in another Contracting State, the sheriff shall not grant decree in absence until it has been shown that the defender has been able to receive the initial writ in sufficient time to arrange for his defence or that all necessary steps have been taken to that end; and for the purposes of this paragraph—

(a) the question whether a person is domiciled in another part of the United Kingdom shall be determined in accordance with sections 41 and 42 of the Civil Jurisdiction and Judgments Act 1982;
(b) the question whether a person is domiciled in another Contracting State shall be determined in accordance with Article 52 of Schedule 1 or 3C to that Act; and
(c) the term "Contracting State" has the meaning assigned in section 1 of that Act.

(4) Where an initial writ has been served in a country to which the Hague Convention on the Service Abroad of Judicial and Extra-Judicial Documents in Civil and Commercial Matters dated 15th November 1965 applies, decree shall not be granted until it is established to the satisfaction of the sheriff that the requirements of Article 15 of that Convention have been complied with.

Applications for time to pay directions in undefended causes

7.3—(1) This rule applies to a cause in which a time to pay direction may be applied for under the Debtors (Scotland) Act 1987.

(2) A defender in a cause which is otherwise undefended, who wishes to apply for a time to pay direction, and where appropriate, to have an arrestment recalled or restricted, shall complete and lodge with the sheriff clerk the appropriate part of Form O3 before the expiry of the period of notice.

(3) Where the pursuer does not object to the application of the defender made in accordance with paragraph (2), he shall minute for decree in accordance with rule 7.2; and the sheriff may grant decree or other order in terms of the application and minute.

(4) Where the pursuer objects to the application of the defender made in accordance with paragraph (2), he shall minute for decree in accordance with rule 7.2; and the sheriff clerk shall thereafter fix a hearing on the application of the defender and intimate the hearing to the pursuer and defender.

(5) The sheriff may determine an application in which a hearing has been fixed under paragraph (4) whether or not any of the parties appear.

Decree for expenses

7.4 On granting decree in absence or thereafter, the sheriff may grant decree for expenses.

Finality of decree in absence

7.5 Subject to section 9(7) of the Land Tenure Reform (Scotland) Act 1974 (decree in action of removing for breach of condition of long lease to be final when extract recorded in Register of Sasines), a decree in absence which has not been recalled or brought under review by suspension or by reduction shall become final and shall have effect as a decree *in foro contentioso*—

(a) on the expiry of six months from the date of the decree or from the date of a charge made under it, where the service of the initial writ or of the charge has been personal; and

(b) in any event, on the expiry of 20 years from the date of the decree.

Amendment of initial writ

7.6—(1) In an undefended cause, the sheriff may—

(a) allow the pursuer to amend the initial writ in any way permitted by rule 18.2 (powers of sheriff to allow amendment); and

(b) order the amended initial writ to be re-served on the defender on such period of notice as he thinks fit.

(2) The defender shall not be liable for the expense occasioned by any such amendment unless the sheriff so orders.

(3) Where an amendment has been allowed under paragraph (1), the amendment—

(a) shall not validate diligence used on the dependence of a cause so as to prejudice the rights of creditors, of the party against whom the diligence has been executed, who are interested in defeating such diligence; and

(b) shall preclude any objection to such diligence stated by a party or any person by virtue of a title acquired or in right of a debt contracted by him subsequent to the execution of such diligence.

Chapter 8 Reponing

Reponing

8.1—(1) In any cause other than—

(a) a cause mentioned in rule 33.1(1)(a) to (h) (certain family actions), or

(b) a cause to which Chapter 37 (causes under the Presumption of Death (Scotland) Act 1977) applies,

the defender may apply to be reponed by lodging with the sheriff clerk, before implement in full of a decree in absence, a reponing note setting out his proposed defence and explaining his failure to appear.

(2) A copy of the note lodged under paragraph (1) shall be served on the pursuer.

(3) The sheriff may, on considering the reponing note, recall the decree so far as not implemented subject to such order as to expenses as he thinks fit; and the cause shall thereafter proceed as if the defender had lodged a notice of intention to defend and the period of notice had expired on the date on which the decree in absence was recalled.

(4) A reponing note, when duly lodged with the sheriff clerk and served upon the pursuer, shall have effect to sist diligence.

(5) Any interlocutor or order recalling, or incidental to the recall of, a decree in absence shall be final and not subject to appeal.

Chapter 9 Standard procedure in defended causes

Notice of intention to defend

9.1—(1) Subject to rules 33.34 (notice of intention to defend and defences in family action) and 35.8 (lodging of notice of appearance in action of multiplepoinding), where the defender intends to—

(a) challenge the jurisdiction of the court,
(b) state a defence, or
(c) make a counterclaim,

he shall, before the expiry of the period of notice, lodge with the sheriff clerk a notice of intention to defend in Form O7.

(2) The lodging of a notice of intention to defend shall not imply acceptance of the jurisdiction of the court.

Fixing date for Options Hearing

9.2—(1) On the lodging of a notice of intention to defend, the sheriff clerk shall fix a date and time for an Options Hearing which date shall be on the first suitable court day occurring not sooner than 10 weeks after the expiry of the period of notice.

(2) On fixing the date for the Options Hearing, the sheriff clerk shall—

(a) forthwith intimate to the parties in Form G5—
  (i) the last date for lodging defences;
  (ii) the last date for adjustment; and
  (iii) the date of the Options Hearing; and
(b) prepare and sign an interlocutor recording those dates.

(3) The fixing of the date for the Options Hearing shall not affect the right of parties to make any incidental application to the court.

Return of initial writ

9.3 Subject to rule 9.4 (lodging of pleadings before Options Hearing), the pursuer shall return the initial writ, unbacked and unfolded, to the sheriff clerk within 7 days after the expiry of the period of notice.

Lodging of pleadings before Options Hearing

9.4 Where any hearing, whether by motion or otherwise, is fixed before the Options Hearing, each party shall lodge in process a copy of his pleadings, or, where the pleadings have been adjusted, the pleadings as adjusted, not later than 2 days before the hearing.

Process folder

9.5—(1) On receipt of the notice of intention to defend, the sheriff clerk shall prepare a process folder which shall include—

(a) interlocutor sheets;
(b) duplicate interlocutor sheets;
(c) a production file;
(d) a motion file; and
(e) an inventory of process.

(2) Any production or part of process lodged in a cause shall be placed in the process folder.

Defences

9.6—(1) Where a notice of intention to defend has been lodged, the defender shall lodge defences within 14 days after the expiry of the period of notice.

(2) Subject to rule 19.1(3) (form of defences where counterclaim included), defences shall be in the form of answers in numbered paragraphs corresponding to the articles of the condescendence and shall have appended a note of the pleas-in-law of the defender.

Implied admissions

9.7 Every statement of fact made by a party shall be answered by every other party, and if such a statement by one party within the knowledge of another party is not denied by that other party, that other party shall be deemed to have admitted that statement of fact.

Adjustment of pleadings

9.8—(1) Parties may adjust their pleadings until 14 days before the date of the Options Hearing or any continuation of it.

(2) Any adjustments shall be exchanged between parties and not lodged in process.

(3) Parties shall be responsible for maintaining a record of adjustments made during the period for adjustment.

(4) No adjustments shall be permitted after the period mentioned in paragraph (1) except with leave of the sheriff.

Effect of sist on adjustment

9.9—(1) Where a cause has been sisted, any period for adjustment before the sist shall be reckoned as a part of the period for adjustment.

(2) On recall of the sist of a cause, the sheriff clerk shall—

(a) fix a new date for the Options Hearing;
(b) prepare and sign an interlocutor recording that date; and
(c) intimate that date to each party.

Open record

9.10 The sheriff may, at any time before the closing of the record in a cause to which this Chapter applies, of his own motion or on the motion of a party, order any party to lodge a copy of the pleadings in the form of an open record containing any adjustments and amendments made as at the date of the order.

Record for Options Hearing

9.11—(1) The pursuer shall, at the end of the period for adjustment referred to in rule 9.8(1) and before the Options Hearing, make a copy of the pleadings and any adjustments and amendments in the form of a record.

(2) Not later than 2 days before the Options Hearing, the pursuer shall lodge a certified copy of the record in process.

Options Hearing

9.12—(1) At the Options Hearing the sheriff shall seek to secure the expeditious progress of the cause by ascertaining from the parties the matters in dispute and information about any other matter referred to in paragraph (3).

(2) It shall be the duty of the parties to provide the sheriff with sufficient information to enable him to conduct the hearing as provided for in this rule.

(3) At the Options Hearing the sheriff shall, except where the cause is ordered to proceed under the procedure in Chapter 10 (additional procedure), close the record and—

- (a) appoint the cause to a proof and make such orders as to the extent of proof, the lodging of a joint minute of admissions or agreement, or such other matter as he thinks fit;
- (b) after having heard parties and considered any note lodged under rule 22.1 (note of basis of preliminary plea), appoint the cause to a proof before answer and make such orders as to the extent of proof, the lodging of a joint minute of admissions or agreements, or such other matter as he thinks fit; or
- (c) after having heard parties and considered any note lodged under rule 22.1, appoint the cause to a debate if satisfied that there is a preliminary matter of law which justifies a debate.

(4) At the Options Hearing the sheriff may, having heard parties—

- (a) of his own motion or on the motion of any party, and
- (b) on being satisfied that the difficulty or complexity of the cause makes it unsuitable for the procedure under this Chapter,

order that the cause proceed under the procedure in Chapter 10 (additional procedure).

(5) The sheriff may, on cause shown, of his motion or on the motion of any party, allow a continuation of the Options Hearing on one occasion only for a period not exceeding 28 days or to the first suitable court day thereafter.

(6) On closing the record—

- (a) where there are no adjustments made since the lodging of the record under rule 9.11(2), that record shall become the closed record; and
- (b) where there are such adjustments, the sheriff may order that a closed record including such adjustments be lodged within 7 days after the date of the interlocutor closing the record.

(7) For the purposes of rules 16.2 (decrees where party in default) and 33.37 (decree by default in family action), an Options Hearing shall be a diet in accordance with those rules.

Inspection and recovery of documents

9.13—(1) Each party shall, within 14 days after the date of the interlocutor allowing proof or proof before answer, intimate to every other party a list of the documents, which are or have been in his possession or control which he intends to use or put in evidence at the proof, including the whereabouts of those documents.

(2) A party who has received a list of documents from another party under paragraph (1) may inspect those documents which are in the possession or control of the party intimating the list at a time and place fixed by that party which is reasonable to both parties.

(3) A party who seeks to use or put in evidence at a proof a document not on his list intimated under paragraph (1) shall, if any other party objects to such document being used or put in evidence, seek leave of the sheriff to do so; and such leave may be granted on such conditions, if any, as the sheriff thinks fit.

(4) Nothing in this rule shall affect—

(a) the law relating, or the right of a party to object, to the inspection of a document on the ground of privilege or confidentiality; or

(b) the right of a party to apply under rule 28.2 for a commission and diligence for recovery of documents or an order under section 1 of the Administration of Justice (Scotland) Act 1972.

Exchange of lists of witnesses

9.14—(1) Within 14 days after the date of the interlocutor allowing a proof or proof before answer, each party shall intimate to every other party a list of witnesses, including any skilled witnesses, whom he intends to call to give evidence.

(2) A party who seeks to call as a witness a person not on his list intimated under paragraph (1) shall, if any other party objects to such a witness being called, seek leave of the sheriff to call that person as a witness; and such leave may be granted on such conditions, if any, as the sheriff thinks fit.

(3) The list of witnesses intimated under paragraph (1) shall include the name, occupation (where known) and address of each intended witness.

Applications for time to pay directions

9.15 An application for a time to pay direction under section 1(1) of the Debtors (Scotland) Act 1987 or for the recall or restriction of an arrestment under section 2(3) or 3(1) of that Act in a cause which is defended shall be made by motion lodged before the sheriff grants decree.

Chapter 10 Additional procedure

Additional period for adjustment

10.1—(1) Where, under rule 9.12(4) (order at Options Hearing to proceed under Chapter 10), the sheriff orders that a cause shall proceed in accordance with the procedure in this Chapter, he shall continue the cause for adjustment for a period of 8 weeks.

(2) Paragraphs (2) and (3) of rule 9.8 (exchange and record of adjustments) shall apply to a cause in which a period for adjustment under paragraph (1) of this rule has been allowed as they apply to the period for adjustment under that rule.

Effect of sist on adjustment period

10.2 Where a cause has been sisted, any period for adjustment before the sist shall be reckoned as part of the period for adjustment.

Variation of adjustment period

10.3—(1) At any time before the expiry of the period for adjustment the sheriff may close the record if parties, of consent or jointly, lodge a motion seeking such an order.

(2) The sheriff may, if satisfied that there is sufficient reason for doing so, extend the period for adjustment for such period as he thinks fit, if any party—

(a) lodges a motion seeking such an order; and

(b) lodges a copy of the record adjusted to the date of lodging of the motion.

(3) A motion lodged under paragraph (2) shall set out—

(a) the reasons for seeking an extension of the period for adjustment; and

(b) the period for adjustment sought.

Order for open record

10.4 The sheriff may, at any time before the closing of the record in a cause to which this Chapter applies, of his own motion or on the motion of a party, order any party to lodge a copy of the pleadings in the form of an open record containing any adjustments and amendments made as at the date of the order.

Closing record

10.5—(1) On the expiry of the period for adjustment, the record shall be closed and, without the attendance of parties, the sheriff clerk shall forthwith—

(a) prepare and sign an interlocutor recording the closing of the record and fixing the date of the Procedural Hearing under rule 10.6, which date shall be on the first suitable court day occurring not sooner than 21 days after the closing of the record; and

(b) intimate the date of the hearing to each party.

(2) The pursuer shall, within 14 days after the date of the interlocutor closing the record, lodge a certified copy of the closed record in process.

(3) The closed record shall contain only the pleadings of the parties.

Procedural Hearing

10.6—(1) At the Procedural Hearing, the sheriff shall seek to secure the expeditious progress of the cause by ascertaining from the parties the matters in dispute and information about any other matter referred to in paragraph (3).

(2) It shall be the duty of the parties to provide the sheriff with sufficient information to enable him to conduct the hearing as provided for in this rule.

(3) At the Procedural Hearing the sheriff shall—

(a) appoint the cause to a proof and make such orders as to the extent of proof, the lodging of a joint minute of admissions or agreement, or such other matter as he thinks fit;

(b) after having heard the parties and considered any note lodged under rule 22.1 (note of basis of preliminary plea), appoint the cause to a proof before answer and make such orders as to the extent of proof, the lodging of a joint minute of admissions or agreement, or such other matter as he thinks fit; or

(c) after having heard the parties and considered any note lodged under rule 22.1, appoint the cause to a debate if satisfied that there is a preliminary matter of law which justifies a debate.

(4) For the purposes of rule 33.37 (decree by default in family action), a Procedural Hearing shall be a diet in accordance with that rule.

Chapter 11 The process

Form and lodging of parts of process

11.1 All parts of process shall be written, typed or printed on A4 size paper of durable quality and shall be lodged, unbacked and unfolded, with the sheriff clerk.

Custody of process

11.2—(1) The initial writ, and all other parts of process lodged in a cause, shall be placed by the sheriff clerk in the process folder.

(2) The initial writ, interlocutor sheets, borrowing receipts and the process folder shall remain in the custody of the sheriff clerk.

(3) The sheriff clerk, may on cause shown, authorise the initial writ to be borrowed by the pursuer, his solicitor or the solicitor's authorised clerk.

Borrowing and returning of process

11.3—(1) Subject to paragraph (3), a process, or any part of a process which may be borrowed, may be borrowed only by a solicitor or by his authorised clerk.

(2) All remedies competent to enforce the return of a borrowed process may proceed on the warrant of the court from the custody of which the process was obtained.

(3) A party litigant—

(a) may borrow a process only—

(i) with leave of the sheriff; and

(ii) subject to such conditions as the sheriff may impose; or

(b) may inspect a process and obtain copies, where practicable, from the sheriff clerk.

(4) The sheriff may, on the motion of any party, ordain any other party who has borrowed a part of process to return it within such time as the sheriff thinks fit.

Failure to return parts of process

11.4—(1) Where a solicitor or party litigant has borrowed any part of process and fails to return it for any diet or hearing at which it is required, the sheriff may impose on such solicitor or party litigant a fine not exceeding £50, which shall be payable to the sheriff clerk; but an order imposing a fine may, on cause shown, be recalled by the sheriff.

(2) An order made under this rule shall not be subject to appeal.

Replacement of lost documents

11.5 Where any part of process is lost or destroyed, a copy of it, authenticated in such manner as the sheriff thinks fit, may be substituted for and shall, for the purposes of the cause to which the process relates, be treated as having the same force and effect as the original.

Intimation of parts of process and adjustments

11.6—(1) After a notice of intention to defend has been lodged, any party lodging a part of process or making an adjustment to his pleadings shall intimate such lodging or adjustment to every other party who has entered the process by delivering to every other party a copy of each part of process or adjustment, including, where practicable, copies of any documentary production.

(2) Unless otherwise provided in these Rules, the party required to give intimation under paragraph (1) shall deliver to every other party who has entered the process a copy of the part of process or adjustment or other document, as the case may be, by—

(a) any of the methods of service provided for in Chapter 5 (citation, service and intimation); or

(b) where intimation is to a party represented by a solicitor—

(i) personal delivery,

(ii) facsimile transmission,

(iii) first class ordinary post,

(iv) delivery to a document exchange,

to that solicitor.

(3) Subject to paragraph (4), where intimation is given under—

(a) paragraph (2)(b)(i) or (ii), it shall be deemed to have been given—

(i) on the day of transmission or delivery where it is given before 5.00 pm on any day; or

(ii) on the day after transmission or delivery where it is given after 5.00 pm on any day; or

(b) paragraph (2)(b)(iii) or (iv), it shall be deemed to have been given on the day after posting or delivery.

(4) Where intimation is given on a Saturday, Sunday or public or court holiday, it shall be deemed to have been given on the next day on which the sheriff clerk's office is open for civil court business.

Retention and disposal of parts of process by sheriff clerk

11.7—(1) Where any cause has been finally determined and the period for marking an appeal has expired without an appeal having been marked, the sheriff clerk shall—

- (a) retain—
  - (i) the initial writ;
  - (ii) any closed record;
  - (iii) the interlocutor sheets;
  - (iv) any joint minute;
  - (v) an offer and acceptance of tender;
  - (vi) any report from a person of skill;
  - (vii) any affidavit; and
  - (viii) any extended shorthand notes of the proof; and
- (b) dispose of all other parts of process (except productions) in such a manner as seems appropriate.

(2) Where an appeal has been marked on the final determination of the cause, the sheriff clerk shall exercise his duties mentioned in paragraph (1) after the final disposal of the appeal and any subsequent procedure.

Uplifting of productions from process

11.8—(1) Each party who has lodged productions in a cause shall—

- (a) within 14 days after the final determination of the cause, where no subsequent appeal has been marked, or
- (b) within 14 days after the disposal of any appeal marked on the final determination of the cause,

uplift the productions from process.

(2) Where any production has not been uplifted as required by paragraph (1), the sheriff clerk shall intimate to—

- (a) the solicitor who lodged the production, or
- (b) where no solicitor is acting, the party himself or such other party as seems appropriate,

that if he fails to uplift the production within 28 days after the date of such intimation, it will be disposed of in such a manner as the sheriff directs.

Chapter 12 Interlocutors

Signature of interlocutors by sheriff clerk

12.1 In accordance with any directions given by the sheriff principal, any interlocutor other than a final interlocutor may be written and signed by the sheriff clerk and—

- (a) any interlocutor written and signed by a sheriff clerk shall be treated for all purposes as if it had been written and signed by the sheriff; and

(b) any extract of such an interlocutor shall not be invalid by reason only of its being written and signed by a sheriff clerk.

Further provisions in relation to interlocutors

12.2—(1) The sheriff may sign an interlocutor when furth of his sheriffdom.

(2) At any time before extract, the sheriff may correct any clerical or incidental error in an interlocutor or note attached to it.

(3) In any cause other than a family action within the meaning of rule 33.1(1) which has proceeded as undefended, the sheriff shall—

(a) in the final interlocutor on the merits, include findings in fact and law; and

(b) append to that interlocutor a note setting out the reasons for his decision.

(4) In any interlocutor other than an interlocutor disposing of the merits, the sheriff may, and shall when requested by a party, append a note setting out the reasons for his decision.

(5) Where the sheriff reserves his decision and gives his decision at a date later than the date of the hearing outwith the presence of the parties—

(a) the date of the interlocutor of the sheriff shall be the date on which it is received by the sheriff clerk; and

(b) the sheriff clerk shall—

(i) enter that date in the interlocutor; and

(ii) forthwith send a copy of the interlocutor and any note attached to it free of charge to each party.

Chapter 13 Party minuter procedure

Person claiming title and interest to enter process as defender

13.1—(1) A person who has not been called as a defender or third party may apply by minute for leave to enter a process as a party minuter and to lodge defences.

(2) A minute under paragraph (1) shall specify—

(a) the applicant's title and interest to enter the process; and

(b) the grounds of the defence he proposes to state.

(3) Subject to paragraph (4), after hearing the applicant and any party, the sheriff may—

(a) if he is satisfied that the applicant has shown title and interest to enter the process, grant the applicant leave to enter the process as a party minuter and to lodge defences; and

(b) make such order as to expenses or otherwise as he thinks fit.

(4) Where an application under paragraph (1) is made after the closing of the record, the sheriff shall only grant leave under paragraph (3) if he is satisfied as to the reason why earlier application was not made.

Procedure following leave to enter process

13.2—(1) Where a party minuter lodges answers, the sheriff clerk shall fix a date and time under rule 9.2 for a hearing under rule 9.12 (Options Hearing) as if the party minuter had lodged a notice of intention to defend and the period of notice had expired on the date for lodging answers.

(2) At the Options Hearing, or at any time thereafter, the sheriff may grant such decree or other order as he thinks fit.

(3) A decree or other order against the party minuter shall have effect and be extractable in the same way as a decree or other order against a defender.

Chapter 14 Applications by minute

Application of this Chapter

14.1—(1) Where an application may be made by minute, the form of the minute and the procedure to be adopted shall, unless otherwise provided in these Rules, be in accordance with this Chapter.

(2) This Chapter shall not apply to—

(a) a minute of amendment; or
(b) a minute of abandonment.

Form of minute

14.2 A minute to which this Chapter applies shall contain—

(a) a crave;
(b) where appropriate, a condescendence in the form of a statement of facts supporting the crave; and
(c) where appropriate, pleas-in-law.

Procedure in minutes

14.3—(1) Where the minute includes a crave seeking leave—

(a) for a person—
  (i) to be sisted as a party to the action,
  (ii) to appear in the proceedings, or
(b) for the cause to be transferred against the representatives of a party who has died or is under a legal incapacity,

the minuter may also seek leave for a date for a hearing under rule 9.12 (Options Hearing) to be fixed.

(2) Where leave is granted under paragraph (1), the sheriff clerk shall fix a date and time for a hearing under rule 9.12.

(3) For the purpose of fixing the date for the Options Hearing referred to in paragraph (1), the date of granting the minute shall be deemed to be the date of expiry of the period of notice.

(4) Where the minute includes a crave for any order including the variation or recall of an existing order or makes any application by minute, as provided in these Rules, the minuter may also seek leave for the lodging of answers within a period specified in the minute.

(5) Rules 15.2 (intimation of motions), 15.3 (opposition to motions) and 15.4 (hearing of motions) shall, with the necessary modifications, apply to the intimation of, opposition to, or hearing of, a minute as they apply to a motion.

Chapter 15 Motions

Lodging of motions

15.1—(1) A motion may be made—

(a) orally with leave of the court during any hearing of a cause; or

(b) by lodging a written motion in Form G6.

(2) Any document referred to in the motion and not already lodged in process shall, so far as practicable, be lodged with the written motion.

(3) On the lodging of a motion in accordance with paragraph (1)(b), the sheriff clerk shall fix a hearing of the motion and shall advise the party lodging the motion of the date, time and place of the hearing.

Intimation of motions

15.2—(1) Subject to paragraph (7), the party lodging a motion in accordance with rule 15.1(1)(b) shall intimate the motion in Form G7, and a copy of any document referred to in the motion, to every other party.

(2) Unless a period of intimation of a motion is otherwise specified in these Rules, intimation under paragraph (1) shall be made not less than 7 days before the date fixed for the hearing of the motion.

(3) Subject to paragraph (4), intimation of a motion may be given by—

(a) any of the methods of service provided for in Chapter 5 (citation, service and intimation); or

(b) where intimation is to a party represented by a solicitor, by—

(i) personal delivery

(ii) facsimile transmission,

(iii) first class ordinary post, or

(iv) delivery to a document exchange,

to that solicitor.

(4) Subject to paragraph (5), where intimation is given—

(a) under paragraph (3)(b)(i) or (ii), it shall be deemed to have been given—

(i) on the day of transmission or delivery where it is given before 5.00 pm on any day; or

(ii) on the day after transmission or delivery where it is given after 5.00 pm on any day; or

(b) under paragraph 3(b)(iii) or (iv), it shall be deemed to have been given on the day after posting or delivery.

(5) Where intimation is given on a Saturday, Sunday or public or court holiday, it shall be deemed to have been given on the next day on which the sheriff clerk's office is open for civil court business.

(6) Where intimation has been given, a certificate of intimation of the motion in Form G8 shall be returned to the sheriff clerk not later than 2 days, or such period as the sheriff has determined, before the date fixed for the hearing of that motion.

(7) The sheriff may, on cause shown, dispense with or reduce the period of intimation specified in paragraph (2) or the period specified in paragraph (6).

Opposition to motions

15.3—(1) Where a party seeks to oppose a motion lodged under rule 15.1(1)(b), he shall—

(a) complete a notice of opposition in Form G9;
(b) forthwith intimate a copy of that notice to every other party; and
(c) lodge the notice with the sheriff clerk not later than 2 days before the date fixed for the hearing of the motion.

(2) Paragraphs (3), (4) and (5) of rule 15.2 (methods and time of intimation of motions) shall apply to the intimation of opposition to a motion under paragraph (1)(b) of this rule as they apply to intimation under that rule.

(3) The sheriff may, on cause shown, dispense with or reduce the period for lodging the notice mentioned in paragraph (1)(c).

Hearing of motions

15.4—(1) Subject to paragraph (2), where no notice of opposition is lodged, the motion shall be determined by the sheriff in chambers without the attendance of parties, unless the sheriff otherwise directs.

(2) In accordance with any directions given by the sheriff principal, the sheriff clerk may determine any motion other than a motion which seeks a final interlocutor.

(3) Where the sheriff clerk considers that a motion dealt with by him under paragraph (2) should not be granted, he shall refer that motion to the sheriff who shall deal with it in accordance with paragraph (1).

(4) Where the sheriff requires to hear a party on a motion, the sheriff clerk shall inform that party that the motion will be heard on the date fixed under rule 15.1(3).

(5) Where a notice of opposition is intimated and lodged, the motion shall be heard by the sheriff on the date fixed under rule 15.1(3).

Chapter 16 Decrees by default

Application of this Chapter

16.1 This rule applies to any cause other than—

(a) an action to which rule 33.37 (decree by default in family action) applies;
(b) an action of multiplepoinding; or
(c) a cause under the Presumption of Death (Scotland) Act 1977.

Decrees where party in default

16.2—(1) In a cause to which this Chapter applies, where a party fails—

(a) to lodge, or intimate the lodging of, any production or part of process within the period required under a provision in these Rules or an order of the sheriff,
(b) to implement an order of the sheriff within a specified period, or
(c) to appear or be represented at any diet,

that party shall be in default.

(2) Where a party is in default, the sheriff may grant decree as craved, decree of absolvitor or dismiss the cause, as the case may be, with expenses.

(3) Where no party appears at a diet, the sheriff may dismiss the cause.

(4) In this rule, "diet" includes—

(a) a hearing under rule 9.12 (Options Hearing);
(b) a hearing under rule 10.6 (Procedural Hearing);
(c) a proof or proof before answer; and
(d) a debate.

Prorogation of time where party in default

16.3 In an action to which this Chapter applies, the sheriff may, on cause shown, prorogate the time for lodging any production or part of process or for giving intimation or for implementing any order.

Chapter 17 Summary decrees

Application of this Chapter

17.1 This Chapter applies to any action other than—

(a) a family action within the meaning of rule 33.1(1);
(b) an action of multiplepoinding; or
(c) a cause under the Presumption of Death (Scotland) Act 1977.

Applications for summary decree

17.2—(1) Subject to paragraphs (2) to (5) of this rule, a pursuer may, at any time after a defender has lodged defences, apply by motion for summary decree against that defender on the ground that there is no defence to the action, or part of it, disclosed in the defences.

(2) In applying for summary decree, the pursuer may move the sheriff—

(a) to grant decree in terms of all or any of the craves of the initial writ;
(b) to pronounce an interlocutor sustaining or repelling a plea-in-law; or
(c) to dispose of the whole or part of the subject-matter of the cause.

(3) The pursuer shall intimate a motion under paragraph (1) by registered post or the first class recorded delivery service to every other party not less than 14 days before the date fixed for the hearing of the motion.

(4) On a motion under paragraph (1), the sheriff may—

(a) if satisfied that there is no defence to the action or to any part of it to which the motion relates, grant the motion for summary decree in whole or in part, as the case may be; or
(b) ordain any party, or a partner, director, officer or office-bearer of, any party—
    (i) to produce any relevant document or article; or
    (ii) to lodge an affidavit in support of any assertion of fact made in the pleadings or at the hearing of the motion.

(5) Notwithstanding the refusal of all or part of a motion for summary decree, a subsequent motion may be made where there has been a change of circumstances.

Application of summary decree to counterclaims, etc.

17.3—(1) Where a defender has lodged a counterclaim—

(a) he may apply by motion for summary decree against the pursuer on that counterclaim on the ground that there is no defence to the counterclaim, or a part of it, disclosed in the answers to it; and

(b) paragraphs (2) to (5) of rule 17.2 shall, with the necessary modifications, apply to a motion by a defender under this paragraph as they apply to a motion by a pursuer under paragraph (1) of that rule.

(2) Where a defender or third party has made a claim against another defender or third party who has lodged defences or answers, as the case may be—

(a) he may apply by motion for summary decree against that other defender or third party on the ground that there is no defence to the claim, or a part of it, disclosed in the defences or answers, as the case may be; and

(b) paragraphs (2) to (5) of rule 17.2 shall, with the necessary modifications, apply to a motion by a defender or third party under this paragraph as they apply to a motion by a pursuer under paragraph (1) of that rule.

Chapter 18 Amendment of pleadings

Alteration of sum sued for

18.1—(1) In a cause in which all other parties have lodged defences or answers, the pursuer may, before the closing of the record, alter any sum sued for by amending the crave of the initial writ, the certified copy of the initial writ and any record.

(2) The pursuer shall forthwith intimate any such amendment in writing to every other party.

Powers of sheriff to allow amendment

18.2—(1) The sheriff may, at any time before final judgment, allow an amendment mentioned in paragraph (2).

(2) Paragraph (1) applies to the following amendments:—

(a) an amendment of the initial writ which may be necessary for the purpose of determining the real question in controversy between the parties, notwithstanding that in consequence of such amendment—

(i) the sum sued for is increased or restricted after the closing of the record; or

(ii) a different remedy from that originally craved is sought;

(b) an amendment which may be necessary—

(i) to correct or supplement the designation of a party to the cause;

(ii) to enable a party who has sued or has been sued in his own right to sue or be sued in a representative capacity;

(iii) to enable a party who has sued or has been sued in a representative capacity to sue or be sued in his own right or in a different representative capacity;

(iv) to add the name of an additional pursuer or person whose concurrence is necessary;

(v) where the cause has been commenced or presented in the name of the wrong person, or it is doubtful whether it has been commenced or presented in the name of the right person, to allow any other person to be sisted in substitution for, or in addition to, the original person; or

(vi) to direct a crave against a third party brought into an action under Chapter 20 (third party procedure);

(c) an amendment of a condescendence, defences, answers, pleas-in-law or other pleadings which may be necessary for determining the real question in controversy between the parties; and

(d) where it appears that all parties having an interest have not been called or that the cause has been directed against the wrong person, an amendment inserting in the initial writ an additional or substitute party and directing existing or additional craves, averments and pleas-in-law against that party.

Applications to amend

18.3—(1) A party seeking to amend shall lodge a minute of amendment in process setting out his proposed amendment and, at the same time, lodge a motion—

(a) to allow the minute of amendment to be received; and

(b) to allow

(i) amendment in terms of minute of amendment and, where appropriate, to grant an order under rule 18.5(1)(a) (service of amendment for additional or substitute party); or

(ii) where the minute of amendment may require to be answered, any other person to lodge answers within a specified period.

(2) Where the sheriff has pronounced an interlocutor allowing a minute of amendment to be received and answered, he may allow a period for adjustment of the minute of amendment and answers and, on so doing, shall fix a date for parties to be heard on the minute of amendment and answers as adjusted.

Applications for diligence on amendment

18.4—(1) Where a minute of amendment is lodged by a pursuer under rule 18.2(2)(d) (all parties not, or wrong person, called), he may apply by motion for warrant to use any form of diligence which could be used on the dependence of a separate action.

(2) A copy certified by the sheriff clerk of the interlocutor granting warrant for diligence on the dependence applied for under paragraph (1) shall be sufficient authority for the execution of that diligence.

Service of amended pleadings

18.5—(1) Where an amendment under rule 18.2(2)(d) (all parties not, or wrong person, called) has been made—

(a) the sheriff shall order that a copy of the initial writ or record, as the case may be, as so amended be served by the party who made the amendment on that additional or substitute party with—

(i) in a cause in which a time to pay direction under the Debtors

(Scotland) Act 1987 may be applied for, a notice in Form O8 specifying the date by which a notice of intention to defend must be lodged in process, a notice in Form O3 and a notice of intention to defend in Form O7; or

(ii) in any other cause, a notice in Form O9 specifying the date by which a notice of intention to defend must be lodged in process and a notice of intention to defend in Form O7; and

(b) the party who made the amendment shall lodge in process—

(i) a copy of the initial writ or record as amended;

(ii) a copy of the notice sent in Form O8 or Form O9; and

(iii) a certificate of service.

(2) When paragraph (1) has been complied with, the cause as so amended shall proceed in every respect as if that party had originally been made a party to the cause.

(3) Where a notice of intention to defend is lodged by virtue of paragraph (1)(a), the sheriff clerk shall fix a date and time for a hearing under rule 9.12 (Options Hearing).

Expenses and conditions of amendment

18.6 The sheriff shall find the party making an amendment liable in the expenses occasioned by the amendment unless it is shown that it is just and equitable that the expenses occasioned by the amendment should be otherwise dealt with, and may attach such other conditions as he thinks fit.

Effect of amendment on diligence

18.7 Where an amendment has been allowed, the amendment—

(a) shall not validate diligence used on the dependence of a cause so as to prejudice the rights of creditors, of the party against whom the diligence has been executed, who are interested in defeating such diligence; and

(b) shall preclude any objection to such diligence stated by a party or any person by virtue of a title acquired or in right of a debt contracted by him subsequent to the execution of such diligence.

Preliminary pleas inserted on amendment

18.8—(1) Where a party seeks to add a preliminary plea by amendment or answers to an amendment, or by adjustment thereto, a note of the basis for the plea shall be lodged at the same time as the minute, answers or adjustment, as the case may be.

(2) If a party fails to comply with paragraph (1), that party shall be deemed to be no longer insisting on the preliminary plea and the plea shall be repelled by the sheriff.

Chapter 19 Counterclaims

Counterclaims

19.1—(1) In any action other than a family action within the meaning of rule 33.1(1) or an action of multiplepoinding, a defender may counterclaim against a pursuer—

(a) where the counterclaim might have been made in a separate action in which it would not have been necessary to call as defender any person other than the pursuer; and

(b) in respect of any matter—

(i) forming part, or arising out of the grounds, of the action by the pursuer;

(ii) the decision of which is necessary for the determination of the question in controversy between the parties; or

(iii) which, if the pursuer had been a person not otherwise subject to the jurisdiction of the court, might have been the subject-matter of an action against that pursuer in which jurisdiction would have arisen by reconvention.

(2) A counterclaim shall be made in the defences—

(a) when the defences are lodged or during the period for adjustment;

(b) by amendment at any other stage, with the leave of the sheriff and subject to such conditions, if any, as to expenses or otherwise as the sheriff thinks fit.

(3) Defences which include a counterclaim shall commence with a crave setting out the counterclaim in such form as, if the counterclaim had been made in a separate action, would have been appropriate in the initial writ in that separate action and shall include—

(a) answers to the condescendence of the initial writ as required by rule 9.6(2) (form of defences);

(b) a statement of facts in numbered paragraphs setting out the facts on which the counterclaim is founded, incorporating by reference, if necessary, any matter contained in the defences; and

(c) appropriate pleas-in-law.

Warrants for diligence on counterclaims

19.2—(1) A defender who makes a counterclaim may apply for a warrant for arrestment on the dependence which would have been permitted had the warrant been sought in an initial writ in a separate action.

(2) An application for a warrant under paragraph (1) shall be made—

(a) at the time of making the counterclaim, by inserting before the crave of the counterclaim the words "Warrant for arrestment on the dependence applied for."; or

(b) after the counterclaim has been made, for a precept of arrestment.

(3) An application for a warrant under paragraph (2)(a) may be granted by the sheriff clerk writing on the defences, defences as adjusted or minute of amendment, as the case may be, the words, "Warrant granted as craved." after the warrant sought, and adding his signature and the date below those words.

(4) A warrant granted under paragraph (3) shall have the same effect as if the warrant had been in an initial writ.

Effect of abandonment of cause

19.3—(1) The right of a pursuer to abandon a cause under rule 23.1 shall not be affected by a counterclaim; and any expenses for which the pursuer is found liable as a condition of, or in consequence of, such abandonment shall not include the expenses of the counterclaim.

(2) Notwithstanding abandonment by the pursuer, a defender may insist in his counterclaim; and the proceedings in the counterclaim shall continue in dependence as if the counterclaim were a separate action.

Disposal of counterclaims

19.4 The sheriff may—

(a) deal with a counterclaim as if it had been stated in a separate action;

(b) regulate the procedure in relation to the counterclaim as he thinks fit; and

(c) grant decree for the counterclaim in whole or in part or for the difference between it and the sum sued for by the pursuer.

Chapter 20 Third party procedure

Applications for third party notice

20.1—(1) Where, in an action, a defender claims that—

(a) he has in respect of the subject-matter of the action a right of contribution, relief or indemnity against any person who is not a party to the action, or

(b) a person whom the pursuer is not bound to call as a defender should be made a party to the action along with the defender in respect that such person is—

(i) solely liable, or jointly or jointly and severally liable with the defender, to the pursuer in respect of the subject-matter of the action, or

(ii) liable to the defender in respect of a claim arising from or in connection with the liability, if any, of the defender to the pursuer,

he may apply by motion for an order for service of a third party notice on that other person in Form O10 for the purpose of convening that other person as a third party to the action.

(2) Where—

(a) a pursuer against whom a counterclaim has been made, or

(b) a third party convened in the action,

seeks, in relation to the claim against him, to make against a person who is not a party, a claim mentioned in paragraph (1) as a claim which could be made by a defender against a third party, he shall apply by motion for an order for service of a third party notice in Form O10 in the same manner as a defender under that paragraph; and rules 20.2 to 20.7 shall, with the necessary modifications, apply to such a claim as they apply in relation to such a claim by a defender.

Averments where order for service of third party notice sought

20.2—(1) Where a defender intends to apply by motion for an order for service of a third party notice before the closing of the record, he shall, before lodging the motion, set out in his defences, by adjustment to those defences, or in a separate statement of facts annexed to those defences—

(a) averments setting out the grounds on which he maintains that the proposed third party is liable to him by contribution, relief or indemnity or should be made a party to the action; and
(b) appropriate pleas-in-law.

(2) Where a defender applies by motion for an order for service of a third party notice after the closing of the record, he shall, on lodging the motion, lodge a minute of amendment containing—

(a) averments setting out the grounds on which he maintains that the proposed third party is liable to him by contribution, relief or indemnity or should be made a party to the action, and
(b) appropriate pleas-in-law,

unless those grounds and pleas-in-law have been set out in the defences in the closed record.

(3) A motion for an order for service of a third party notice shall be lodged before the commencement of the hearing of the merits of the cause.

Warrants for diligence on third party notice

20.3—(1) A defender who applies for an order for service of a third party notice may apply for a warrant for arrestment to found jurisdiction or for arrestment on the dependence which would have been permitted had the warrant been sought in an initial writ in a separate action.

(2) Averments in support of the application for such a warrant shall be included in the defences or the separate statement of facts referred to in rule 20.2(1).

(3) An application for a warrant under paragraph (1) shall be made by motion—

(a) at the time of applying for the third party notice; or
(b) if not applied for at that time, at any stage of the cause thereafter.

(4) A certified copy of the interlocutor granting warrant for diligence applied for under paragraph (2) shall be sufficient authority for execution of the diligence.

Service on third party

20.4—(1) A third party notice shall be served on the third party within 14 days after the date of the interlocutor allowing service of that notice.

(2) Where service of a third party notice has not been made within the period specified in paragraph (1), the order for service of it shall cease to have effect; and no service of the notice may be made unless a further order for service of it has been applied for and granted.

(3) There shall be served with a third party notice a copy of the pleadings (including any adjustments and amendments).

(4) A copy of the third party notice, with a certificate of service attached to it, shall be lodged in process by the defender.

Answers to third party notice

20.5—(1) An order for service of a third party notice shall specify 28 days, or such other period as the sheriff on cause shown may specify, as the period within which the third party may lodge answers.

(2) Answers for a third party shall be headed "Answers for [E.F.], Third Party in the action at the instance of [A.B.], Pursuer against [C.D.], Defender" and shall include—

(a) answers to the averments of the defender against him in the form of numbered paragraphs corresponding to the numbered articles of the condescendence in the initial writ and incorporating, if the third party so wishes, answers to the averments of the pursuer; or

(b) where a separate statement of facts has been lodged by the defender under rules 20.2(1), answers to the statement of facts in the form of numbered paragraphs corresponding to the numbered paragraphs of the statement of facts; and

(c) appropriate pleas-in-law.

Procedure following answers

20.6—(1) Where a third party lodges answers, the sheriff clerk shall fix a date and time under rule 9.2 for a hearing under rule 9.12 (Options Hearing) as if the third party had lodged a notice of intention to defend and the period of notice had expired on the date for lodging answers.

(2) At the Options Hearing, or at any time thereafter, the sheriff may grant such decree or other order as he thinks fit.

(3) A decree or other order against the third party shall have effect and be extractable in the same way as a decree or other order against a defender.

Chapter 21 Documents founded on or adopted in pleadings

Lodging documents found on or adopted

21.1—(1) Subject to any other provision in these Rules, any document founded on by a party, or adopted as incorporated, in his pleadings shall, so far as in his possession or within his control, be lodged in process as a production by him—

(a) when founded on or adopted in an initial writ, at the time of returning the initial writ under rule 9.3;

(b) when founded on or adopted in a minute, defences, counterclaim or answers, at the time of lodging that part of process; and

(c) when founded on or adopted in an adjustment to any pleadings, at the time when such adjustment is intimated to any other party.

(2) Paragraph (1) shall be without prejudice to any power of the sheriff to order the production of any document or grant a commission and diligence for recovery of it.

Consequences of failure to lodge documents founded on or adopted

21.2 Where a party fails to lodge a document in accordance with rule 21.1(1), he may be found liable in the expenses of any order for production or recovery of it obtained by any other party.

Objection to documents founded on

21.3—(1) Where a deed or writing is founded on by a party, any objection to it by any other party may be stated and maintained by exception without its being reduced.

(2) Where an objection is stated under paragraph (1) and an action of reduction would otherwise have been competent, the sheriff may order the party stating the objection to find caution or give such other security as the sheriff thinks fit.

Chapter 22 Preliminary pleas

Note of basis of preliminary plea

22.1—(1) A party intending to insist on a preliminary plea shall, not later than 3 days before the Options Hearing under rule 9.12 or the Procedural Hearing under rule 10.6—

(a) lodge in process a note of the basis for the plea; and
(b) intimate a copy of it to every other party.

(2) If a party fails to comply with paragraph (1), he shall be deemed to be no longer insisting on the preliminary plea; and the plea shall be repelled by the sheriff at the Options Hearing or Procedural Hearing.

(3) At any proof before answer to debate, parties may raise matters in addition to those set out in the note mentioned in paragraph (1).

Chapter 23 Abandonment

Abandonment of causes

23.1—(1) A pursuer may abandon a cause at any time before decree of absolvitor or dismissal by lodging a minute of abandonment and—

(a) consenting to a decree of absolvitor; or
(b) seeking decree of dismissal.

(2) The sheriff shall not grant decree of dismissal under paragraph (1)(b) unless full judicial expenses have been paid to the defender, and any third party against whom he has directed any crave, within 28 days after the date of taxation.

(3) If the pursuer fails to pay the expenses referred to in paragraph (2) to the party to whom they are due within the period specified in that paragraph, that party shall be entitled to decree of absolvitor with expenses.

Application of abandonment to counterclaims

23.2 Rule 23.1 shall, with the necessary modifications, apply to the abandonment by a defender of his counterclaim as it applies to the abandonment of a cause.

Chapter 24 Withdrawal of solicitors

Intimation of withdrawal to court

24.1—(1) Where a solicitor withdraws from acting on behalf of a party, he shall intimate his withdrawal by letter to the sheriff clerk and to every other party.

(2) The sheriff clerk shall lodge such letter in process.

Intimation to party whose solicitor has withdrawn

24.2—(1) The sheriff shall, of his own motion, or on the motion of any other party, pronounce an interlocutor ordaining the party whose solicitor has withdrawn from acting to appear or be represented at a specified diet fixed by the sheriff to state whether or not he intends to proceed, under certification that if he fails to do so the sheriff may grant decree or make such other order or finding as he thinks fit.

(2) The diet fixed in the interlocutor under paragraph (1) shall not be less than 14 days after the date of the interlocutor unless the sheriff otherwise orders.

(3) The party who has lodged the motion under paragraph (1), or any other party appointed by the sheriff, shall forthwith serve on the party whose solicitor has withdrawn a copy of the interlocutor and a notice in Form G10; and a certificate of service shall be lodged in process.

Consequences of failure to intimate intention to proceed

24.3 Where a party on whom a notice and interlocutor has been served under rule 24.2(2) fails to appear or be represented at a diet fixed under rule 24.2(1) and to state his intention as required by that paragraph, the sheriff may grant decree or make such other order or finding as he thinks fit.

Chapter 25 Minutes of sist and transference

Minutes of sist

25.1 Where a party dies or comes under legal incapacity while a cause is depending, any person claiming to represent that party or his estate may apply by minute to be sisted as a party to the cause.

Minutes of transference

25.2—(1) Where a party dies or comes under legal incapacity while a cause is depending and the provisions of rule 25.1 are not invoked, any other party may apply by minute to have the cause transferred in favour of or against, as the case may be, any person who represents that party or his estate.

(2) The party intimating a minute of transference on a person referred to in paragraph (1) of this rule in accordance with rule 15.2 by virtue of rule 14.3(5) (intimation of minutes) shall at the same time intimate a copy of the pleadings (including any adjustments and amendments) to that person.

Chapter 26 Transfer and remit of causes

Transfer to another sheriff court

26.1—(1) The sheriff may, on cause shown, remit any cause to another sheriff court.

(2) Subject to paragraph (4), where a cause in which there are two or more defenders has been brought in the sheriff court of the residence or place of business of one of them, the sheriff may transfer the cause to any other sheriff court which has jurisdiction over any of the defenders.

(3) Subject to paragraph (4), where a plea of no jurisdiction is sustained, the sheriff may transfer the cause to the sheriff court before it appears to him the cause ought to have been bought.

(4) The sheriff shall not transfer a cause to another sheriff court under paragraph (2) or (3) except—

(a) on the motion of a party; and
(b) where he considers it expedient to do so having regard to the convenience of the parties and their witnesses.

(5) On making an order under paragraph (1), (2) or (3), the sheriff—

(a) shall state his reasons for doing so in the interlocutor; and
(b) may make the order on such conditions as to expenses or otherwise as he thinks fit.

(6) The court to which a cause is transferred under paragraph (1), (2) or (3) shall accept the cause.

(7) A transferred cause shall proceed in all respects as if it had been originally brought in the court to which it is transferred.

(8) An interlocutor transferring a cause may, with leave of the sheriff, be appealed to the sheriff principal but shall not be subject to appeal to the Court of Session.

Remit to Court of Session

26.2—(1) The sheriff clerk shall, within four days after the sheriff has pronounced an interlocutor remitting a cause to the Court of Session, transmit the process to the Deputy Principal Clerk of Session.

(2) The sheriff clerk shall, within the period specified in paragraph (1), send written notice of the remit to each party and certify on the interlocutor sheet that he has done so.

(3) Failure by a sheriff clerk to comply with paragraph (2) shall not affect the validity of a remit made under paragraph (1).

Remit from Court of Session

26.3 On receipt of the process in an action which has been remitted from the Court of Session under section 14 of the Law Reform (Miscellaneous Provisions) (Scotland) Act 1985, the sheriff clerk shall—

(a) record the date of receipt on the interlocutor sheet;
(b) fix a hearing to determine further procedure on the first suitable court day occurring not earlier than 14 days after the date of receipt of the process; and

(c) forthwith send written notice of the date of the hearing fixed under sub-paragraph (b) to each party.

Chapter 27 Caution and security

Application of this Chapter

27.1 This Chapter applies to—

(a) any cause in which the sheriff has power to order a person to find caution or give other security; and

(b) security for expenses ordered to be given by the election court or the sheriff under section 136(2)(i) of the Representation of the People Act 1983 in an election petition.

Form of applications

27.2—(1) An application for an order for caution or other security, or for variation or recall of such an order, shall be made by motion.

(2) The grounds on which such an application is made shall be set out in the motion.

Orders

27.3 Subject to section 726(2) of the Companies Act 1985 (expenses by certain limited companies), an order to find caution or give other security shall specify the period within which such caution is to be found or such security given.

Methods of finding caution or giving security

27.4—(1) A person ordered—

(a) to find caution, shall do so by obtaining a bond of caution; or

(b) to consign a sum of money into court, shall do so by consignation under the Sheriff Court Consignations (Scotland) Act 1893 in the name of the sheriff clerk.

(2) The sheriff may approve a method of security other than one mentioned in paragraph (1), including a combination of two or more methods of security.

(3) Subject to paragraph (4), any document by which an order to find caution or give other security is satisfied shall be lodged in process.

(4) Where the sheriff approves a security in the form of a deposit of a sum of money in the joint names of the agents of parties, a copy of the deposit receipt, and not the principal, shall be lodged in process.

(5) Any document lodged in process, by which an order to find caution or give other security is satisfied, shall not be borrowed from process.

Cautioners and guarantors

27.5 A bond of caution or other security obtained from an insurance company shall be given only by a company authorised under section 3 or 4 of the Insurance Companies Act 1982 to carry on insurance business of class 15(b) in Schedule 2 to that Act.

Forms of bonds of caution and other securities

27.6—(1) A bond of caution shall oblige the cautioner, his heirs and executors to make payment of the sums for which he has become cautioner to the party to whom he is bound, as validity and in the same manner as the party and his heirs and successors, for whom he is cautioner, are obliged.

(2) A bond of caution or other security document given by an insurance company shall state whether the company is authorised under section 3 or 4 of the Insurance Companies Act 1982 to carry on insurance business of class 15(b) in Schedule 2 to that Act.

Sufficiency of caution or security and objections

27.7—(1) The sheriff clerk shall satisfy himself that any bond of caution, or other document lodged in process under the rule 27.4(3), is in proper form.

(2) A party who is dissatisfied with the sufficiency or form of the caution or other security offered in obedience to an order of the court may apply by motion for an order under rule 27.9 (failure to find caution or give security).

Insolvency or death of cautioner or guarantor

27.8 Where caution has been found by bond of caution or security has been given by guarantee and the cautioner or guarantor, as the case may be—

- (a) becomes apparently insolvent within the meaning assigned by section 7 of the Bankruptcy (Scotland) Act 1985 (constitution of apparent insolvency),
- (b) calls a meeting of his creditors to consider the state of his affairs,
- (c) dies unrepresented, or
- (d) is a company and—
  - (i) an administration or winding up order has been made, or a resolution for a voluntary winding up has been passed, with respect to it,
  - (ii) a receiver of all or any part of its undertaking has been appointed, or
  - (iii) a voluntary arrangement (within the meaning assigned by section 1(1) of the Insolvency Act 1986) has been approved under Part I of that Act,

the party entitled to benefit from the caution or guarantee may apply by motion for a new security or further security to be given.

Failure to find caution or give security

27.9 Where a party fails to find caution or give other security (in this rule referred to as "the party in default"), any other party may apply by motion—

- (a) where the party in default is a pursuer, for decree of absolvitor; or
- (b) where the party in default is a defender or a third party, for decree by default or for such other finding or order as the sheriff thinks fit.

Chapter 28 Recovery of evidence

Application and interpretation of this Chapter

28.1—(1) This Chapter applies to the recovery of any evidence in a cause depending before the sheriff.

(2) In this Chapter, "the Act of 1972" means the Administration of Justice (Scotland) Act 1972.

Applications for commission and diligence for recovery of documents or for orders under section 1 of the Act of 1972

28.2—(1) An application by a party for—

(a) a commission and diligence for the recovery of a document, or

(b) an order under section 1 of the Act of 1972,

shall be made by motion.

(2) At the time of lodging a motion under paragraph (1), a specification of—

(a) the document or other property sought to be inspected, photographed, preserved, taken into custody, detained, produced, recovered, sampled or experimented on or with, as the case may be, or

(b) the matter in respect of which information is sought as to the identity of a person who might be a witness or a defender,

shall be lodged in process.

(3) A copy of the specification lodged under paragraph (2) and intimation of the motion made under paragraph (1) shall be sent by the applicant to every other party, any third party haver and where necessary, the Lord Advocate.

(4) Where the sheriff grants a motion made under paragraph (1) in whole or in part, he may order the applicant to find such caution or give such other security as he thinks fit.

(5) The Lord Advocate may appear at the hearing of any motion under paragraph (1).

Optional procedure before executing commission and diligence

28.3—(1) The party who has obtained a commission and diligence for the recovery of a document on an application made under rule 28.2(1)(a), may at any time before executing it against a haver, serve on the haver an order in Form G11 (in this rule referred to as "the order"); and if so, the provisions of this rule shall apply.

(2) The order shall be served on the haver or his known solicitor and shall be complied with by the haver in the manner and within the period specified in the order.

(3) Not later than the day after the date on which the order, a certificate in Form G12 and any document is received by the sheriff clerk from a haver, he shall intimate that fact to each party.

(4) No party, other than the party who served the order, may uplift such a document until after the expiry of 7 days after the date of intimation under paragraph (3).

(5) Where the party who served the order fails to uplift such a document within 7 days after the date of intimation under paragraph (3), the sheriff clerk shall

intimate that failure to every other party.

(6) Where no party has uplifted such a document within 14 days after the date of intimation under paragraph (5), the sheriff clerk shall return it to the haver who delivered it to him.

(7) Where a party who has uplifted such a document does not wish to lodge it, he shall return it to the sheriff clerk who shall—

(a) intimate the return of the document to every other party; and
(b) if no other party uplifts the document within 14 days after the date of intimation, return it to the haver.

(8) If the party who served the order is not satisfied—

(a) that full compliance has been made with the order, or
(b) that adequate reasons for non-compliance have been given,

he may execute the commission and diligence under rule 28.4.

(9) Where an extract from a book of any description (whether the extract is certified or not) is produced under the order, the sheriff may, on the motion of the party who served the order, direct that that party shall be allowed to inspect the book and take copies of any entries falling within the specification.

(10) Where any question of confidentiality arises in relation to a book directed to be inspected under paragraph (9), the inspection shall be made, and any copies shall be taken, at the sight of the commissioner appointed in the interlocutor granting the commission and diligence.

(11) The sheriff may, on cause shown, order the production of any book (not being a banker's book or book of public record) containing entries falling under a specification, notwithstanding the production of a certificated extract.

Execution of commission and diligence for recovery of documents

28.4—(1) The party who seeks to execute a commission and diligence for recovery of a document obtained on an application made under rule 28.2(1)(a) shall—

(a) provide the commissioner with a copy of the specification, a copy of the pleadings (including any adjustments and amendments) and a certified copy of the interlocutor of his appointment; and
(b) instruct the clerk and any shorthand writer considered necessary by the commissioner or any party; and
(c) be responsible for the fees of the commissioner and his clerk, and of any shorthand writer.

(2) The commissioner shall, in consultation with the parties, fix a diet for the execution of the commission.

(3) The interlocutor granting such a commission and diligence shall be sufficient authority for citing a haver to appear before the commissioner.

(4) A citation in Form G13 shall be served on the haver with a copy of the specification and, where necessary for a proper understanding of the specification, a copy of the pleadings (including any adjustments and amendments).

(5) The parties and the haver shall be entitled to be represented by a solicitor or person having a right of audience before the sheriff at the execution of the commission.

(6) At the commission, the commissioner shall—

(a) administer the oath *de fideli administratione* to any shorthand writer appointed for the commission; and

(b) administer to the haver the oath in Form G14, or, where the haver elects to affirm, the affirmation in Form G15.

(7) The report of the execution of the commission and diligence, any document recovered and an inventory of that document, shall be sent by the commissioner to the sheriff clerk.

(8) Not later than the day after the date on which such a report, document and inventory, if any, are received by the sheriff clerk, he shall intimate to the parties that he has received them.

(9) No party, other than the party who served the order, may uplift such a document until after the expiry of 7 days after the date of intimation under paragraph (8).

(10) Where the party who served the order fails to uplift such a document within 7 days after the date of intimation under paragraph (8), the sheriff clerk shall intimate that failure to every other party.

(11) Where no party has uplifted such a document within 14 days after the date of intimation under paragraph (10), the sheriff clerk shall return it to the haver.

(12) Where a party who has uplifted such a document does not wish to lodge it, he shall return it to the sheriff clerk who shall—

(a) intimate the return of the document to every other party; and

(b) if no other party uplifts the document within 14 days of the date of intimation, return it to the haver.

Execution of orders for production or recovery of documents or other property under section 1(1) of the Act of 1972

28.5—(1) An order under section 1(1) of the Act of 1972 for the production or recovery of a document or other property shall grant a commission and diligence for the production or recovery of that document or other property.

(2) Rules 28.3 (optional procedure before executing commission and diligence) and 28.4 (execution of commission and diligence for recovery of documents) shall apply to an order to which paragraph (1) applies as they apply to a commission and diligence for the recovery of a document.

Execution of orders for inspection etc. of documents or other property under section 1(1) of the Act of 1972

28.6—(1) An order under section 1(1) of the Act of 1972 for the inspection or photographing of a document or other property, the taking of samples or the carrying out of any experiment thereon or therewith, shall authorise and appoint a specified person to photograph, inspect, take samples of, or carry out any experiment on or with any such document or other property, as the case may be, subject to such conditions, if any, as the sheriff thinks fit.

(2) A certified copy of the interlocutor granting such an order shall be sufficient authority for the person specified to execute the order.

(3) When such an order is executed, the party who obtained the order shall serve on the haver a copy of the interlocutor granting it, a copy of the specification and, where necessary for a proper understanding of the specification, a copy of the pleadings (including any adjustments and amendments).

Execution of orders for preservation etc. of documents or other property under section 1(1) of the Act of 1972

28.7—(1) An order under section 1(1) of the Act of 1972 for the preservation, custody and detention of a document or other property, other than in the hands of a haver, shall grant a commission and diligence for the detention and custody of that document or other property.

(2) The party who has obtained an order under paragraph (1) shall—

(a) provide the commissioner with a copy of the specification, a copy of the pleadings (including any adjustments and amendments) and a certified copy of the interlocutor of his appointment;

(b) be responsible for the fees of the commissioner and his clerk; and

(c) serve a copy of the order on the haver.

(3) The report of the execution of the commission and diligence, any document or other property taken by the commissioner and an inventory of such property, shall be sent by the commissioner to the sheriff clerk for the further order of the sheriff.

Confidentiality

28.8—(1) Where confidentiality is claimed for any evidence sought to be recovered under any of the following rules, such evidence shall be enclosed in a sealed packet:—

28.3 (optional procedure before executing commission and diligence),

28.4 (execution of commission and diligence for recovery of documents),

28.5 (execution of orders for production or recovery of documents or other property under section 1(1) of the Act of 1972),

28.7 (execution of orders for preservation etc. of documents or other property under section 1(1) of the Act of 1972).

(2) A motion to have such a sealed packet opened up may be lodged by—

(a) the party who obtained the commission and diligence; or

(b) any other party after the date of intimation by the sheriff clerk under the rule 28.3(5) or 28.4(10) (intimation of failure to uplift documents).

(3) In addition to complying with rule 15.2 (intimation of motions), the party lodging such a motion shall intimate the terms of the motion to the haver by post by the first class recorded delivery service.

(4) The person claiming confidentiality may oppose a motion made under paragraph (2).

Warrants for production of original documents from public records

28.9—(1) Where a party seeks to obtain from the keeper of any public record production of the original of any register or deed in his custody for the purpose of a cause, he shall apply to the sheriff by motion.

(2) Intimation of a motion under paragraph (1) shall be given to the keeper of the public record concerned at least 7 days before the motion is lodged.

(3) In relation to a public record kept by the Keeper of the Registers of Scotland or the Keeper of the Records of Scotland, where it appears to the sheriff that it is necessary for the ends of justice that a motion under this rule should be granted, he shall pronounce an interlocutor containing a certificate to that effect; and the party applying for production may apply by letter (enclosing a copy of the interlocutor duly certified by the sheriff clerk), addressed to the Deputy Principal Clerk of Session, for an order from the Court of Session authorising the Keeper of the Registers or the Keeper of the Records, as the case may be, to exhibit the original of any register or deed to the sheriff.

(4) The Deputy Principal Clerk of Session shall submit the application sent to him under paragraph (3) to the Lord Ordinary in chambers who, if satisfied, shall grant a warrant for production or exhibition of the original register or deed sought.

(5) A certified copy of the warrant granted under paragraph (4) shall be served on the keeper of the public record concerned.

(6) The expense of the production or exhibition of such an original register or deed shall be met, in the first instance, by the party who applied by motion under paragraph (1).

Commission for examination of witnesses

28.10—(1) This rules applies to a commission—

(a) to take the evidence of a witness who—

(i) is resident beyond the jurisdiction of the court;

(ii) although resident within the jurisdiction of the court, resides at some place remote from that court; or

(iii) by reason of age, infirmity or sickness, is unable to attend the diet of proof; or

(b) in respect of the evidence of a witness which is in danger of being lost, to take the evidence to lie *in retentis*.

(2) An application by a party for a commission to examine a witness shall be made by motion; and that party shall specify in the motion the name and address of at least one proposed commissioner for approval and appointment by the sheriff.

(3) The interlocutor granting such a commission shall be sufficient authority for citing the witness to appear before the commissioner.

(4) At the commission, the commissioner shall—

(a) administer the oath *de fideli administratione* to any shorthand writer appointed for the commission; and

(b) administer to the witness the oath in Form G14, or where the witness elects to affirm, the affirmation in Form G15.

(5) Where a commission is granted for the examination of a witness, the commission shall proceed without interrogatories unless, on cause shown, the sheriff otherwise directs.

Commissions on interrogatories

28.11—(1) Where interrogatories have not been dispensed with, the party who obtained the commission to examine a witness under rule 28.10 shall lodge draft interrogatories in process.

(2) Any other party may lodge cross-interrogatories.

(3) The interrogatories and any cross-interrogatories, when adjusted, shall be extended and returned to the sheriff clerk for approval and the settlement of any dispute as to their contents by the sheriff.

(4) The party who has obtained the commission shall—

(a) provide the commissioner with a copy of the pleadings (including any adjustments and amendments), the approved interrogatories and any cross-interrogatories and a certified copy of the interlocutor of his appointment;

(b) instruct the clerk; and

(c) be responsible, in the first instance, for the fee of the commissioner and his clerk.

(5) The commissioner shall, in consultation with the parties, fix a diet for the execution of the commission to examine the witness.

(6) The executed interrogatories, any document produced by the witness and an inventory of that document, shall be sent by the commissioner to the sheriff clerk.

(7) Not later than the day after the date on which the executed interrogatories, any document and an inventory of that document, are received by the sheriff clerk, he shall intimate to each party that he has received them.

(8) The party who obtained the commission to examine the witness shall lodge in process—

(a) the report of the commission; and

(b) the executed interrogatories and any cross-interrogatories.

Commissions without interrogatories

28.12—(1) Where interrogatories have been dispensed with, the party who has obtained a commission to examine a witness under rule 28.10 shall—

(a) provide the commissioner with a copy of the pleadings (including any adjustments and amendments) and a certified copy of the interlocutor of his appointment;

(b) fix a diet for the execution of the commission in consultation with the commissioner and every other party;

(c) instruct the clerk and any shorthand writer; and

(d) be responsible for the fees of the commissioner, his clerk and any shorthand writer.

(2) All parties shall be entitled to be present and represented at the execution of the commission.

(3) The report of the execution of the commission, any document produced by the witness and an inventory of that document, shall be sent by the commissioner to the sheriff clerk.

(4) Not later than the day after the date on which such a report, any document and an inventory of that document are received by the sheriff clerk, he shall intimate to each party that he has received them.

(5) The party who obtained the commission to examine the witness shall lodge the report in process.

Evidence taken on commission

28.13—(1) Subject to the following paragraphs of this rule and to all questions of relevancy and admissibility, evidence taken on commission under rule 28.11 or 28.12 may be used as evidence at any proof of the cause.

(2) Any party may object to the use of such evidence at a proof; and the objection shall be determined by the sheriff.

(3) Such evidence shall not be used at a proof if the witness becomes available to attend the diet of proof.

(4) A party may use such evidence in accordance with the preceding paragraphs of this rule notwithstanding that it was obtained at the instance of another party.

Letters of request

28.14—(1) This rule applies to an application for a letter of request to a court or tribunal outside Scotland to obtain evidence of the kind specified in paragraph (2), being evidence obtainable within the jurisdiction of that court or tribunal, for the purposes of a cause depending before the sheriff.

(2) An application to which paragraph (1) applies may be made in relation to a request—

- (a) for the examination of a witness;
- (b) for the inspection, photographing, preservation, custody, detention, production or recovery of, or the taking of samples of, or the carrying out of any experiment on or with, a document or other property, as the case may be.

(3) Such an application shall be made by minute in Form G16 together with a proposed letter of request in Form G17.

(4) It shall be a condition of granting a letter of request that any solicitor for the applicant shall become personally liable for the whole expenses which may become due and payable in respect of the letter of request to the court or tribunal obtaining the evidence and to any witness who may be examined for the purpose; and he shall consign into court such sum in respect of such expenses as the sheriff thinks fit.

(5) Unless the court or tribunal to which a letter of request is addressed is a court or tribunal in a country or territory—

- (a) where English is an official language, or
- (b) in relation to which the sheriff clerk certifies that no translation is required,

then the applicant shall, before the issue of the letter of request, lodge in process a translation of that letter and any interrogatories and cross-interrogatories into the official language of that court or tribunal.

(6) The letter of request when issued, any interrogatories and cross-interrogatories adjusted as required by rule 28.11 and the translations (if any), shall be forwarded by the sheriff clerk to the Foreign and Commonwealth Office or to such person and in such manner as the sheriff may direct.

Citation of witnesses and havers

28.15 The following rules shall apply to the citation of a witness or haver to a commission under this Chapter as they apply to the citation of a witness for a proof:—

rule 29.7 (citation of witnesses), except paragraph (4),
rule 29.9 (second diligence against a witness),
rule 29.10 (failure of witness to attend).

Chapter 29 Proof

Reference to oath

29.1—(1) Where a party intends to refer any matter to the oath of his opponent he shall lodge a motion to that effect.

(2) If a party fails to appear at the diet for taking his deposition on the reference to his oath, the sheriff may hold him as confessed and grant decree accordingly.

Remit to person of skill

29.2—(1) The sheriff may, on a motion by any party or on a joint motion, remit to any person of skill, or other person, to report on any matter of fact.

(2) Where a remit under paragraph (1) is made by joint motion or of consent of all parties, the report of such person shall be final and conclusive with respect to the subject-matter of the remit.

(3) Where a remit under paragraph (1) is made—

(a) on the motion of one of the parties, the expenses of the remit shall, in the first instance, be met by that party; and

(b) on a joint motion or of consent of all parties, the expenses shall, in the first instance, be met by the parties equally, unless the sheriff otherwise orders.

Evidence generally

29.3—(1) A party may apply by motion for the evidence of a witness to be received by way of affidavit; and the sheriff, after consisting the affidavit, may make such order as he thinks fit.

(2) A party may apply by motion for a specified statement or document to be admitted as evidence without calling as a witness the maker of the statement or document; and the sheriff, after considering the statement or document, may make such order on such conditions, if any, as he thinks fit.

Renouncing probation

29.4—(1) Where, on or at any time after, the closing of the record, the parties seek to renounce probation, they shall lodge in process a joint minute to that effect with or without a statement of admitted facts and any productions.

(2) On the lodging of a joint minute under paragraph (1), the sheriff may order a debate.

Orders for proof

29.5. Where proof is necessary in any cause, the sheriff shall fix a date for taking the proof and may limit the mode of proof.

Hearing parts of proof separately

29.6—(1) In action with pecuniary conclusions, the sheriff may—

(a) of his own motion, or

(b) on the motion of any party,

order that proof on liability or any specified issue be heard separately from proof on the question of the amount for which decree may be pronounced and determine the order in which the proofs shall be heard.

(2) The sheriff shall pronounce such interlocutor as he thinks fit at the conclusion of the first proof of any cause ordered to be heard in separate parts under paragraph (1).

Citation of witnesses

29.7—(1) A witness shall be cited for a proof—

(a) by registered post or the first class recorded delivery service by the solicitor for the party on whose behalf he is cited; or

(b) by a sheriff officer—

(i) personally;

(ii) by a citation being left with a resident at the person's dwelling place or an employee at his place of business;

(iii) by depositing it in that person's dwelling place or place of business;

(iv) by affixing it to the door of that person's dwelling place or place of business; or

(v) by registered post or the first class recorded delivery service.

(2) Where service is executed under paragraph (1)(b)(iii) or (iv), the sheriff officer shall, as soon as possible after such service, send, by ordinary post to the address at which he thinks it most likely that the person may be found, a letter containing a copy of the citation.

(3) A certified copy of the interlocutor allowing a proof shall be sufficient warrant to a sheriff officer to cite a witness on behalf of a party.

(4) A witness shall be cited on a period of notice of 7 days in Form G13 and the party citing the witness shall lodge a certificate of citation in Form G12.

(5) A solicitor who cites a witness shall be personally liable for his fees and expenses.

(6) In the event of a solicitor intimating to a witness that his citation is cancelled, the solicitor shall advise him that the cancellation is not to affect any other citation which he may have received from another party.

Citation of witnesses by party litigants

29.8—(1) Where a party to a cause is a party litigant, he shall—

(a) not later than 4 weeks before the diet of proof, apply to the sheriff by motion to fix caution in such sum as the sheriff considers reasonable having regard to the number of witnesses he proposes to cite and the period for which they may be required to attend court; and

(b) before instructing a sheriff officer to cite a witness, find caution for such expenses as can reasonably be anticipated to be incurred by the witness in answering the citation.

(2) A party litigant who does not intend to cite all the witnesses referred to in his application under paragraph (1)(a), may apply by motion for variation of the amount of caution.

Second diligence against a witness

29.9—(1) The sheriff may, on the motion of a party, grant a second diligence to compel the attendance of a witness under pain of arrest and imprisonment until caution can be found for his due attendance.

(2) The warrant for a second diligence shall be effective without endorsation and the expenses of such a motion and diligence may be decerned for against the witness.

Failure of witness to attend

29.10—(1) Where a witness fails to answer a citation after having been duly cited, the sheriff may, on the motion of a party and on production of a certificate of citation, grant warrant for the apprehension of the witness and for bringing him to court; and the expenses of such a motion and apprehension may be decerned for against the witness.

(2) Where a witness duly cited and after having demanded and been paid for his travelling expenses fails to attend a diet, either before the sheriff or before a commissioner, the sheriff may—

(a) ordain the witness to forfeit and pay penalty not exceeding £250 unless a reasonable excuse be offered and sustained; and

(b) grant decree for that penalty in favour of the party on whose behalf the witness was cited.

Lodging productions

29.11—(1) Where a proof has been allowed, all productions which are intended to be used at the proof shall be lodged in process not later than 14 days before the diet of proof.

(2) A production which is not lodged in accordance with paragraph (1) shall not be used or put in evidence at a proof unless—

(a) by consent of parties; or

(b) with leave of the sheriff on cause shown and on such conditions, if any, as to expenses or otherwise as the sheriff thinks fit.

Copy productions

29.12—(1) A copy of every production, marked with the appropriate number of process of the principal production, shall be lodged for the use of the sheriff at a proof not later than 48 hours before the diet of proof.

(2) Each copy production consisting of more than one sheet shall be securely fastened together by the party lodging it.

Returning borrowed parts of process and productions before proof

29.13 All parts of process and productions which have been borrowed shall be returned to process before 12.30 pm on the day preceding the diet of proof.

Notices to admit and notices of non-admission

29.14—(1) At any time after a proof has been allowed, a party may intimate to any other party a notice or notices calling on him to admit for the purposes of that cause only—

(a) such facts relating to an issue averred in the pleadings as may be specified in the notice;

(b) that a particular document lodged in process and specified in the notice is—

(i) an original and properly authenticated document; or

(ii) a true copy of an original and properly authenticated document.

(2) Where a party on whom a notice is intimated under paragraph (1)—

(a) does not admit a fact specified in the notice, or

(b) does not admit, or seeks to challenge, the authenticity of a document specified in the notice, he shall, within 21 days after the date of intimation of the notice under paragraph (1), intimate a notice of non-admission to the party intimating the notice to him under paragraph (1) stating that he does not admit the fact or document specified.

(3) A party who fails to intimate a notice of non-admission under paragraph (2) shall be deemed to have admitted the fact or document specified in the notice intimated to him under paragraph (1); and such fact or document may be used in evidence at a proof if otherwise admissible in evidence, unless the sheriff, on special cause shown, otherwise directs.

(4) A party who fails to intimate a notice of non-admission under paragraph (2) within 14 days after the notice to admit intimated to him under paragraph (1) shall be liable to the party intimating the notice to admit for the expenses of proving the fact or document specified in that notice unless the sheriff, on special cause shown, otherwise directs.

(5) The party serving a notice under paragraph (1) or (2) shall lodge a copy of it in process.

(6) A deemed admission under paragraph (3) shall not be used against the party by whom it was deemed to be made other than in the cause for the purpose for which it was deemed to be made or in favour of any person other than the party by whom the notice was given under paragraph (1).

Instruction of shorthand writer

29.15 Where a shorthand writer is to record evidence at a proof, the responsibility for instructing a shorthand writer shall lie with the pursuer.

Administration of oath or affirmation to witnesses

29.16 The sheriff shall administer the oath to a witness in Form G14 or, where the witness elects to affirm, the affirmation in Form G15.

Proof to be taken continuously

29.17 A proof shall be taken continuously so far as possible; but the sheriff may adjourn the diet from time to time.

Recording of evidence

29.18—(1) Evidence in a cause shall be recorded by—

(a) a shorthand writer, to whom the oath *de fideli administratione* in connection with the sheriff court service generally has been administered, or

(b) tape recording or other mechanical means approved by the court,

unless the parties, by agreement and with the approval of the sheriff, dispense with the recording of evidence.

(2) Where a shorthand writer is employed to record evidence, he shall, in the first instance, be paid by the parties equally.

(3) Where evidence is recorded by tape recording or other mechanical means, any fee payable shall, in the first instance, be paid by the parties in equal proportions.

(4) The solicitors for the parties shall be personally liable for the fees payable under paragraph (2) or (3), and the sheriff may make an order directing payment to be made.

(5) The record of the evidence at a proof shall include—

(a) any objection taken to a question or to the line of evidence;

(b) any submission made in relation to such an objection; and

(c) the ruling of the court in relation to the objection and submission.

(6) A transcript of the record of the evidence shall be made only on the direction of the sheriff; and the cost shall, in the first instance, be borne—

(a) in an undefended cause, by the solicitor for the pursuer; and

(b) in a defended cause, by the solicitor for the parties in equal proportions.

(7) The transcript of the record of the evidence provided for the use of the court shall be certified as a faithful record of the evidence by—

(a) the shorthand writer who recorded the evidence; or

(b) where the evidence was recorded by tape recording or other mechanical means, by the persons who transcribed the record.

(8) The sheriff may make such alterations to the transcript of the record of the evidence as appear to him to be necessary after hearing the parties; and, where such alterations are made, the sheriff shall authenticate the alterations.

(9) Where a transcript of the record of the evidence has been made for the use of the sheriff, copies of it may be obtained by any party from the person who transcribed the record on payment of his fee.

(10) Except with leave of the sheriff, the transcript of the record of the evidence may be borrowed from process only for the purpose of enabling a party to consider whether to appeal against the interlocutor of the sheriff on the proof.

(11) Where a transcript of the record of the evidence is required for the purpose of an appeal but has not been directed to be transcribed under paragraph (6), the appellant—

(a) may request such a transcript from the shorthand writer or as the case may be, the cost of the transcript being borne by the solicitor for the appellant in the first instance; and

(b) shall lodge the transcript in process;

and copies of it may be obtained by any party from the shorthand writer or as the case may be, on payment on his fee.

(12) Where the recording of evidence has been dispensed with under paragraph (1), the sheriff, if called upon to do so, shall—

(a) in the case of an objection to—

(i) the admissibility of evidence on the ground of confidentiality, or

(ii) the production of a document on any ground,

note the terms in writing of such objections and his decisions on the objection; and

(b) in the case of any other objection, record, in the note to his interlocutor disposing of the merits of the cause, the terms of the objection and his decision on the objection.

(13) This rule shall, with the necessary modifications, apply to the recording of evidence at a commission as it applies to the recording of evidence at a proof.

Incidental appeal against rulings on confidentiality of evidence and production of documents

29.19—(1) Where a party or any other person objects to the admissibility of oral or documentary evidence on the ground of confidentiality or to the production of a document on any ground, he may, if dissatisfied with the ruling of the sheriff on the objection, express immediately his formal dissatisfaction with the ruling and, with leave of the sheriff, appeal to the sheriff principal.

(2) The sheriff principal shall dispose of an appeal under paragraph (1) with the least possible delay.

(3) Except as provided in paragraph (1), no appeal may be made during a proof against any decision of the sheriff as to the admissibility of evidence or the production of documents.

(4) The appeal referred to in paragraph (1) shall not remove the cause from the sheriff who may proceed with the cause in relation to any issue which is not dependent on the ruling appealed against.

Parties to be heard at close of proof

29.20 At the close of the proof, or at an adjourned diet if for any reason the sheriff has postponed the hearing, the sheriff shall hear parties on the evidence and thereafter shall pronounce judgment with the least possible delay.

Chapter 30 Decrees, extracts and execution

Interpretation of this Chapter

30.1 In this Chapter, "decree" includes any judgment, deliverance, interlocutor, act, order, finding or authority which may be extracted.

Taxes on money under control of the court

30.2—(1) Subject to paragraph (2), in a cause in which money has been consigned into court under the Sheriff Court Consignations (Scotland) Act 1893, no decree, warrant or order for payment to any person shall be granted until there has been lodged with the sheriff clerk a certificate by an authorised officer of the Inland Revenue stating that all taxes or duties payable to the Commissioners of Inland Revenue have been paid or satisfied.

(2) In an action of multiplepoinding, it shall not be necessary for the grant of a decree, warrant or order for payment under paragraph (1) that all of the taxes or duties payable on the estate of a decreased claimant have been paid or satisfied.

Decrees for payment in foreign currency

30.3—(1) Where decree has been granted for payment of a sum of money in a foreign currency or the sterling equivalent, a party requesting extract of the decree shall do so by minute endorsed on or annexed to the initial writ stating the rate of exchange prevailing on the date of the decree sought to be extracted or the date, or within 3 days before the date, on which the extract is ordered, and the sterling equivalent at that rate for the principal sum and interest decerned for.

(2) A certificate in Form G18, from the Bank of England or a bank which is an institution authorised under the Banking Act 1987 certifying the rate of exchange and the sterling equivalent shall be lodged with the minute requesting extract of the decree.

(3) The extract decree issued by the sheriff clerk shall mention any certificate referred to in paragraph (2).

When decrees extractable

30.4—(1) Subject to the following paragraphs:—

- (a) a decree in absence may be extracted after the expiry of 14 days from the date of decree;
- (b) any decree pronounced in a defended cause may be extracted at any time after whichever is the later of the following:
  - (i) the expiry of the period within which an application for leave to appeal may be made and no such application has been made;
  - (ii) the date on which leave to appeal has been refused and there is no right of appeal from such refusal;
  - (iii) the expiry of the period within which an appeal may be marked and no appeal has been marked; or
  - (iv) the date on which an appeal has been finally disposed of; and
- (c) where the sheriff has, in pronouncing decree, reserved any question of expenses, extract of that decree may be issued only after the expiry of 14 days from the date of the interlocutor disposing of the question of expenses unless the sheriff otherwise directs.

(2) The sheriff may, on cause shown, grant a motion to allow extract to be applied for and issued earlier than a date referred to in paragraph (1).

(3) In relation to a decree referred to in paragraph (1)(b) or (c), paragraph (2) shall not apply unless—

- (a) the motion under that paragraph is made in the presence of parties; or
- (b) the sheriff is satisfied that proper intimation of the motion has been

made in writing to every party not present at the hearing of the motion.

(4) Nothing in this rule shall affect the power of the sheriff to supersede extract.

Extract of certain awards notwithstanding appeal

30.5 The sheriff clerk may issue an extract of an award of custody, access or aliment notwithstanding that an appeal had been made against an interlocutor containing such an award unless an order under rule 31.5 (appeals in connection with custody, access or aliment) has been made excusing obedience to or implement of that interlocutor.

Form of extract decree

30.6—(1) The extract of a decree mentioned in Appendix 2 shall be in the appropriate form for that decree in Appendix 2.

(2) In the case of a decree not mentioned in Appendix 2, the extract of the decree shall be modelled on a form in that Appendix with such variation as circumstances may require.

Form of warrant for execution

3.7 An extract of a decree on which execution may proceed shall include a warrant for execution in the following terms:— "This extract is warrant for all lawful execution hereon.".

Date of decree in extract

30.8—(1) Where the sheriff principal has adhered to the decision of the sheriff following an appeal, the date to be inserted in the extract decree as the date of decree shall be the date of the decision of the sheriff principal.

(2) Where a decree has more than one date it shall not be necessary to specify in an extract what was done on each date.

Service of charge where address of defender not known

30.9—(1) Where the address of a defender is not known to the pursuer, a charge shall be deemed to have been served on the defender if it is—

(a) served on the sheriff clerk of the sheriff court district where the defender's last known address is located; and

(b) displayed by the sheriff clerk on the walls of court for the period of the charge.

(2) On receipt of such a charge, the sheriff clerk shall display it on the walls of court and it shall remain displayed for the period of the charge.

(3) The period specified in the charge shall run from the first date on which it was displayed on the walls of court.

(4) On the expiry of the period of charge, the sheriff clerk shall endorse a certificate on the charge certifying that it has been displayed in accordance with this rule and shall thereafter return it to the sheriff officer by whom service was executed.

Chapter 31 Appeals

Time limit for appeal

31.1 Subject to the provisions of any other enactment, an interlocutor which may be appealed against may be appealed within 14 days after the date of the interlocutor unless it has been extracted following a motion under rule 30.4(2) (early extract).

Applications for leave to appeal

31.2—(1) Where leave to appeal is required, applications for leave to appeal against an interlocutor of a sheriff shall be made within 7 days after the date of the interlocutor against which it is sought to appeal unless the interlocutor has been extracted following a motion under rule 30.4(2) (early extract).

(2) Subject to the provisions of any other enactment, where leave to appeal has been granted, an appeal shall be made within 7 days after the date on which leave was granted.

(3) An application for leave to appeal from a decision in relation to a time to pay direction made under section 1 of the Debtors (Scotland) Act 1987 or the recall or restriction of an arrestment made under section 3(4) of that Act shall specify the question of law on which the appeal is made.

Form of appeal and notice to parties

31.3—(1) An appeal shall be marked by writing a note of appeal on the interlocutor sheet, or other written record containing the interlocutor appealed against, or on a separate sheet lodged with the sheriff clerk, in the following terms:— "The pursuer [*or* applicant, claimant, defender, respondent *or other party, as the case may be*] appeals to the sheriff principal [*or* the Court of Sessions].".

(2) A note of appeal shall be—

(a) signed by the appellant;
(b) bear the date on which it is signed; and
(c) where the appeal is to the Court of Session and the appellant is represented, specify the name and address of the solicitor or other agent who will be acting for him in the appeal.

(3) The sheriff clerk shall transmit the process of a cause within 4 days after the appeal is marked—

(a) in an appeal to the sheriff principal, to him;
(b) in an appeal to the Court of Session, to the Deputy Principal Clerk of Session.

(4) Within the period specified in paragraph (3), the sheriff clerk shall—

(a) send written notice of the appeal to every other party; and
(b) certify on the interlocutor sheet that he has done so.

(5) Failure of the sheriff clerk to comply with paragraph (4) shall not invalidate the appeal.

Reclaiming petition or oral hearing ordered or dispensed with

31.4 In an appeal to him, the sheriff principal may—

(a) order a reclaiming petition and answers;
(b) hear parties orally; or
(c) on the motion of the parties, if he thinks fit, dispose of the appeal without ordering either a reclaiming petition and answers or an oral hearing.

Appeals in connection with custody, access or aliment

31.5 Where an appeal is marked against an interlocutor containing an award of custody, access or aliment, the marking of that appeal shall not excuse obedience to or implement of the award of custody, access or aliment unless by order to the sheriff, the sheriff principal or the Court of Session, as the case may be.

Interim possession etc. pending appeal

31.6—(1) Notwithstanding an appeal, the sheriff or sheriff principal from whose decision an appeal has been taken shall have power—

(a) to regulate all matters relating to interim possession;
(b) to make any order for the preservation of any property to which the action relates or its sale if perishable;
(c) to make provision for the preservation of evidence; or
(d) to make any interim order which a due regard to the interests of the parties may require.

(2) An order made under paragraph (1) may be reviewed—

(a) by the sheriff principal, on an appeal to him; or
(b) the Court of Session, on an appeal to it.

Abandonment of appeal

31.7 After an appeal to the sheriff principal has been marked, the appellant shall not be entitled to abandon his appeal unless—

(a) of consent of all other parties; or
(b) with leave of the sheriff principal.

Chapter 32 Taxation of expenses

Taxation before decree for expenses

32.1 Expenses allowed in any cause, whether in absence or *in foro contentioso*, unless modified at a fixed amount, shall be taxed before decree is granted for them.

Decree for expenses in name of solicitor

32.2 The sheriff may allow a decree for expenses to be extracted in the name of the solicitor who conducted the cause.

Procedure for taxation

32.3—(1) Where an account of expenses awarded in a cause is lodged for taxation, the account and process shall be transmitted by the sheriff clerk to the auditor of court.

(2) The auditor of court shall—

(a) assign a diet of taxation not earlier than 7 days from the date he receives the account from the sheriff clerk; and

(b) intimate that diet forthwith to the party who lodged the account.

(3) The party who lodged the account of expenses shall, on receiving intimation from the auditor of court under paragraph (2)—

(a) send a copy of the account, and

(b) intimate the date, time and place of the diet of taxation,

to every other party.

(4) After the account has been taxed, the auditor of court shall transmit the process with the account and his report to the sheriff clerk.

(5) Where the auditor of court has reserved consideration of the account at the diet of taxation, he shall intimate his decision to the parties who attended the taxation.

(6) Where no objections are lodged under rule 32.4 (objections to auditor's report), the sheriff may grant decree for the expenses as taxed.

Objections to auditor's report

32.4—(1) A party may lodge a note of objections to an account as taxed only where he attended the diet of taxation.

(2) Such a note shall be lodged within 7 days after—

(a) the diet of taxation; or

(b) where the auditor of court reserved consideration of the account under paragraph (5) of rule 32.3, the date on which the auditor of court intimates his decision under that paragraph.

(3) The sheriff shall dispose of the objection in a summary manner, with or without answers.

Special provisions in relation to particular causes

Chapter 33 Family actions

PART I GENERAL PROVISIONS

Interpretation of this Chapter

33.1—(1) In this Chapter, "family action" means—

(a) an action of divorce;

(b) an action of separation;

(c) an action of declarator of legitimacy;

(d) an action of declarator of illegitimacy;

(e) an action of declarator of parentage;

(f) an action of declarator of non-parentage;
(g) an action of declarator of legitimation;
(h) an action or application for any parental rights;
(i) an action of affiliation and aliment;
(j) an action of, or application for or in respect of, aliment;
(k) an action or application for financial provision after a divorce or annulment in an overseas country within the meaning of Part IV of the Matrimonial and Family Proceedings Act 1984;
(l) an action or application for an order under the Act of 1981;
(m) an application for the variation or recall of an order mentioned in section 8(1) of the Law Reform (Miscellaneous Provisions) (Scotland) Act 1966.

(2) In this Chapter, unless the context otherwise requires—
"the Act of 1975" means the Children Act 1975;
"the Act of 1976" means the Divorce (Scotland) Act 1976;
"the Act of 1981" means the Matrimonial Homes (Family Protection) (Scotland) Act 1981;
"the Act of 1985" means the Family Law (Scotland) Act 1985;
"child" means a person under the age of 16 years;
"local authority" means a regional or islands council;
"mental disorder" means mental illness or mental handicap however caused or manifested;
"order for financial provision" means, except in Part VII of this Chapter (financial provision after overseas divorce or annulment), an order mentioned in section 8(1) of the Act of 1985;
"parental rights" has the meaning assigned in section 8 of the Law Reform (Parent and Child) (Scotland) Act 1986.

(3) For the purposes of rules 33.2 (averments in actions of divorce or separation about other proceedings) and 33.3 (averments where custody sought) and, in relation to proceedings in another jurisdiction, Schedule 3 to the Domicile and Matrimonial Proceedings Act 1973 (sisting of consistorial actions in Scotland), proceedings are continuing at any time after they have commenced and before they are finally disposed of.

Averments in actions of divorce or separation about other proceedings

33.2—(1) This rule applies to an action of divorce or separation.

(2) In an action to which this rule applies, the pursuer shall state in the condescendence of the initial writ—
(a) whether to his knowledge any proceedings are continuing in Scotland or in any other country in respect of the marriage to which the initial writ relates or are capable of affecting its validity or subsistence; and
(b) where such proceedings are continuing—
  (i) the court, tribunal or authority before which the proceedings have been commenced;
  (ii) the date of commencement;
  (iii) the names of the parties;

(iv) the date, or expected date of any proof (or its equivalent) in the proceedings; and

(v) such other facts as may be relevant to the question of whether or not the action before the sheriff should be sisted under Schedule 3 to the Domicile and Matrimonial Proceedings Act 1973.

(3) Where—

(a) such proceedings are continuing;

(b) the action before the sheriff is defended; and

(c) either—

(i) the initial writ does not contain the statement referred to in paragraph (2)(a), or

(ii) the particulars mentioned in paragraph (2)(b) as set out in the initial writ are incomplete or incorrect,

any defences or minute, as the case may be, lodged by any person to the action shall include that statement and, where appropriate, the further or correct particulars mentioned in paragraph (2)(b).

Averments where custody sought

33.3—(1) A party to a family action, who makes an application in that action for a custody order (within the meaning assigned in section 1(1)(b) of the Family Law Act 1986) in respect of a child shall include in his pleadings—

(a) where that action is an action of divorce or separation, averments giving particulars of any other proceedings known to him, whether in Scotland or elsewhere and whether concluded or not, which relate to the child in respect of whom the custody order is sought;

(b) in any other family action—

(i) the averments mentioned in paragraph (a); and

(ii) averments giving particulars of any proceedings known to him which are continuing, whether in Scotland or elsewhere, and which relate to the marriage of the parents of that child.

(2) Where such other proceedings are continuing or have taken place and the averments of the applicant for such a custody order—

(a) do not contain particulars of the other proceedings, or

(b) contain particulars which are incomplete or incorrect,

any defences or minute, as the case may be, lodged by any person to the family action shall include such particulars or such further or correct particulars as are known to him.

(3) In paragraph 1(b)(ii), "child" includes a child of the family within the meaning assigned in section 42(4) of the Family Law Act 1986.

Averments where identity or address of person not known

33.4 In a family action, where the identity or address of any person referred to in rule 33.7 as a person in respect of whom a warrant for intimation requires to be applied for is not known and cannot reasonably be ascertained, the party required to apply for the warrant shall include in his pleadings an averment of that fact and averments setting out what steps have been taken to ascertain the identity or address, as the case may be, of that person.

Averments about maintenance orders

33.5 In a family action in which an order for aliment or periodical allowance is sought, or is sought to be varied or recalled, by any party, the pleadings of that party shall contain an averment stating whether and, if so, when and by whom, a maintenance order (within the meaning of section 106 of the Debtors (Scotland) Act 1987) has been granted in favour of or against that party or of any other person in respect of whom the order is sought.

Averments where aliment or financial provision sought

33.6—(1) In this rule—

"the Act of 1991" means the Child Support Act 1991;

"child" has the meaning assigned in section 55 of the Act of 1991;

"crave relating to aliment" means—

(a) for the purposes of paragraph (2), a crave for decree of aliment in relation to a child or for recall or variation of such a decree; and

(b) for the purpose of paragraph (3), a crave for decree of aliment in relation to a child or for recall or variation of such a decree or for the variation or termination of an agreement on aliment in relation to a child;

"maintenance assessment" has the meaning assigned in section 55 of the Act of 1991.

(2) A family action containing a crave relating to aliment and to which section 8(6), (7), (8) or (10) of the Act of 1991 (top up maintenance orders) applies shall—

(a) include averments stating, where appropriate—

(i) that a maintenance assessment under section 11 of that Act (maintenance assessments) is in force;

(ii) the date of the maintenance assessment;

(iii) the amount and frequency of periodical payments of child support maintenance fixed by the maintenance assessment; and

(iv) the grounds on which the sheriff retains jurisdiction under section 8(6), (7), (8) or (10) of that Act; and

(b) unless the sheriff on cause shown otherwise directs, be accompanied by any document issued by the Secretary of State to the party intimating the making of the maintenance assessment referred to in sub-paragraph (a).

(3) A family action containing a crave relating to aliment, and to which section 8(6), (7), (8) or (10) of the Act of 1991 does not apply, shall include averments stating—

(a) that the habitual residence of the absent parent, person with care or qualifying child, within the meaning of section 3 of that Act, is furth of the United Kingdom;

(b) that the child is not a child within the meaning of section 55 of that Act; or

(c) where the action is lodged for warranting before 7th April 1997, the grounds on which the sheriff retains jurisdiction.

(4) In an action for declarator of non-parentage or illegitimacy—

(a) the initial writ shall include an article of condescendence stating whether the pursuer previously has been alleged to be the parent in an application for a maintenance assessment under section 4, 6 or 7 of the

Act of 1991 (applications for maintenance assessment); and

(b) where an allegation of paternity has been made against the pursuer, the Secretary of State shall be named as a defender in the action.

(5) A family action involving parties in respect of whom a decision has been made in any application, review or appeal under the Act of 1991 relating to any child of those parties, shall—

(a) include averments stating that such a decision has been made and giving details of that decision; and

(b) unless the sheriff on cause shown otherwise directs, be accompanied by any document issued by the Secretary of State to the parties intimating that decision.

Warrants and forms for intimation

33.7—(1) In the initial writ in a family action, the pursuer shall include a crave for a warrant for intimation—

(a) in an action where the address of the defender is not known to the pursuer and cannot reasonably be ascertained, to—

(i) every child of the marriage between the parties who has reached the age of 16 years, and

(ii) one of the next-of-kin of the defender who has reached that age,

unless the address of such a person is not known to the pursuer and cannot reasonably be ascertained, and a notice of intimation in Form F1 shall be attached to the copy of the initial writ intimated to any such person;

(b) in an action where the pursuer alleges that the defender has committed adultery with another person, to that person, unless—

(i) that person is not named in the initial writ and, if the adultery is relied on for the purposes of section 1(2)(a) of the Act of 1976 (irretrievable breakdown of marriage by reason of adultery), the initial writ contains an averment that his or her identity is not known to the pursuer and cannot reasonably be ascertained, or

(ii) the pursuer alleges that the defender has been guilty of rape upon or incest with, that named person,

and a notice of intimation in Form F2 shall be attached to the copy of the initial writ intimated to any such person;

(c) in an action where the defender is a person who is suffering from a mental disorder, to—

(i) those persons mentioned in sub-paragraph (a)(i) and (ii), unless the address of such person is not known to the pursuer and cannot reasonably be ascertained, and

(ii) the *curator bonis* to the defender, if one has been appointed,

and a notice of intimation in Form F3 shall be attached to the copy of the initial writ intimated to any such person;

(d) in an action relating to a marriage which was entered into under a law which permits polygamy where—

(i) one of the decrees specified in section 2(2) of the Matrimonial Proceedings (Polygamous Marriages) Act 1972 is sought, and

(ii) either party to the marriage in question has any spouse additional to the other party,

to any such additional spouse, and a notice of intimation in Form F4 shall be attached to the initial writ intimated to any such person;

(e) in an action of divorce or separation where the sheriff may make an order for any parental rights in respect of a child—
   (i) who is in the care of a local authority, to that authority and a notice of intimation in Form F5 shall be attached to the initial writ intimated to that authority;
   (ii) who, being a child of one party to the marriage, has been accepted as a child of the family by the other party to the marriage and who is liable to be maintained by a third party, to that third party, and a notice of intimation in Form F5 shall be attached to the initial writ intimated to that third party; or
   (iii) in respect of whom a third party exercises such rights *de facto*, to that third party, and a notice of intimation in Form F6 shall be attached to the initial writ intimated to that third party;

(f) in an action where the pursuer craves the custody of a child, to any parent or guardian of the child who is not a party to the action, and a notice of intimation in Form F7 shall be attached to the initial writ intimated to any such parent or guardian;

(g) in an action where the pursuer craves the custody of a child and he is—
   (i) not a parent of that child, and
   (ii) resident in Scotland when the initial writ is lodged,

   to the local authority within which area the pursuer resides, and a notice of intimation in Form F8 shall be attached to the initial writ intimated to that authority;

(h) in an action which affects a child, to that child if not a party to the action, and a notice of intimation in Form F9 shall be attached to the initial writ intimated to that child;

(i) in action where the pursuer makes an application for an order under section 8(1)(aa) of the Act of 1985 (transfer of property) and—
   (i) the consent of a third party to such a transfer is necessary by virtue of an obligation, enactment or rule of law, or
   (ii) the property is subject to a security,

   to the third party or creditor, as the case may be, and a notice of intimation in Form F10 shall be attached to the initial writ intimated to any such person;

(j) in an action where the pursuer makes an application for an order under section 18 of the Act of 1985 (which relates to avoidance transactions), to—
   (i) any third party in whose favour the transfer of, or transaction involving, the property is to be or was made, and
   (ii) any other person having an interest in the transfer of, or transactions involving, the property, and a notice of intimation in Form F11 shall be attached to the initial writ intimated to any such person; and

(k) in an action where the pursuer makes an application for an order under the Act of 1981—
  (i) where he is a non-entitled partner and the entitled partner has a spouse, to that spouse, or
  (ii) where the application is under section 2(1)(e), 2(4)(a), 3(1), 3(2), 4, 7, 13 or 18 of that Act, and the entitled spouse or entitled partner is a tenant or occupies the matrimonial home by permission of a third party, to the landlord or the third party, as the case may be,

and a notice of intimation in Form F12 shall be attached to the initial writ intimated to any such person.

(2) Expressions used in paragraph (1)(k) which are also used in the Act of 1981 have the same meaning as in that Act.

(3) A notice of intimation under paragraph (1) shall be on a period of notice of 21 days unless the sheriff otherwise orders; but the sheriff shall not order a period of notice of less than 2 days.

(4) In a family action, where the pursuer—
(a) craves for the custody of a child, and
(b) is not resident in Scotland when the initial writ is lodged for warranting,

he shall include a crave for an order for intimation in Form F8 to such local authority as the sheriff thinks fit.

(5) Where the address of a person mentioned in paragraph (1)(b), (d), (e), (f), (h), (i), (j) or (k) is not known and cannot reasonably be ascertained, the pursuer shall include a crave in the initial writ to dispense with intimation; and the sheriff may grant that crave or make such other order as he thinks fit.

(6) Where the identity or address of a person to whom intimation of a family action is required becomes known during the course of the action, the party who would have been required to insert a warrant for intimation to that person shall lodge a motion for a warrant for intimation to that person or to dispense with such intimation.

Intimation where improper association

33.8—(1) In a family action where the pursuer alleges an improper association between the defender and another named person, the pursuer shall, immediately after the expiry of the period of notice, lodge a motion for an order for intimation to that person or to dispense with such intimation.

(2) In determining a motion under paragraph (1), the sheriff may—
(a) make such order for intimation as he thinks fit; or
(b) dispense with intimation; and
(c) where he dispenses with intimation, order that the name of that person be deleted from the condescendence of the initial writ.

(3) Where intimation is ordered under paragraph (2), a copy of the initial writ and an intimation in Form F13 shall be intimated to the named person.

(4) In paragraph (1), "improper association" means sodomy, incest or any homosexual relationship.

Productions in action of divorce or where order for custody may be made

33.9 Unless the sheriff otherwise directs—

(a) in an action of divorce, a warrant for citation shall not be granted without there being produced with the initial writ an extract of the relevant entry in the register of marriages or an equivalent document; and

(b) in an action where the sheriff may make an order in respect of the custody of a child, a warrant for citation shall not be granted without there being produced with the initial writ an extract of the relevant entry in the register of births or an equivalent document.

Warrant of citation

33.10 The warrant of citation in a family action shall be in Form F14.

Form of citation and certificate

33.11—(1) Subject to rule 5.6 (service where address of person is not known), citation of a defender shall be in Form F15, which shall be attached to a copy of the initial writ and warrant of citation and shall have appended to it a notice of intention to defend in Form F26.

(2) The certificate of citation shall be in Form F16 which shall be attached to the initial writ.

Execution of service on, or intimation to, local authority

33.12—(1) Where a local authority referred to in rule 33.7(1)(g) (custody sought by non-parent resident in Scotland) or 33.7(4) (custody sought by pursuer not resident in Scotland) is named as a defender in an initial writ at the time it is lodged, service of the initial writ on that local authority shall be executed within 7 days after the date of granting of the warrant of citation.

(2) Where in a family action—

(a) to which rule 33.7(1)(g) applies, or

(b) in which a motion under rule 33.7(4) is required,

the local authority referred to in that provision is named as a defender in the initial writ at the time it is lodged, a notice in Form F8 shall be attached to the copy of the initial writ served on that local authority.

(3) Where, by virtue of rule 33.7(1)(g), 33.7(4) or 33.15(2), intimation of an application for custody is to be made to a local authority, intimation to that local authority shall be given within 7 days after the date on which a warrant of citation, or an order for intimation, as the case may be, has been granted.

Service in cases of mental disorder of defender

33.13—(1) In a family action where the defender suffers or appears to suffer from mental disorder and is resident in a hospital or other similar institution, citation shall be executed by registered post or the first class recorded delivery service addressed to the medical officer in charge of that hospital or institution; and there shall be included with the copy of the initial writ—

(a) a citation in Form F15;
(b) any notice required by rule 33.14(1);
(c) a request in Form F17;
(d) a form of certificate in Form F18 requesting the medical officer to—
  (i) deliver and explain the initial writ, citation and any notice or form of notice of consent required under rule 33.14(1) personally to the defender; or
  (ii) certify that such delivery or explanation would be dangerous to the health or mental condition of the defender; and
(e) a stamped envelope addressed for return of that certificate to the pursuer or his solicitor, if he has one.

(2) The medical officer referred to in paragraph (1) shall send the certificate in Form F18 duly completed to the pursuer or his solicitor, as the case may be.

(3) The certificate mentioned in paragraph (2) shall be attached to the certificate of citation.

(4) Where such a certificate bears that the initial writ has not been delivered to the defender, the sheriff may, at any time before decree—
(a) order such further medical inquiry, and
(b) make such order for further service or intimation,
as he thinks fit.

Notices in certain actions of divorce or separation

33.14—(1) In the following actions of divorce or separation there shall be attached to the copy of the initial writ served on the defender—
(a) in an action relying on section 1(2)(d) of the Act of 1976 (no cohabitation for two years with consent of defender to decree)—
  (i) which is an action of divorce, a notice in Form F19 and a notice of consent in Form F20;
  (ii) which is an action of separation, a notice in Form F21 and a form of notice of consent in Form F2;
(b) in an action relying on section 1(2)(e) of the Act of 1976 (no cohabitation for five years)—
  (i) which is an action of divorce, a notice in Form F23;
  (ii) which is an action of separation, a notice in Form F24.

(2) The certificate of service of an initial writ in an action mentioned in paragraph (1) shall state which notice or form mentioned in paragraph (1) has been attached to the initial writ.

Orders for intimation by sheriff

33.15—(1) In any family action, the sheriff may order intimation to be made to such person as he thinks fit.

(2) Where a party makes an application or averment in a family action which, had it been made in an initial writ, would have required a warrant for intimation under rule 33.7, that party shall lodge a motion for a warrant for intimation or to dispense with such intimation.

Appointment of curators *ad litem* to defenders

33.16—(1) This rule applies to an action of divorce or separation where it appears to the court that the defender is suffering from a mental disorder.

(2) In an action to which this rule applies, the sheriff shall—

(a) appoint a curator *ad litem* to the defender;

(b) where the facts set out in section 1(2)(d) of the Act of 1976 (no cohabitation for two years with consent of defender to decree) are relied on—

(i) make an order for intimation of the ground of the action to the Mental Welfare Commission for Scotland; and

(ii) include in such an order a requirement that the Commission sends to the sheriff clerk a report indicating whether in its opinion the defender is capable of deciding whether or not to give consent to the granting of decree.

(3) Within 7 days after the appointment of a curator *ad litem* under paragraph (2)(a), the pursuer shall send to him—

(a) a copy of the initial writ and any defences (including any adjustments and amendments) lodged; and

(b) a copy of the notice in Form G5 sent to him by the sheriff clerk.

(4) On receipt of a report required under paragraph (2)(b)(ii), the sheriff clerk shall—

(a) lodge the report in process; and

(b) intimate that this has been done to—

(i) the pursuer;

(ii) the solicitor for the defender, if known; and

(iii) the curator *ad litem*.

(5) The curator *ad litem* shall lodge in process one of the writs mentioned in paragraph (6)—

(a) within 14 days after the report required under paragraph (2)(b)(ii) has been lodged in process; or

(b) where no such report is required, within 21 days after the date of his appointment under paragraph (2)(a).

(6) The writs referred to in paragraph (5) are—

(a) a notice of intention to defend;

(b) defences to the action;

(c) a minute adopting defences already lodged; and

(d) a minute stating that the curator *ad litem* does not intend to lodge defences.

(7) Notwithstanding that he has lodged a minute stating that he does not intend to lodge defences, a curator *ad litem* may appear at any stage of the action to protect the interests of the defender.

(8) If, at any time, it appears to the curator *ad litem* that the defender is not suffering from mental disorder, he may report that fact to the court and seek his own discharge.

(9) The pursuer shall be responsible, in the first instance, for payment of the fees and outlays of the curator *ad litem* incurred during the period from his appointment until—

(a) he lodges a minute stating that he does not intend to lodge defences;
(b) he decides to instruct the lodging of defences or a minute adopting defences already lodged; or
(c) being satisfied after investigation that the defender is not suffering from mental disorder, he is discharged.

Applications for sist

33.17 An application for a sist, or the recall of a sist, under Schedule 3 to the Domicile and Matrimonial Proceedings Act 1973 shall be made by written motion.

Notices of consent to divorce or separation

33.18—(1) Where, in an action of divorce or separation in which the facts in section 1(2)(d) of the Act of 1976 (no cohabitation for two years with consent of defender to decree) are relied on, the defender wishes to consent to the grant of decree of divorce or separation he shall do so by giving notice in writing in Form F20 (divorce) or Form F22 (separation), as the may be, to the sheriff clerk.

(2) The evidence of one witness shall be sufficient for the purpose of establishing that the signature on a notice of consent under paragraph (1) is that of the defender.

(3) In an action of divorce or separation where the initial writ includes, for the purposes of section 1(2)(d) of the Act of 1976, an averment that the defender consents to the grant of decree, the defender may give notice by letter sent to the sheriff clerk stating that he has not so concerned or that he withdraws any consent which he has already given.

(4) On receipt of a letter under paragraph (3), the sheriff clerk shall intimate the terms of the letter to the pursuer.

(5) On receipt of any intimation under paragraph (4), the pursuer may, within 14 days after the date of the intimation, if none of the other facts mentioned in section 1(2) of the Act of 1976 is averred in the initial writ, lodge a motion for the action to be sisted.

(6) If no such motion is lodged, the pursuer shall be deemed to have abandoned the action and the action shall be dismissed.

(7) If a motion under paragraph (5) is granted and the sist is not recalled or renewed within a period of 6 months from the date of the interlocutor granting the sist, the pursuer shall be deemed to have abandoned the action and the action shall be dismissed.

Consents to grant of custody

33.19—(1) Where a party who requires a consent under section 47(2) of the Act of 1975 to the grant of custody, executes service on, or gives intimation to, a person who may give such consent, he shall—
(a) include with the copy of the initial writ or other pleadings, as the case may be—
  (i) a notice in Form F7; and
  (ii) a form of notice of consent in Form F25; and
(b) in the certificate of service or intimation, as the case may be, state expressly that such notice and form of notice of consent was included.

(2) Where a parent or guardian wishes to consent to the grant of an application for custody, he shall—

(i) complete and sign the notice of consent in Form F25;
(ii) have his signature witnessed; and
(iii) send the notice of consent to the sheriff clerk.

(3) Where a person, who has consented under paragraph (2) to the grant of such an application, wishes to withdraw that consent, he shall give notice by letter sent to the sheriff clerk stating that he withdraws his consent.

(4) On receipt of a letter under paragraph (3), the sheriff clerk shall intimate the terms of the letter to the applicant and to every other party.

Reports by local authorities under section 49(2) of the Act of 1975

33.20—(1) On completion of a report made under section 49(2) of the Act of 1975 (reports by local authority on child in certain custody applications), the local authority shall—

(a) send the report, with a copy for each party, to the sheriff clerk; and
(b) where a curator *ad litem* has been appointed to the child in respect of whom the application for custody has been made, send a copy of the report to him.

(2) On receipt of such a report, the sheriff clerk shall send a copy of the report to each party.

(3) Where intimation is given to a local authority under rule 33.7(1)(g) or (4) for the purposes of section 49(2) of the Act of 1975, an application for the custody of the child shall not be determined until the report of the local authority has been lodged.

(4) When disposing of an application for custody, the sheriff shall determine which party or parties are to be liable for the expenses of the local authority incurred in the preparation of any report made under section 49(2) of the Act of 1975.

Appointment of local authority or reporter to report on a child

33.21—(1) This rule applies where, at any stage of a family action, the sheriff appoints—

(a) a local authority under section 11(1) of the Matrimonial Proceedings (Children) Act 1958 or section 12(2)(a) of the Guardianship Act 1973 (which both relate to a report on a child with respect to custody), or
(b) another person (referred to in this rule as a "reporter"), whether under a provision mentioned in sub-paragraph (a) or otherwise,

to investigate and report to the court on the circumstances of a child and on proposed arrangements for the care and upbringing of the child.

(2) On making an appointment referred to in paragraph (1), the sheriff shall direct that the party who sought the appointment or, where the court makes the appointment of its own motion, the pursuer or minuter, as the case may be, shall—

(a) instruct the local authority or reporter; and
(b) be responsible, in the first instance, for the fees and outlays of the local authority or reporter appointed.

(3) Where a local authority or reporter is appointed—

(a) the party who sought the appointment, or

(b) where the sheriff makes the appointment of his own motion, the pursuer or minuter, as the case may be,

shall, within 7 days after the date of the appointment, intimate the name and address of the local authority or reporter to any local authority to which intimation of the family action has been made.

(4) On completion of a report referred to in paragraph (1), the local authority or reporter, as the case may be, shall send the report, with a copy of it for each party, to the sheriff clerk.

(5) On receipt of such a report, the sheriff clerk shall send a copy of the report to each party.

(6) Where a local authority or reporter has been appointed to investigate and report in respect of a child, an application for the custody of that child shall not be determined until the report of the local authority or reporter, as the case may be, has been lodged.

Referral to family mediation and conciliation service

33.22 In any family action in which the custody of, or access to, a child is in dispute, the sheriff may, at any stage of the action, where he considers it appropriate to do so, refer that dispute to a specified family mediation and conciliation service.

Applications for orders to disclose whereabouts of children

33.23—(1) An application for an order under section 33(1) of the Family Law Act 1986 (which relates to the disclosure of the whereabouts of a child) shall be made by motion.

(2) Where the sheriff makes an order under section 33(1) of the Family Law Action 1986, he may ordain the person against whom the order has been made to appear before him or to lodge an affidavit.

Applications in relation to removal of children

33.24—(1) An application for leave under section 51(1) of the Act of 1975 (authority to remove a child from the care and possession of the applicant for custody) or for an order under section 35(3) of the Family Law Act 1986 (application for interdict or interim interdict prohibiting removal of child from jurisdiction) shall be made—

(a) by a party to the action, by motion; or

(b) by a person who is not a party to the action, by minute.

(2) An application under section 35(3) of the Family Law Act 1986 need not be served or intimated.

(3) An application under section 23(2) of the Child Abduction and Custody Act 1985 (declarator that removal of child from United Kingdom was unlawful) shall be made—

(a) in an action depending before the sheriff—

(i) by a party, in the initial writ, defences or minute, as the case may be, or by motion; or

(ii) by any person, by minute; or

(b) after final decree, by minute in the process of the action to which the application relates.

Intimation to local authority before supervised access

33.25 Where the sheriff, of his own motion or on the motion of a party, is considering making an award of access or interim access subject to supervision by the social work department of a local authority, he shall ordain the party moving for access or interim access to intimate to the chief executive of that local authority (where not already a party to the action and represented at the hearing at which the issues arises)—

(a) the terms of any relevant motion;

(b) the intention of the sheriff to order that access be supervised by the social work department of that local authority; and

(c) that the local authority shall, within such period as the sheriff has determined—

(i) notify the sheriff clerk whether it intends to make representations to the sheriff; and

(ii) where it intends to make representations in writing, to do so within that period.

Joint minutes

33.26 Where any parties have reached agreement in relation to—

(a) any parental rights in respect of a child,

(b) aliment for a child, or

(c) an order for financial provision,

a joint minute may be entered into expressing that agreement; and the sheriff may grant decree in respect of those parts of the joint minute in relation to which he could otherwise make an order, whether or not such a decree would include a matter for which there was no crave.

Affidavits

33.27 The sheriff may accept evidence by affidavit at any hearing for an order or interim order.

PART II UNDEFENDED FAMILY ACTIONS

Evidence in certain undefended family actions

33.28—(1) This rule—

(a) subject to sub-paragraph (b), applies to all family actions in which no notice of intention to defend has been lodged, other than a family action—

(i) for any parental rights or aliment;

(ii) of affiliation and aliment;

(iii) for financial provision after an overseas divorce or annulment within the meaning of Part IV of the Matrimonial and Family Proceedings Act 1984; or

(iv) for an order under the Act of 1981;

(b) applies to a family action in which a curator *ad litem* has been appointed under rule 33.16 where the curator *ad litem* to the defender has lodged a minute intimating that he does not intend to lodge defences;

(c) applies to any family action which proceeds at any stage as undefended where the sheriff so directs;

(d) applies to the merits of a family action which is undefended on the merits where the sheriff so directs, notwithstanding that the action is defended on an ancillary matter.

(2) Unless the sheriff otherwise directs, evidence shall be given by affidavit.

(3) Unless the sheriff otherwise directs, evidence relating to the welfare of a child shall be given by affidavit, at least one affidavit being emitted by a person other than a parent or party to the action.

(4) Evidence in the form of a written statement bearing to be the professional opinion of a duly qualified medical practitioner, which has been signed by him and lodged in process, shall be admissible in place of parole evidence by him.

Procedure for decree in actions under rule 33.28

33.29—(1) In an action to which rule 33.28 (evidence in certain undefended family actions) applies, the pursuer shall at any time after the expiry of the period for lodging a notice of intention to defend—

(a) lodge in process the affadavit evidence; and

(b) endorse a minute in Form F27 on the initial writ.

(2) The sheriff may, at any time after the pursuer has complied with paragraph (1), without requiring the appearance of parties—

(a) grant decree in terms of the motion for decree; or

(b) remit the cause for such further procedure, if any, including proof by parole evidence, as the sheriff thinks fit.

Extracts of undefended decree

33.30 In an action to which rule 33.28 (evidence in certain undefended family actions) applies, the sheriff clerk shall, after the expiry of 14 days after the grant of decree under rule 33.29 (procedure for decree in actions under rule 33.28), issue to the pursuers and the defender an extract decree.

Procedure in undefended family action for parental rights

33.31—(1) Where no notice of intention to defend has been lodged in a family action for any parental rights or any right or authority relating to the welfare or upbringing of a child, any proceedings in the cause shall be dealt with by the sheriff in chambers.

(2) In an action to which paragraph (1) applies, decree may be pronounced after such inquiry as the sheriff thinks fit.

No recording of evidence

33.32 It shall not be necessary to record the evidence in any proof in a family action which is not defended.

Disapplication of Chapter 15

33.33 Chapter 15 (motions) shall not apply to a family action in which no notice of intention to defend has been lodged.

PART III DEFENDED FAMILY ACTIONS

Notice of intention to defend and defences

33.34—(1) This rule applies where the defender in a family action seeks—

(a) to oppose any crave in the initial writ;

(b) to make a claim for—

(i) aliment;

(ii) an order for financial provision within the meaning of section 8(3) of the Act of 1985; or

(iii) an order relating to parental rights; or

(c) an order—

(i) under section 16(1)(b) or (3) of the Act of 1985 (setting aside or varying agreement as to financial provision);

(ii) under section 18 of the Act of 1985 (which relates to avoidance transactions); or

(iii) under the Act of 1981; or

(d) to challenge the jurisdiction of the court.

(2) In an action to which this rule applies, the defender shall—

(a) lodge a notice of intention to defend in Form F26 before the expiry of the period of notice; and

(b) make any claim or seek any order referred to in paragraph (1), as the case may be, in those defences by setting out in his defences—

(i) craves;

(ii) averments in the answers to the condescendence in support of those craves; and

(iii) appropriate pleas-in-law.

Abandonment by pursuer

33.35 Notwithstanding abandonment by a pursuer, the court may allow a defender to pursue an order or claim sought in his defences; and the proceedings in relation to that order or claim shall continue in dependence as if a separate cause.

Attendance of parties at Options Hearing

33.36 All parties shall, except on cause shown, attend personally the hearing under rule 9.12 (Options Hearing).

Decree by default

33.37—(1) In a family action in which the defender has lodged a notice of intention to defend, where a party fails—

(a) to lodge, or intimate the lodging of, any production or part of process,

(b) to impiement an order of the sheriff within a specified period, or

(c) to appear to be represented at any diet,

that party shall be in default.

(2) Where a party is in default under paragraph (1), the sheriff may—

(a) where the family action is one mentioned in rule 33.1(1)(a) to (h), allow that action to proceed as undefended under Part II of this Chapter; or

(b) where the family action is one mentioned in rule 33.1(1)(i) to (m), grant decree as craved; or

(c) grant decree of absolvitor; or

(d) dismiss the family action or any claim made or order sought; and

(e) award expenses.

(3) Where no party appears at a diet in a family action, the sheriff may dismiss that action.

(4) In a family action, the sheriff may, on cause shown, prorogate the time for lodging any production or part of process, or for intimating or implementing any order.

PART IV APPLICATIONS AND ORDERS RELATING TO CHILDREN IN CERTAIN ACTIONS

Application and interpretation of this Part

33.38—(1) This Part applies to an action of divorce or separation.

(2) In this Part, "the Act of 1958" means the Matrimonial Proceedings (Children) Act 1958.

Applications in actions to which this Part applies

33.39—(1) An application for an order mentioned in paragraph (2) shall be made—

(a) by a crave in the initial writ or defences, as the case may be, in an action to which this Part applies; or

(b) where the application is made by a person other than the pursuer or defender, by minute in that action.

(2) The orders referred to in paragraph (1) are:—

(a) an order for any parental rights; and

(b) an order for aliment for a child.

Intimation before committal to care or supervision

33.40 Where the sheriff is considering making an order under section 10(1) of the Act of 1958 (committal of care of child to an individual other than one of the parties to the marriage or to a local authority) or under section 12(1) of that Act (placing child under supervision of a local authority), he shall ordain one of the parties to intimate to that person or to the chief executive of the appropriate local authority, as the case may be, where not already a party to the action and represented at the hearing at which the issue arises—

(a) a copy of the pleadings (including any adjustments and amendments);

(b) the terms of any relevant motion; and

(c) notice of intimation in Form F28 requiring any representations which that person or that local authority wishes to make to the sheriff to be made by minute in the process of the action within the period specified.

Care or supervision orders

33.41 Where the sheriff makes, varies or recalls an order under section 10(1) (committal of care of child to an individual other than one of the parties to the marriage or to a local authority), or section 12(1) (placing child under supervision of a local authority), of the Act of 1958, the sheriff clerk shall send a copy of the interlocutor making the order and a notice of intimation in Form F29 to the chief executive of the local authority or other person concerned.

Intimation of certain applications to local authorities or other persons

33.42 Where a child is subject to an order under section 10(1) (committal of care of child to an individual other than one of the parties to the marriage or to a local authority), or section 12(1) (placing child under supervision of a local authority), of the Act of 1958, any motion or minute lodged which relates to that child shall be intimated to the chief executive of the local authority or other person concerned.

Applications in depending actions by motion

33.43 An application by a party in an action depending before the court to which this Part applies—

- (a) for, or for variation of, an order—
  - (i) for interim aliment for a child under the age of 18 years, or
  - (ii) for interim custody of, or interim access to, a child, or
- (b) for variation or recall of an order under section 10(1) (committal of care of child to an individual other than one of the parties to the marriage or to a local authority), or section 12(1) (placing child under supervision of a local authority), of the Act of 1958,

shall be made by motion.

Applications after decree relating to parental rights, care or supervision

33.44—(1) An application after final decree—

- (a) for, or for the variation or recall of, an order relating to parental rights,
- (b) for an order under section 10(1) of the Act of 1958 (committal of care of child to an individual other than one of the parties to the marriage or to a local authority), or
- (c) an order under section 12(1) of the Act of 1958 (placing child under supervision of a local authority),

shall be made by minute in the process of the action to which the application relates.

(2) Where a minute has been lodged under paragraph (1), any party may apply by motion for any interim order which may be made pending the determination of the application.

Applications after decree relating to aliment

33.45—(1) An application after final decree for, or for the variation or recall of, an order for aliment for a child shall be made by minute in the process of the action to which the application relates.

(2) Where a minute has been lodged under paragraph (1), any party may lodge a motion for any interim order which may be made pending the determination of the application.

Applications after decree by persons over 18 years for aliment

33.46—(1) A person—

(a) to whom an obligation of aliment is owed under section 1 of the Act of 1985,

(b) in whose favour an order for aliment while under the age of 18 years was made in an action to which this Part applies, and

(c) who seeks, after attaining that age, an order for aliment against the person in that action against whom the order for aliment in his favour was made,

shall apply by minute in the process of that action.

(2) An application for interim aliment pending the determination of an application under paragraph (1) shall be made by motion.

(3) Where a decree has been pronounced in an application under paragraph (1) or (2), any application for variation or recall of any such decree shall be made by minute in the process of the action to which the application relates.

PART V ORDERS RELATING TO FINANCIAL PROVISION

Application and interpretation of this Part

33.47—(1) This Part applies to an action of divorce.

(2) In this Part, "incidental order" has the meaning assigned in section 14(2) of the Act of 1985.

Applications in actions to which this Part applies

33.48—(1) An application for an order mentioned in paragraph (2) shall be made—

(a) by a crave in the initial writ or defences, as the case may be, in an action to which this Part applies; or

(b) where the application is made by a person other than the pursuer or defender, by minute in that action.

(2) The orders referred to in paragraph (1) are:—

(a) an order for financial provision within the meaning of section 8(3) of the Act of 1985;

(b) an order under section 16(1)(b) or (3) of the Act of 1985 (setting aside or varying agreement as to financial provision);

(c) an order under section 18 of the Act of 1985 (which relates to avoidance transactions); and

(d) an order under section 13 of the Act of 1981 (transfer or vesting of tenancy).

Applications in depending actions relating to incidental orders

33.49—(1) In an action depending before the sheriff to which this Part applies—

(a) the pursuer or defender, notwithstanding rules 33.34(2) (application by defender for order for financial provision) and 33.48(1)(a) (application for order for financial provision in initial writ or defences), may apply by motion for an incidental order; and

(b) the sheriff shall not be bound to determine such a motion if he considers that the application should properly be by a crave in the initial writ or defences, as the case may be.

(2) In an action depending before the sheriff to which this Part applies, an application under section 14(4) of the Act of 1985 for the variation or recall of an incidental order shall be made by minute in the process of the action to which the application relates.

Applications relating to interim aliment

33.50 An application for, or for the variation or recall of, an order for interim aliment for the pursuer or defender shall be made by motion.

Applications relating to orders for financial provision

33.51—(1) An application—

(a) after final decree under any of the following provisions of the Act of 1985—
  - (i) section 8(1) for periodical allowances,
  - (ii) section 12(1)(b) (payment of capital sum or transfer of property),
  - (iii) section 12(4) (variation of date or method of payment of capital sum or date of transfer of property), or
  - (iv) section 13(4) (variation, recall, backdating or conversion of periodical allowance), or

(b) after the grant or refusal of an application under—
  - (i) section 8(1) or 14(3) for an incidental order, or
  - (ii) section 14(4) (variation or recall of incidental order),

shall be made by minute in the process of the action to which the application relates.

(2) Where a minute is lodged under paragraph (1), any party may lodge a motion for any interim order which may be made pending the determination of the application.

Applications after decree relating to agreements and avoidance transactions

33.52 An application for an order—

(a) under section 16(1)(a) or (3) of the Act of 1985 (setting aside or varying agreements as to financial provision), or

(b) under section 18 of the Act of 1985 (which relates to avoidance transactions),

made after final decree shall be made by minute in the process of the action to which the application relates.

PART VI APPLICATIONS RELATING TO AVOIDANCE TRANSACTIONS

Form of applications

33.53—(1) An application for an order under section 18 of the Act of 1985 (which relates to avoidance transactions) by a party to an action shall be made by including in the initial writ, defences or minute, as the case may be, appropriate craves, averments and pleas-in-law.

(2) An application for an order under section 18 of the Act of 1985 after final decree in an action, shall be made by minute in the process of the action to which the application relates.

PART VII FINANCIAL PROVISION AFTER OVERSEAS DIVORCE OR ANNULMENT

Interpretation of this Part

33.54 In this Part—

"the Act of 1984" means the Matrimonial and Family Proceedings Act 1984;

"order for financial provision" has the meaning assigned in section 30(1) of the Act of 1984;

"overseas country" has the meaning assigned in section 30(1) of the Act of 1984.

Applications for financial provision

33.55—(1) An application under section 28 of the Act of 1984 for an order for financial provision after a divorce or annulment in an overseas country shall be made by initial writ.

(2) An application for an order in an action to which paragraph (1) applies made before final decree under—

(a) section 13 of the Act of 1981 (transfer of tenancy of matrimonial home),
(b) section 29(4) of the Act of 1984 for interim periodical allowance, or
(c) section 14(4) of the Act of 1985 (variation or recall of incidental order),

shall be made by motion.

(3) An application for an order in an action to which paragraph (1) applies made after final decree under—

(a) section 12(4) of the Act of 1985 (variation of date or method of payment of capital sum or date of transfer of property),
(b) section 13(4) of the Act of 1985 (variation, recall, backdating or conversion of periodical allowance), or
(c) section 14(4) of the Act of 1985 (variation or recall of incidental order),

shall be made by minute in the process of the action to which the application relates.

(4) Where a minute has been lodged under paragraph (3), any party may apply by motion for an interim order pending the determination of the application.

PART VIII ACTIONS OF ALIMENT

Interpretation of this Part

33.56 In this Part, "action of aliment" means a claim for aliment under section 2(1) of the Act of 1985.

Undefended actions of aliment

33.57—(1) Where a motion for decree in absence under Chapter 7 (undefended causes) is lodged in an action of aliment, the pursuer shall, on lodging the motion, lodge all documentary evidence of the means of the parties available to him in support of the amount of aliment sought.

(2) Where the sheriff requires the appearance of parties, the sheriff clerk shall fix a hearing.

Applications relating to aliment

33.58—(1) An application for, or for variation of, an order for interim aliment in a depending action of aliment shall be made by motion.

(2) An application after final decree for the variation or recall of an order for aliment in an action of aliment shall be made by minute in the process of the action to which the application relates.

(3) A person—

(a) to whom an obligation of aliment is owned under section 1 of the Act of 1985,

(b) in whose favour an order for aliment while under the age of 18 years was made in an action of aliment, or

(c) who seeks, after attaining that age, an order for aliment against the person in that action against whom the order for aliment in his favour was made,

shall apply by minute in the process of that action.

(4) An application for interim aliment pending the determination of an application under paragraph (2) or (3) shall be made by motion.

(5) Where a decree has been pronounced in an application under paragraph (2) or (3), any application for variation or recall of any such decree shall be made by minute in the process of the action to which the application relates.

Applications relating to agreements on aliment

33.59—(1) Subject to paragraph (2), an application under 7(2) of the Act of 1985 (variation or termination of agreement on aliment) shall be made by summary application.

(2) In a family action in which a crave for aliment may be made, an application under section 7(2) of the Act of 1985 shall be made by a crave in the initial writ or in defences, as the case may be.

PART IX ACTIONS RELATING TO PARENTAL RIGHTS

Application and interpretation of this Part

33.60—(1) This Part applies to an application for any parental rights in a family action other than in an action of divorce or separation.

(2) In this Part, "the Act of 1973" means the Guardianship Act 1973.

Form of applications

33.61 Subject to any other provision in this Chapter, an application for an order for any parental rights in respect of a child shall be made—

(a) by an action for parental rights;
(b) by a crave in the initial writ or defences, as the case may be, in any other family action to which this Part applies; or
(c) where the application is made by a person other than a party to an action mentioned in paragraph (a) or (b), by minute in that action.

Defences in actions for parental rights

33.62 In an action for parental rights, the pursuer shall call as a defender—

(a) the parents or other parent of the child in respect of whom the order is sought;
(b) any guardian of the child;
(c) any person who has accepted the child into his family;
(d) any person having the *de facto* custody of the child;
(e) any local authority in whose care or under whose supervision the child is; and
(f) in any case where there is no person falling within paragraphs (a) to (e), the Lord Advocate.

Applications relating to interim orders in depending actions

33.63 An application, in an action depending before the sheriff to which this Part applies, for, or for the variation or recall of, an order for interim custody or interim access shall be made—

(a) by a party to the action, by motion; or
(b) by a person who is not a party to the action, by minute.

Care and supervision by local authorities

33.64—(1) Where the sheriff is considering making an order under section 11(1) of the Act of 1973 (committal of care of child to a local authority or order that child be under supervision of a local authority), he shall ordain one of the parties to intimate to the chief executive of the appropriate local authority unless a party to the cause and represented at the hearing at which the issue arises—

(a) a copy of the pleadings (including any adjustments and amendments);
(b) the terms of any relevant motion;
(c) a notice of intimation in Form F28 requiring any representations which the local authority wishes to make to the court to be made by minute in the process of the action within the period specified.

(2) Where the sheriff makes, varies or recalls an order placing a child under the supervision of a local authority under section 11(1) of the Act of 1973, the sheriff clerk shall send a copy of the interlocutor making the order and a notice of intimation in Form F29 to the chief executive of that authority.

(3) Where a child is subject to an order made under section 11(1) of the Act of 1973, any motion or minute lodged which relates to that child shall be intimated to the chief executive of the local authority concerned.

Applications after decree

33.65—(1) An application after final decree—

(a) for variation or recall of an order relating to parental rights, or

(b) for, or for variation or recall of, an order under section 11(1) of the Act of 1973 (committal of care of child to a local authority or order that child be under the supervision of a local authority),

shall be made by minute in the process of the action to which the application relates.

(2) Where a minute has been lodged under paragraph (1), any party may apply by motion for an interim order pending the determination of the application.

PART X ACTIONS UNDER THE MATRIMONIAL HOMES (FAMILY PROTECTION) (SCOTLAND) ACT 1981

Interpretation of this Part

33.66 Unless the context otherwise requires, words and expressions used in this Part which are also used in the Act of 1981 have the same meaning as in that Act.

Form of applications

33.67—(1) Subject to any other provision in this Chapter, an application for an order under the Act of 1981 shall be made—

(a) by an action for such an order;

(b) by a crave in the initial writ or in defences, as the case may be, in any other family action; or

(c) where the application is made by a person other than a party to any action mentioned in paragraph (a) or (b), by minute in that action.

(2) An application under section 7(1) (dispensing with consent of non-entitled spouse to a dealing) or section 11 (application in relation to poinding) shall, unless made in a depending family action, be made by summary application.

Defenders

33.68 The applicant for an order under the Act of 1981 shall call as a defender—

(a) where he is seeking an order as a spouse, the other spouse;

(b) where he is a third party making an application under section 7(1) (dispensing with consent of non-entitled spouse to a dealing), or 8(1) (payment from non-entitled spouse in respect of loan), of the Act of 1981, both spouses; and

(c) where the application is made under section 18 of the Act of 1981 (occupancy rights of cohabiting couples), or is one to which that section applies, the other partner.

Applications by motion

33.69—(1) An application under any of the following provisions of the Act of 1981 shall be made by motion in the process of the depending action to which the application relates:

(a) section 3(4) (interim order for regulation of rights of occupancy, etc.);
(b) section 4(6) (interim order suspending occupancy rights);
(c) section 7(1) (dispensing with consent of non-entitled spouse to a dealing);
(d) section 15(1) (order attaching power of arrest), if made after application for matrimonial interdict; and
(e) the proviso to section 18(1) (extension of period of occupancy rights).

(2) Intimation of a motion under paragraph (1) shall be given—

(a) to the other spouse or partner, as the case may be;
(b) where the motion is under paragraph (1)(a), (b) or (e) and the entitled spouse or partner is a tenant or occupies the matrimonial home by the permission of a third party, to the landlord or third party, as the case may be; and
(c) to any other person to whom intimation of the application was or is to be made by virtue of rule 33.7(1)(k) (warrant for intimation to certain persons in actions for orders under the Act of 1981) or 33.15 (order for intimation by sheriff).

Applications by minute

33.70—(1) An application for an order under—

(a) section 5 of the Act of 1981 (variation and recall of orders regulating occupancy rights and of exclusion order), or
(b) section 15(2) and (5) of the Act of 1981 (variation and recall of matrimonial interdict and power of arrest),

shall be made by minute.

(2) A minute under paragraph (1) shall be intimated—

(a) to the other spouse or partner, as the case may be;
(b) where the entitled spouse or partner is a tenant or occupies the matrimonial home by the permission of a third party, to the landlord or third party, as the case may be; and
(c) to any other person to whom intimation of the application was or is to be made by virtue of rule 33.7(1)(k) (warrant for intimation to certain persons in actions for orders under the Act of 1981) or 33.15 (order for intimation for sheriff).

Sist of actions to enforce occupancy rights

33.71 Unless the sheriff otherwise directs, the sist of an action by virtue of section 7(4) of the Act of 1981 (where action raised by non-entitled spouse to enforce occupancy rights) shall apply only to such part of the action as relates to the enforcement of occupancy rights by a non-entitled spouse.

Certificates of delivery of documents to chief constable

33.72—(1) Where an applicant is required to comply with section 15(4) or (5), as the case may be, of the Act of 1981 (delivery of documents to chief constable where power of arrest attached to matrimonial interdict is granted, varied or recalled), he shall, after such compliance, lodge in process a certificate of delivery in Form F30.

(2) Where a matrimonial interdict to which a power of arrest under section 15(1) of the Act of 1981 has been attached ceases to have effect by reason of a decree of divorce being pronounced by the sheriff, the pursuer shall send—

- (a) to the chief constable of the police area in which the matrimonial home is situated, and
- (b) if the applicant spouse (within the meaning of section 15(6) of the Act 1981) resides in another police area, to the chief constable of that other police area,

a copy of the interlocutor granting decree and lodge in process a certificate of delivery in Form F30.

PART XI SIMPLIFIED DIVORCE APPLICATIONS

Application and interpretation of this Part

33.73—(1) This Part applies to an application for divorce by a party to a marriage made in the manner prescribed in rule 33.74 (form of applications) if, but only if—

- (a) that party relies on the facts set out in section 1(2)(d) (no cohabitation for two years with consent of defender to decree), or section 1(2)(e) (no cohabitation for five years), of the Act of 1976;
- (b) in an application under section 1(2)(d) of the Act of 1976, the other party consents to decree of divorce being granted;
- (c) no other proceedings are pending in any court which could have the effect of bringing the marriage to an end;
- (d) there are no children of the marriage under the age of 16 years;
- (e) neither party to the marriage applies for an order for financial provision on divorce; and
- (f) neither party to the marriage suffers from mental disorder.

(2) If an application ceases to be one to which this Part applies at any time before final decree, it shall be deemed to be abandoned and shall be dismissed.

(3) In this Part "simplified divorce application" means an application mentioned in paragraph (1).

Form of applications

33.74—(1) A simplified divorce application in which the facts set out in section 1(2)(d) of the Act of 1976 (no cohabitation for two years with consent of defender to decree) are relied on shall be made in Form F31 and shall only be of effect if—

- (a) it is signed by the applicant; and
- (b) the form of consent in Part 2 of Form F32 is signed by the party to the marriage giving consent.

(2) A simplified divorce application in which the facts set out in section 1(2)(e) of the Act of 1976 (no cohabitation for five years) are relied on shall be made in Form F33 and shall only be of effect if it is signed by the applicant.

Lodging of applications

33.75 The applicant shall send a simplified divorce application to the sheriff clerk with—

(a) an extract or certified copy of the marriage certificate; and
(b) the appropriate fee.

Citation and intimation

33.76—(1) This rule is subject to rule 33.77 (citation where address not known).

(2) It shall be the duty of the sheriff clerk to cite any person or intimate any document in connection with a simplified divorce application.

(3) The form of citation—

(a) in an application relying on the facts in section 1(2)(d) of the Act of 1976 shall be in Form F34; and
(b) in an application relying on the facts in section 1(2)(e) of the Act of 1976 shall be in Form F35.

(4) The sheriff clerk shall arrange for the citation or intimation required by paragraph (2) to be made—

(a) by registered post or the first class recorded delivery service in accordance with rule 5.3 (postal service or intimation);
(b) on payment of an additional fee, by a sheriff officer in accordance with rule 5.4(1) and (2) (service within Scotland by sheriff officer); or
(c) where necessary, in accordance with rule 5.5 (service on persons furth of Scotland).

Citation where address not known

33.77—(1) In a simplified divorce application in which the facts in section 1(2)(e) of the Act of 1976 (no cohabitation for five years) are relied on and the address of the other party to the marriage is not known and cannot reasonably be ascertained—

(a) citation shall be executed by displaying a copy of the application and a notice in Form F36 on the walls of court on a period of notice of 21 days; and
(b) intimation shall be made to—
    (i) every child of the marriage between the parties who has reached the age of 16 years, and
    (ii) one of the next-of-kin of the other party to the marriage who has reached the age, unless the address of such person is not known and cannot reasonably be ascertained.

(2) Intimation to a person referred to in paragraph (1)(b) shall be given by intimating a copy of the application and a notice of intimation in Form F37.

Opposition to applications

33.78—(1) Any person on whom service or intimation of a simplified divorce application has been made may give notice by letter sent to the sheriff clerk that he challenges the jurisdiction of the court or opposes the grant of decree of divorce and giving the reasons for his opposition to the application.

(2) Where opposition to a simplified divorce application is made under paragraph (1), the sheriff shall dismiss the application unless he is satisfied that the reasons given for the opposition are frivolous.

(3) The sheriff clerk shall intimate the decision under paragraph (2) to the applicant and the respondent.

(4) The sending of a letter under paragraph (1) shall not imply acceptance of the jurisdiction of the court.

Evidence

33.79 Parole evidence shall not be given in a simplified divorce application.

Decree

33.80—(1) The sheriff may grant decree in terms of the simplified divorce application on the expiry of the period of notice if such application has been properly served proved that, when the application has been served in a country to which the Hague Convention on the Service Abroad of Judicial and Extra-Judicial Documents in Civil or Commercial Matters dated 15 November 1965 applies, decree shall not be granted until it is established to the satisfaction of the sheriff that the requirements of article 15 of that Convention have been complied with.

(2) The sheriff clerk shall, not sooner than 14 days after the granting of decree in terms of paragraph (1), issue to each party to the marriage an extract of the decree of divorce in Form F38.

Appeals

33.81 Any appeal against an interlocutor granting decree of divorce under rule 33.80 (decree) may be made, within 14 days after the date of decree, by sending a letter to the court giving reasons for the appeal.

Applications after decree

33.82 Any application to the court after decree of divorce has been granted in a simplified divorce application which could have been made if it had been made in an action of divorce shall be made by minute.

PART XII VARIATION OF COURT OF SESSION DECREES

Application and interpretation of this Part

33.83—(1) This Part applies to an application to the sheriff for variation or recall of any order to which section 8 of the Act of 1966 (variation of certain Court of Session orders) applies.

(2) In this Part, the "Act of 1966" means the Law Reform (Miscellaneous Provisions) (Scotland) Act 1966.

Form of applications and intimation to Court of Session

33.84—(1) An application to which this Part applies shall be made by initial writ.

(2) In such an application there shall be lodged with the initial writ a copy of the interlocutor, certified by a clerk of the Court of Session, which it is sought to vary.

(3) Before lodging the initial writ, a copy of the initial writ certified by the pursuer or his solicitor shall be lodged, or sent by first class recorded delivery post to the Deputy Principal Clerk of Session to be lodged in the process of the cause in the Court of Session in which the original order was made.

(4) The pursuer or his solicitor shall attach a certificate to the initial writ stating that paragraph (3) has been complied with.

(5) The sheriff may, on cause shown, prorogate the time for lodging the certified copy of the interlocutor required under paragraph (1).

Defended actions

33.85—(1) Where a notice of intention to defend has been lodged and no request is made under rule 33.87 (remit of applications to Court of Session), the pursuer shall within 14 days after the date of the lodging of a notice of intention to defend or within such other period as the sheriff may order, lodge in process the following documents (or copies) from the process in the cause in the Court of Session in which the original order was made:—

(a) the pleadings;
(b) the interlocutor sheets;
(c) any opinion of the court; and
(d) any productions on which he seeks to found.

(2) The sheriff may, on the joint motion of parties made at any time after the lodging of the documents mentioned in paragraph (1)—

(a) dispense with proof;
(b) whether defences have been lodged or not, hear the parties; and
(c) thereafter, grant decree or otherwise dispose of the cause as he thinks fit.

Transmission of process to Court of Session

33.86—(1) Where decree has been granted or the cause otherwise disposed of—

(a) and the period for marking an appeal has elapsed without an appeal being marked, or
(b) after the determination of the cause on any appeal,

the sheriff clerk shall transmit to the Court of Session the sheriff court process and the documents from the process of the cause in the Court of Session which have been lodged in the sheriff court process.

(2) A sheriff court process transmitted under paragraph (1) shall form part of the process of the cause in the Court of Session in which the original order was made.

Remit of applications to Court of Session

33.87—(1) A request for a remit to the Court of Session under section 8(3) of the Act of 1966 shall be made by motion.

(2) The sheriff shall, in respect of any such motion, order that the cause be remitted to the Court of Session; and, within four days after the date of such order,

the sheriff clerk shall transmit the whole sheriff court process to the Court of Session.

(3) A cause remitted to the Court of Session under paragraph (2) shall form part of the process of the cause in the Court of Session in which the original order was made.

PART XIII CHILD SUPPORT ACT 1991

Interpretation of this Part

33.88—(1) In this Part—

"the Act of 1991" means the Child Support Act 1991;

"child" has the meaning assigned in section 55 of the Act of 1991;

"maintenance assessment" has the meaning assigned in section 55 of the Act of 1991.

Restriction of expenses

33.89 Where the Secretary of State is named as a defender in an action for declarator of non-parentage or illegitimacy, and the Secretary of State does not defend the action, no expenses shall be awarded against the Secretary of State.

Effect of maintenance assessments

33.90 The sheriff clerk shall, on receiving notification that a maintenance assessment has been made, cancelled or has ceased to have effect so as to affect an order of a kind prescribed for the purposes of section 10 of the Act of 1991, endorse on the interlocutor sheet relating to that order a certificate, in Form F49 or F40, as the case may be.

Effect of maintenance assessments on extracts relating to aliment

33.91—(1) Where an order relating to aliment is affected by a maintenance assessment, any extract of that order issued by the sheriff clerk shall be endorsed with the following certificate:—

"A maintenance assessment having been made under the Child Support Act 1991 on (*insert date*), this order, in so far as it relates to the making or securing of periodical payments to or for the benefit of (*insert name(s) of child/children*), ceases to have effect from (*insert date two days after the date on which the maintenance assessment was made*).".

(2) Where an order relating to aliment has ceased to have effect on the making of a maintenance assessment, and that maintenance assessment is later cancelled or ceases to have effect, any extract of that order issued by the sheriff clerk shall be endorsed also with the following certificate:—

"The jurisdiction of the child support officer under the Child Support Act 1991 having terminated on (*insert date*), this order, in so far as it relates to (*insert name(s) of child/children*), again shall have effect as from (*insert date of termination of child support officer's jurisdiction*).".

Chapter 34 Actions relating to heritable property

PART I SEQUESTRATION FOR RENT

Actions craving payment for rent

34.1—(1) In an action for sequestration and sale—

(a) for non-payment of rent,

(b) for recovery of rent, or

(c) in security of rent,

whether brought before or after the term of payment, payment of rent may be craved; and decree for payment of such rent or part of it, when due and payable, may be pronounced and extracted in common form.

(2) There shall be served on the defender in such an action, with the initial writ, warrant and citation, a notice in Form H1.

Warrant to inventory and secure

34.2—(1) In the first deliverance on an initial writ for sequestration and sale, the sheriff may sequestrate the effects of the tenant, and grant warrant to inventory and secure them.

(2) A warrant to sequestrate, inventory, sell, eject or relet shall include authority to open, shut and lockfast places for the purpose of executing such warrant.

Sale of effects

34.3—(1) In an action for sequestration and sale, the sheriff may order the sequestrated effects to be sold by a sheriff officer or other named person.

(2) Where a sale follows an order under paragraph (1), the sale shall be reported within 14 days after the date of the sale and the pursuer shall lodge with the sheriff clerk the roup rolls or certified copies of them and a state of debt.

(3) In the interlocutor approving the report of sale, or by separate interlocutor, the sheriff may grant decree against the defender for any balance remaining due.

Care of effects

34.4 The sheriff may, at any stage of an action for sequestration and sale appoint a fit person to take charge of the sequestrated effects, or may require the tenant to find caution that they shall be made available.

PART II REMOVING

Actions of removing where fixed term of removal

34.5—(1) Subject to section 21 of the Agricultural Holdings (Scotland) Act 1991 (notice to quit and notice of intention to quit)—

(a) where the tenant has bound himself to remove by writing, dated and signed—

(i) within 12 months after the term of removal, or

(ii) where there is more than one ish, after the ish first in date to remove, an action of removing may be raised at any time; and

(b) where the tenant has not bound himself, an action of removing may be raised at any time, but—

(i) in the case of a lease of lands exceeding two acres in extent for three years and upwards, an interval of not less than one year nor more than two years shall elapse between the date of notice of removal and the term of removal first in date;

(ii) in the case of a lease of lands exceeding two acres in extent, whether written or verbal, held from year to year or under tacit relocation, or for any other period less than three years, an interval of not less than six months shall elapse between the date of notice of removal and the term of removal first in date; and

(iii) in the case of a house let with or without land attached not exceeding two acres in extent, as also of land not exceeding two acres in extent without houses, as also of mills, fishings, shootings, and all other heritable subjects excepting land exceeding two acres in extent, and let for a year or more, 40 days at least shall elapse between the date of notice of removal and the term of removal first in date.

(2) In any defended action of removing the sheriff may order the defender to find caution for violent profits.

(3) In an action for declarator of irritancy and removing by a superior against a vassal, the pursuer shall call as parties the last entered vassal and such heritable creditors and holders of postponed ground burdens as are disclosed by a search for 20 years before the raising of the action, and the expense of the search shall form part of the pursuer's expenses of process.

Form of notice of removal

34.6—(1) A notice under the following sections of this Act shall be in Form H2:—

(a) section 34 (notice in writing to remove where lands exceeding two acres held on probative lease),

(b) section 35 (letter of removal where tenant in possession of lands exceeding two acres), and

(c) section 36 (notice of removal where lands exceeding two acres occupied by tenant without written lease).

(2) A letter of removal shall be in Form H3.

Form of notice under section 37 of this Act

34.7 A notice under section 37 of this Act (notice of termination of tenancy) shall be in Form H4.

Giving notice of removal

34.8—(1) A notice under section 34, 35, 36, 37 or 38 of this Act (which relate to notices of removal) may be given by—

(a) a sheriff officer,

(b) the person entitled to give such notice, or

(c) the solicitor or factor of such person,

posting the notice by registered post or the first class recorded delivery service at any post office within the United Kingdom in time for it to be delivered at the address on the notice before the last date on which by law such notice must be given, addressed to the person entitled to receive such notice, and bearing the address of that person at the time, if known, or, if not known, to the last known address of that person.

(2) A sheriff officer may also give notice under a section of this Act mentioned in paragraph (1) in any manner in which he may serve an initial writ; and, accordingly, rule 5.4 (service within Scotland by sheriff officer) shall, with the necessary modifications, apply to the giving of notice under this paragraph as it applies to service of an initial writ.

Evidence of notice to remove

34.9—(1) A certificate of the sending of notice under rule 34.8 dated and endorsed on the lease or an extract of it, or on the letter of removal, signed by the sheriff officer or the person sending the notice, his solicitor or factor, or an acknowledgement of the notice endorsed on the lease or an extract of it, or on the letter of removal, by the party in possession or his agent, shall be sufficient evidence that notice has been given.

(2) Where there is no lease, a certificate of the sending of such notice shall be endorsed on a copy of the notice or letter of removal.

Applications under Part II of the Conveyancing and Feudal Reform (Scotland) Act 1970

34.10—(1) An application or counter-application to the sheriff under any of the following provisions of Part II of the Conveyancing and Feudal Reform (Scotland) Act 1970 (which relates to the standard security) shall be made by initial writ where any other remedy is craved:—

(a) section 18(2) (declarator that obligations under contract performed);
(b) section 20(3) (application by creditor for warrant to let security subjects);
(c) section 22(1) (objections to notice of default); and
(d) section 22(3) (counter-application for remedies under the Act);
(e) section 24(1) (application by a creditor for warrant to exercise remedies on default); and
(f) section 28(1) (decree of foreclosure).

(2) An interlocutor of the sheriff disposing of an application or counter-application under paragraph (1) shall be final and not subject to appeal except as to a question of title or any other remedy granted.

Chapter 35 Actions of multiplepoinding

Application of this Chapter

35.1 This Chapter applies to an action of multiplepoinding.

Application of Chapters 9 and 10

35.2 Chapter 10 (additional procedure) and the following rules in Chapter 9 (standard procedure in defended causes) shall not apply to an action of multiplepoinding:—

rule 9.1 (notice of intention to defend),
rule 9.2 (fixing date for Options Hearing),
rule 9.4 (lodging of pleadings before Options Hearing),
rule 9.8 (adjustment of pleadings),
rule 9.9 (effect of sist on adjustment),
rule 9.10 (open record),
rule 9.11 (record for Option Hearing),
rule 9.12 (Option Hearing),
rule 9.15 (applications for time to pay directions).

Parties

35.3—(1) An action of multiplepoinding may be brought by any person holding, or having an interest in, or claim on, the fund *in medio* in his own name.

(2) The pursuer shall call as defenders to such an action—

(a) all persons so far as known to him as having an interest in the fund *in medio*; and

(b) where he is not the holder of the fund, the holder of that fund.

Condescendence of fund *in medio*

35.4—(1) Where the pursuer is the holder of the fund *in medio*, he shall include a detailed statement of the fund in the condescendence in the initial writ.

(2) Where the pursuer is not the holder of the fund *in medio*, the holder shall, before the expiry of the period of notice—

(a) lodge in process—

(i) a condescendence of the fund *in medio*, stating any claim or lien which he may profess to have on that fund;

(ii) a list of all persons known to him as having an interest in the fund; and

(b) intimate a copy of the condescendence and list to any other party.

Warrant of citation in multiplepoindings

35.5 The warrant of citation of the initial writ in an action of multiplepoinding shall be in Form M1.

Citation

35.6—(1) Subject to rule 5.6 (service where address of person is not known), citation of any person in an action of multiplepoinding shall be in Form M2 which shall be attached to a copy of the initial writ and warrant of citation and shall have appended to it a notice of appearance in Form M4.

(2) The certificate of citation shall be in Form M3 and shall be attached to the initial writ.

Advertisement

35.7 The sheriff may make an order for advertisement of the action in such newspapers as he thinks fit.

Lodging of notice of appearance

35.8 Where a party intends to lodge—
(a) defences to challenge the jurisdiction of the court or the competency of the action,
(b) objections to the condescendence of the fund *in medio*, or
(c) a claim on the fund,
he shall, before the expiry of the period of notice, lodge a notice of appearance in Form M4.

Fixing date of first hearing

35.9 Where a notice of appearance, or a condescendence on the fund *in medio* and a list under rule 35.4(2)(a) has been lodged, the sheriff clerk shall—
(a) fix a date and time for the first hearing, which date shall be the first suitable court day occurring not sooner than four weeks after the expiry of the period of notice;
(b) on fixing the date for the first hearing forthwith intimate that date in Form M5 to each party; and
(c) prepare and sign an interlocutor recording the date of the first hearing.

Hearings

35.10—(1) The sheriff shall conduct the first, and any subsequent hearing, with a view to securing the expeditious progress of the cause by ascertaining from the parties the matters in dispute.

(2) The parties shall provide the sheriff with sufficient information to enable him to conduct the hearing as provided for in this Chapter.

(3) At the first, or any subsequent hearing, the sheriff shall fix a period within which defences, objections or claims shall be lodged, and appoint a date for a second hearing.

(4) Where the list lodged under rule 35.4(2)(a) contains any person who is not a party to the action, the sheriff shall order—
(a) the initial writ to be amended to add that person as a defender;
(b) service of the pleadings so amended to be made on that person, with a citation in Form M6; and
(c) intimation to that person of any condescendence of the fund *in medio* lodged by a holder of the fund who is not the pursuer.

(5) Where a person to whom service has been made under paragraph (4) lodges a notice of appearance under rule 35.8, the sheriff clerk shall intimate to him in Form M5 the date of the next hearing fixed in the action.

Lodging defences, objections and claims

35.11—(1) Defences, objections and claims by a party shall be lodged with the sheriff clerk in a single document under separate headings.

(2) Each claimant shall lodge with his claim any documents founded on in his claim, so far as they are within his custody or power.

Disposal of defences

35.12—(1) Where defences have been lodged, the sheriff may order the initial writ and defences to be adjusted and thereafter close the record and regulate further procedure.

(2) Unless the sheriff otherwise directs, defences shall be disposed of before any further procedure in the action.

Objections to fund *in medio*

35.13—(1) Where objections to the fund *in medio* have been lodged, the sheriff may, after disposal of any defences, order the condescendence of the fund and objections to be adjusted; and thereafter close the record and regulate further procedure.

(2) If no objections to the fund *in medio* have been lodged, or if objections have been lodged and disposed of, the sheriff may, on the motion of the holder of the fund, and without ordering intimation to any party approve the condescendence of the fund and find the holder liable only in one single payment.

Preliminary pleas in multiplepoindings

35.14—(1) A party intending to insist on a preliminary plea shall, not later than 3 days before any hearing to determine further procedure following the lodging of defences, objections or claims, lodge with the sheriff clerk a note of the basis of the plea.

(2) Where a party fails to comply with the provisions of paragraph (1), he shall be deemed to be no longer insisting on the plea and the plea shall be repelled by the sheriff at the hearing referred to in paragraph (1).

(3) If satisfied that there is a preliminary matter of law which justifies a debate, the sheriff shall, after having heard parties and considered the note lodged under this rule, appoint the action to debate.

Consignation of the fund and discharge of holder

35.15—(1) At any time after the condescendence of the fund *in medio* has been approved, the sheriff may order the whole or any part of the fund to be sold and the proceeds of the sale consigned into court.

(2) After such consignation the holder of the fund *in medio* may apply for his exoneration and discharge.

(3) The sheriff may allow the holder of the fund *in medio*, on his exoneration and discharge, his expenses out of the fund as a first charge on the fund.

Further service or advertisement

35.16 The sheriff may at any time, of his own motion or on the motion of any party, order further service on any person of advertisement.

Ranking of claims

35.17—(1) After disposal of any defences, and approval of the condescendence of the fund *in medio*, the sheriff may, where there is no competition on the fund, rank and prefer the claimants and grant decree in terms of that ranking.

(2) Where there is competition on the fund, the sheriff may order claims to be adjusted and thereafter close the record and regulate further procedure.

Remit to reporter

35.18—(1) Where several claims have been lodged, the sheriff may remit to a reporter to prepare a scheme of division and report.

(2) The expenses of such remit, when approved by the sheriff, shall be made a charge on the fund, to be deducted before division.

Chapter 36 Actions of Damages

PART I INTIMATION TO CONNECTED PERSONS IN CERTAIN ACTIONS OF DAMAGES

Application and interpretation of this Part

36.1—(1) This Part applies to an action of damages in which, following the death of any person from personal injuries, damages are claimed—

(a) by the executor of the deceased, in respect of the injuries from which the deceased died; or

(b) by any relative of the deceased, in respect of the death of the deceased.

(2) In this Part—

"connected person" means a person, not being a party to the action, who has title to sue the defender in respect of the personal injuries from which the deceased died or in respect of his death;

"relative" has the meaning assigned to it in Schedule 1 to the Damages (Scotland) Act 1976.

Averments

36.2 In an action to which this Part applies, the pursuer shall aver in the condescendence, as the case may be—

(a) that there are no connected persons;

(b) that there are connected persons, being the persons specified in the crave for intimation;

(c) that there are connected persons in respect of whom intimation should be dispensed with on the ground that—

(i) the names or whereabouts of such persons are not known to, and cannot reasonably be ascertained by, the pursuer; or

(ii) such persons are unlikely to be awarded more than £200 each.

Warrants for intimation

36.3—(1) Where the pursuer makes averments under rule 36.2(b) (existence of connected persons), he shall include a crave in the initial writ for intimation to any person who is believed to have title to sue the defender in an action in respect of the death of the deceased or the personal injuries from which the deceased died.

(2) A notice of intimation in Form D1 shall be attached to the copy of the initial writ where intimation is given on a warrant under paragraph (1).

Applications to dispense with intimation

36.4—(1) Where the pursuer makes averments under rule 36.2(c) (dispensing with intimation to connected persons), he shall apply by crave in the initial writ for an order to dispense with intimation.

(2) In determining an application under paragraph (1), the sheriff shall have regard to—

- (a) the desirability of avoiding a multiplicity of actions; and
- (b) the expense, inconvenience or difficulty likely to be involved in taking steps to ascertain the name or whereabouts of the connected person.

(3) Where the sheriff is not satisfied that intimation to a connected person should be dispensed with, he may—

- (a) order intimation to a connected person whose name and whereabouts are known;
- (b) order the pursuer to take such further steps as he may specify in the interlocutor to ascertain the name or whereabouts of any connected person; and
- (c) order advertisement in such manner, place and at such times as he may specify in the interlocutor.

Subsequent disclosure of connected persons

36.5 Where the name or whereabouts of a person, in respect of whom the sheriff has dispensed with intimation on a ground specified in rule 36.2(c) (dispensing with intimation to connected persons), subsequently becomes known to the pursuer, the pursuer shall apply to the sheriff by motion for a warrant for intimation to such a person; and such intimation shall be made in accordance with rule 36.3(2).

Connected persons entering process

36.6—(1) A connected person may apply by minute craving leave to be sisted as an additional pursuer to the action.

(2) Such a minute shall also crave leave of the sheriff to adopt the existing grounds of action, and to amend the craves, condescendence and pleas-in-law.

(3) The period within which answers to a minute under this rule may be lodged shall be 14 days from the date of intimation of the minute.

(4) Paragraphs (1) to (4) of rule 14.3 (procedure in minutes) shall not apply to a minute to which this rule applies.

Failure to enter process

36.7 Where a connected person to whom intimation is made in accordance with this Part—

(a) does not apply to be sisted as an additional pursuer to the action,

(b) subsequently raises a separate action against the same defender in respect of the same personal injuries or death, and

(c) would, apart from this rule, be awarded the expenses or part of the expenses of that action,

he shall not be awarded those expenses except on cause shown.

PART II INTERIM PAYMENTS OF DAMAGES

Application and interpretation of this Part

36.8—(1) This Part applies to an action of damages for personal injuries or the death of a person in consequence of personal injuries.

(2) In this Part—

"defender" includes a third party against whom the pursuer has a crave for damages;

"personal injuries" includes any disease or impairment of a physical or mental condition.

Applications for interim payment of damages

36.9—(1) In an action to which this Part applies, a pursuer may, at any time after defences have been lodged, apply by motion for an order for interim payment of damages to him by the defender or, where there are two or more of them, by any one or more of them.

(2) The pursuer shall intimate a motion under paragraph (1) to every other party on a period of notice of 14 days.

(3) On a motion under paragraph (1), the sheriff may, if satisfied that—

(a) the defender has admitted liability to the pursuer in the action, or

(b) if the action proceeded to proof, the pursuer would succeed in the action on the question of liability without any substantial finding of contributory negligence on his part, or on the part of any person in respect of whose injury or death the claim of the pursuer arises, and would obtain decree for damages against any defender,

ordain that defender to make an interim payment to the pursuer of such amount as the sheriff thinks fit, not exceeding a reasonable proportion of the damages which, in the opinion of the sheriff, are likely to be recovered by the pursuer.

(4) Any such payment may be ordered to be made in one lump sum or otherwise as the sheriff thinks fit.

(5) No order shall be made against a defender under this rule unless it appears to the sheriff that the defender is—

(a) a person who is insured in respect of the claim of the pursuer;

(b) a public authority; or

(c) a person whose means and resources are such as to enable him to make the interim payment.

(6) Notwithstanding the grant or refusal of a motion for an interim payment, a subsequent motion may be made where there has been a range of circumstances.

(7) Subject to Part IV (management of damages payable to persons under legal disability), an interim payment shall be made to the pursuer unless the sheriff otherwise directs.

(8) This rule shall, with the necessary modifications, apply to a counterclaim for damages for personal injuries made by a defender as it applies to an action in which the pursuer may apply for an order for interim payment of damages.

Adjustment on final decree

36.10 Where a defender has made an interim payment under rule 36.9, the sheriff may, when final decree is pronounced, make such order with respect to the interim payment as he thinks fit to give effect to the final liability of that defender to the pursuer; and in particular may order—

(a) repayment by the pursuer of any sum by which the interim payment exceeds the amount which that defender is liable to pay to the pursuer; or

(b) payment by any other defender or a third party, of any part of the interim payment which the defender who made it is entitled to recover from him by way of contribution or indemnity or in respect of any remedy or relief relating to, or connected with, the claim of the pursuer.

PART III PROVISIONAL DAMAGES FOR PERSONAL INJURIES

Application and interpretation of this Part

36.11—(1) This Part applies to an action of damages for personal injuries.

(2) In this Part—

"the Act of 1982" means the Administration of Justice Act 1982;

"further damages" means the damages referred to in section 12(4)(b) of the Act of 1982;

"provisional damages" means the damages referred to in section 12(4)(a) of the Act of 1982.

Applications for provisional damages

36.12 An application under section 12(2)(a) of the Act of 1982 for provisional damages for personal injuries shall be made by including in the initial writ—

(a) a crave for provisional damages;

(b) averments in the condescendence supporting the crave, including averments—

  (i) that there is a risk that, at some definite or indefinite time in the future, the pursuer will, as a result of the act or omission which gave rise to the cause of action, develop some serious disease or suffer some serious deterioration of his physical or mental condition; and

  (ii) that the defender was, at the time of the act or omission which gave rise to the cause of action, a public authority, public corporation or insured or otherwise indemnified in respect of the claim; and

(c) an appropriate plea-in-law.

Applications for further changes

36.13—(1) An application for further damages by a pursuer in respect of whom an order under section 12(2)(b) of the Act of 1982 has been made shall be made by minute in the process of the action to which it relates and shall include—

(a) a crave for further damages;
(b) averments in the statement of facts supporting that crave; and
(c) appropriate pleas-in-law.

(2) On lodging such a minute in process, the pursuer shall apply by motion for warrant to serve the minute on—

(a) every other party; and
(b) where such other party is insured or otherwise indemnified, his insurer or indemnifier, if known to the pursuer.

(3) Any such party, insurer or indemnifier may lodge answers to such a minute in process within 28 days after the date of service on him.

(4) Where answers have been lodged under paragraph (3), the sheriff may, on the motion of any party, make such further order as to procedure as he thinks fit.

PART IV MANAGEMENT OF DAMAGES PAYABLE TO PERSONS UNDER LEGAL DISABILITY

Orders for payment and management of money

36.14—(1) In an action of damages in which a sum of money becomes payable, by virtue of a decree or an extra-judicial settlement, to or for the benefit of a person under legal disability, the sheriff shall make such order regarding the payment and management of that sum for the benefit of that person as he thinks fit.

(2) An order under paragraph (1) shall be made on the granting of decree for payment or of absolvitor.

Methods of management

36.15 In making an order under rule 36.14(1), the sheriff may—

(a) appoint a judicial factor to apply, invest or otherwise deal with the money for the benefit of the person under legal disability;
(b) order the money to be paid to—
 (i) the Accountant of Court, or
 (ii) the guardian of the person under legal disability,
 as trustee, to be applied, invested or otherwise dealt with and administered under the directions of the sheriff for the benefit of the person under legal disability;
(c) order the money to be paid to the sheriff clerk of the sheriff court district in which the person under legal disability resides, to be applied, invested or otherwise dealt with and administered, under the directions of the sheriff of that district, for the benefit of the person under legal disability; or
(d) order the money to be paid directly to the person under legal disability.

Subsequent orders

36.16—(1) Where the sheriff has made an order under rule 36.14(1), any person having an interest may apply for an appointment or order under rule 36.15, or any other order for the payment or management of the money, by minute in the process of the cause to which the application relates.

(2) An application for directions under rule 36.15(b) or (c) may be made by any person having an interest by minute in the process of the cause to which the application relates.

Management of money paid to sheriff clerk

36.17—(1) A receipt in Form D2 by the sheriff clerk shall be a sufficient discharge in respect of the amount paid to him under this Part.

(2) The sheriff clerk shall, at the request of any competent court, accept custody of any sum of money in an action of damages ordered to be paid to, applied, invested or otherwise dealt with by him, for the benefit of a person under legal disability.

(3) Any money paid to the sheriff clerk under this Part shall be paid out, applied, invested or otherwise dealt with by the sheriff clerk only after such intimation, service and enquiry as the sheriff may order.

(4) Any sum of money invested by the sheriff clerk under this Part shall be best invested in a manner in which trustees are authorised to invest by virtue of the Trustee Investments Act 1961.

PART V SEX DISCRIMINATION ACT 1975

Causes under section 66 of the Act of 1975

36.18—(1) In a cause in which a breach of statutory duty under section 66(1) of the Sex Discrimination Act 1975 (proceedings for act of discrimination) is averred, the sheriff may, of his own motion or on the motion of any party, appoint an assessor.

(2) An assessor appointed under paragraph (1) shall be a person who the sheriff considers has special qualifications to be of assistance in determining an action referred to in that paragraph.

(3) In a cause referred to in paragraph (1), the pursuer should send a copy of the initial writ by post by the first class recorded delivery service to the Equal Opportunities Commission.

Chapter 37 Causes under the Presumption of Death (Scotland) Act 1977

Interpretation of this Chapter

37.1 In this Chapter—

"the Act of 1977" means the Presumption of Death (Scotland) Act 1977;
"action of declarator" means an action under section 1(1) of the Act of 1977;
"missing person" has the meaning assigned in section 1(1) of the Act of 1977.

Parties to, and service and intimation of, actions of declarator

37.2—(1) The missing person shall be named as the defender in an action of declarator and, subject to paragraph (2), service on that person shall be executed in accordance with rule 5.6 (service where address of person is not known).

(2) In the application of rule 5.6(1)(a) (advertisement where address of person not known) to service under paragraph (1) of this rule, for the reference to Form G3 there shall be substituted a reference to Form P1.

(3) Subject to paragraph (5), in an action of declarator, the pursuer shall include a crave for a warrant for intimation to—

- (a) the missing person's—
  - (i) spouse, and
  - (ii) children, or, if he has no children, his nearest relative known to the pursuer,
- (b) any person, including any insurance company, who so far as known to the pursuer has an interest in the action, and
- (c) the Lord Advocate,

in the following terms:— "For intimation to (*name and address*) as [husband *or* wife, child *or* nearest relative] [a person having an interest in the presumed death] of (*name and last known address of the missing person*) and to the Lord Advocate.".

(4) A notice of intimation in Form P2 shall be attached to the copy of the summons where intimation is given on a warrant under paragraph (3).

(5) The sheriff may, on the motion of the pursuer, dispense with intimation on a person mentioned in paragraph (3)(a) or (b).

(6) An application by minute under section 1(5) of the Act of 1977 (person interested in seeking determination or appointment not sought by pursuer) shall contain a crave for the determination or appointment sought, averments in the answers to the condescendence in support of that crave and an appropriate plea-in-law.

(7) On lodging a minute under paragraph (6), the minuter shall—

- (a) send a copy of the minute by registered post or the first class recorded delivery service to each person to whom intimation of the action has been made under paragraph (2); and
- (b) lodge in process the Post Office receipt or certificate of posting of that minute.

Further advertisement

37.3 Where no minute has been lodged indicating knowledge of the present whereabouts of the missing person, at any time before the determination of the action, the sheriff may, of his own motion or on the motion of a party, make such order for further advertisement as he thinks fit.

Applications for proof

37.4—(1) In an action of declarator where no minute has been lodged, the pursuer shall, after such further advertisement as may be ordered under rule 37.3, apply to the sheriff by motion for an order for proof.

(2) A proof ordered under paragraph (1) shall be by affidavit evidence unless the sheriff otherwise directs.

Applications for variation or recall of decree

37.5—(1) An application under section 4(1) of the Act of 1977 (variation or recall of decree) shall be made by minute in the process of the action to which it relates.

(2) On the lodging of such a minute, the sheriff shall make an order—

(a) for service on the missing person, where his whereabouts have become known;

(b) for intimation to those persons mentioned in rule 37.2(3) or to dispense with intimation to a person mentioned in rule 37.2(3)(a) or (b); and

(c) for any answers to the minute to be lodged in process within such period as the sheriff thinks fit.

(3) An application under section 4(3) of the Act of 1977 (person interested seeking determination or appointment not sought by applicant for variation order) shall be made by lodging answers containing a crave for the determination or appointment sought.

(4) A person lodging answers containing a crave under paragraph (3) shall, as well as sending a copy of the answers to the minuter—

(a) send a copy of the answers by registered post or the first class recorded delivery service to each person on whom service or intimation of the minute was ordered; and

(b) lodge in process the Post Office receipt or certificate of posting of those answers.

Appointment of judicial factors

37.6—(1) The Act of Sederunt (Judicial Factors Rules) 1992 shall apply to an application for the appointment of a judicial factor under section 2(2)(c) or section 4(2) of the Act of 1977 as it applies to a petition for the appointment of a judicial factor.

(2) In the application of rule 37.5 (applications for variation or recall of decree) to an application under section 4(1) of the Act of 1977 in a cause in which variation or recall of the appointment of a judicial factor is sought, for references to a minute there shall be substituted references to a note.

Chapter 38 European Court

Interpretation of this Chapter

38.1—(1) In this Chapter—

"appeal" includes an application for leave to appeal;

"the European Court" means the Court of Justice of the European Communities;

"reference" means a reference to the European Court for—

(a) a preliminary ruling under Article 177 of the E.E.C. Treaty, Article 150 of the Euratom Treaty, or Article 41 of the E.C.S.C. Treaty; or

(b) a ruling on the interpretation of the Conventions, as defined in section 1(1) of the Civil Jurisdiction and Judgments Act 1982, under Article 3 of Schedule 2 of that Act.

(2) The expressions "E.E.C. Treaty", "Euratom Treaty" and "E.C.S.C. Treaty" have the meanings assigned respectively in Schedule 1 to the European Communities Act 1972.

Applications for reference

38.2—(1) A reference may be made by the sheriff of his own motion or on the motion of a party.

(2) A reference shall be made in the form of a request for a preliminary ruling of the European Court in Form E1.

Preparation of case for reference

38.3—(1) Where the sheriff decides that a reference shall be made, he shall continue the cause for that purpose and, within 4 weeks after the date of that continuation, draft a reference.

(2) On the reference being drafted, the sheriff clerk shall send a copy to each party.

(3) Within 4 weeks after the date on which copies of the draft have been sent to parties, each party may—

(a) lodge with the sheriff clerk, and
(b) send to every other party,

a note of any adjustments he seeks to have made in the draft reference.

(4) Within 14 days after the date on which any such note of adjustments may be lodged, the sheriff, after considering any such adjustments, shall make and sign the reference.

(5) The sheriff clerk shall forthwith intimate the making of the reference to each party.

Sist of cause

38.4—(1) Subject to paragraph (2), on a reference being made, the cause shall, unless the sheriff when making such a reference otherwise orders, be sisted until the European Court has given a preliminary ruling the question referred to it.

(2) The sheriff may recall a sist made under paragraph (1) for the purpose of making an interim order which a due regard to the interests of the parties may require.

Transmission of reference

38.5—(1) Subject to paragraph (2), a copy of the reference, certified by the sheriff clerk, shall be transmitted by the sheriff clerk to the Registrar of the European Court.

(2) Unless the sheriff otherwise directs, a copy of the reference shall not be sent to the Registrar of the European Court where an appeal against the making of the reference is pending.

(3) For the purpose of paragraph (2), an appeal shall be treated as pending—

(a) until the expiry of the time for making that appeal; or
(b) where an appeal has been made, until that appeal has been determined.

Index